Leap into Darkness

Leap into Darkness

Seven years on the run in wartime Europe

LEO BRETHOLZ AND
MICHAEL OLESKER

Constable · London

First published in the United States of America 1999
by Woodholme House Publishers
First published in Great Britain 1999
by Constable and Company Limited
3 The Lanchesters, 162 Fulham Palace Road
London W6 9ER
Copyright © Leo Bretholz and Michael Olesker 1999
ISBN 0 09 479960 1
The right of Leo Bretholz and Michael Olesker to be identified
as authors of this work has been asserted by them in accordance with
the Copyright, Designs and Patents Act 1988
Printed in Great Britain by
St Edmundsbury Press Ltd
Bury St Edmunds, Suffolk

A CIP catalogue record for this book
is available from the British Library

For my wife Flo; my children Myron, Denise, and Edie; and my grandchildren Andrea, Samantha, Michael, and David. Dedicated to the memory of my mother, my sisters, and all those in my family who were not able to escape the upheaval.

To Selma Olesker and Jacob Gitomer, and to the memory of Anna Gitomer and Lionel Olesker.

The city limits of Vienna, marked with a sign stating, "Jews not desired," 1938
(Kurier Abteilung Bildarchiv, courtesy USHMM Photo Archives).

Despise not any man and carp not at anything; for there is not a man who has not his hour, and there is not a thing that has not its place.

Sayings of the Fathers
Ch. 4, v. 3

Our only hope will lie in the frail web of understanding of one person for the pain of another.

John Dos Passos
December, 1940

Contents

Foreword

by Michael Olesker

One overcast winter day, Leo Bretholz met me for lunch and handed me his death notice. Leo was still among the living, but there was his name, listed among those condemned to ride the German freight transport No. 42 from the holding camp at Drancy, France, to the concentration camp in Oswiecim, Poland, called Auschwitz.

The Germans were painstaking in their record-keeping, but not always accurate. One thousand Jews left Drancy on the raw morning of November 6, 1942. Seven hundred seventy-three were gassed on arrival at Auschwitz or died *en route*. Another one hundred and forty-five men and eighty-two women were selected for forced labor, of whom four men survived. These are the Germans' own numbers.

Leo Bretholz is listed as a non-survivor. He reached across our lunch table on that winter day and handed me a book, *Le Mémorial de la Déportation Des Juifs de France*, published in 1978. It chronicles the murderous arithmetic of the Holocaust that originated at the railroad station at Drancy. There was Leo's name, and his date of birth, and his birthplace of Vienna. He was listed between one Marthe Breitenfeld, formerly of Bienfeld, Germany, and Abram Bronoff, formerly of Novogoriek,

Russia. But two things were wrong: Leo's last name was misspelled as "Breholz" and he was not dead.

"It was," he said in his soft voice, "the day that I was to die. And also, the day on which I was reborn."

Leo Bretholz is a diminutive white-haired man who spent more than six years of his youth running from the Nazis' destruction of the Jews. He escaped, and escaped again, but was arrested in 1942 in Switzerland and transported back to France, where the choreography of annihilation had already begun. In 1940, the Nazis merely wanted to dump German Jews into France. But Marshal Philippe Pétain's Vichy government, controlled by Germany and eager to show compliance, went further. They registered all French Jews and marked their wartime ration cards with *"Juif,"* thus making them easy targets. They enacted laws excluding them from various professions. And then they detained foreign Jews in camps that were the beginning of the end.

Leo lived in Vienna in March, 1938, when Hitler entered the city and found a quarter of a million people rapturously cheering him. The *Anschluss*, the takeover of Hitler's native Austria by the Third Reich, quickly ensued. So did the rule of the mob.

By the fall of that year, Leo's mother insisted that her only son take flight. A bloodlust was in the air. Before the war would end, little Austria would supply nearly half of the staff of all Nazi concentration camps and death camps. Little Austria would supply four-fifths of the entourage of Adolf Eichmann, who was in charge of transporting Jews to the death camps. Little Austria would send sixty-five thousand Jews to their deaths in the camps.

Leo would survive by a series of audacious escapes. He survived one chilly night by swimming fully clothed across the River Sauer out of Germany, and six years later survived when he passed out on a street in Limoges, France, but awoke in the protection of a nun. He escaped the French camp at St. Cyprien by crawling under barbed wire. He crossed the Alps on feet so frozen and bloody that his skin could not be separated from his socks, and reached the Swiss border where he imagined he would find freedom but did not. He hid in an attic in the Pyrénées Mountains with gendarmes at the door and, in the holding camp at Rivesaltes, hid in a ceiling crawlspace with guards below him. And one morning he climbed onto a freight train bound for Auschwitz where he was supposed to die, but he disappeared by leaping blindly into the dark French countryside. Arrested by French gendarmes, he escaped once more. He was sent to prison and beaten by brutal guards. He escaped from a train with armed officers watching. He joined the French Resistance. He was in France when liberation arrived.

From March, 1942, to July, 1944—a time of capitulation and cooperation by French authorities—more than seventy-five thousand Jews were deported from France as part of the German "final solution." Of that total, only about twenty-five hundred Jews survived. Of those who died, two thousand were children under six years old, six thousand were under thirteen, and nine thousand were over sixty. The oldest was a ninety-five-year-old woman. The youngest were children a few days old. Trains that might have transported German soldiers instead took Jews to camps. They altered their own war effort in order to carry out systematic slaughter.

To have survived this is both a gift and an obligation. Leo Bretholz arrived in America in 1947, built a family in Baltimore, and kept silent about the war for the next fourteen years. He was haunted by the past and wanted to move on. He belongs to a traumatized generation who found themselves alive at war's end, but hadn't yet discovered the grammar of their pain. Now, as time takes its inevitable toll, they wish to have their final say.

"Forgetting, or not speaking," Leo said over lunch that day, "means that we've been silenced, which is what Hitler wanted."

Thirty years after the war, I was a newspaper columnist when I met a man named Alexander Bernfes, a survivor of the Warsaw Ghetto massacre who arrived in Baltimore with movies. The Germans had taken mountains of them, conscientiously documenting the day-by-day destruction inside the ghetto, and Bernfes had pieced them together. But the film had never been seen in America. A small group of us watched the old footage and saw children with rifles at their backs, and old men with their beards set afire by laughing German soldiers. A little girl put her arm around her younger brother, whose face was reduced to the outlines of his skull. Dead bodies littered the streets, and were casually flung onto carts. People leaped from burning buildings, and defended themselves with kitchen knives against German tanks and bombs.

How could it be that we in safe America were only dimly aware of such inhumanity, thirty years after the war? A year later, I sat in a federal courtroom in Baltimore where the government attempted to deport a man named Karlis Detlavs, accused of brutalizing and killing Latvian Jews for the Germans. On the witness stand sat a man named Abraham Libchim, a resident of Israel, who said he'd seen Detlavs shoot people in cold blood in the streets of Latvia.

"And when the shooting began," Libchim said, "they started to run and scream...people began to fall. The younger people could run faster and were able to escape. The older ones mostly could not."

He looked at Detlavs and said he'd had a pistol in his hand, "and he shot. More than once. He was pointing at people in front...I saw where he shot, and where he shot, people fell."

Cross-examined by Detlavs' lawyer, Libchim was asked, "How old was the man you saw shooting people?"

"In his thirties or so," said Libchim. "Over thirty."

"How tall was he?"

"Middle height. And broad."

"How tall was he, in centimeters?"

"What do you think, I stood there and measured him?" Libchim asked plaintively. "In anticipation of going to Israel and then coming to America many years later to testify? What do you think, I had time to stand there and measure him?"

"What color were his eyes?" Detlavs' attorney persisted. "Were you close enough to observe?"

"What do you think I did, examine him?" Libchim shot back again. History was finally ready to hear him, and he was being ridiculed in a court of law. "Do you think I thought I would remain alive and come thirty years later to America?"

I wobbled out of the courtroom, imagining his exasperation and rage. How many were like Libchim, finally learning to speak openly only to find the story of their salvation being challenged? It was 1977, and time was starting to get away from us.

I met Leo that year. He ran a bookstore in downtown Baltimore. Infinitely gentle and polite and courtly, he said nothing about the war. We talked about books, about politics.

Then one Sunday I went to a ceremony at the Baltimore Holocaust Memorial, and Leo was there. The memorial had the feel of an outdoor holy place. We stood near the back of a crowd of several hundred people, and Leo quietly removed a yellow Jewish star from his shirt pocket. He'd worn it while behind barbed wire at Drancy.

Over the next twenty years, he patched in little pieces of his story to me. He showed me things he had saved during the war: identity papers, notebooks, calendars, jailhouse scribblings, old letters and photographs, all of them the fragments of a story waiting to be written.

The message of the Holocaust keeps coming back. More than half a century ago came the "final solution" for the Jews; today the phrase in various parts of the world is "ethnic cleansing." Fifty-six years ago, Leo Bretholz sought safety in allegedly neutral Switzerland, but found guards who sent him back to Vichy-France; today, the bankers take their own hard look at Switzerland's war record and see a nation that cashed in on people's desperation. During the war, Jews attempted to change their identity merely to go on living; now, Madeleine Albright becomes the United States Secretary of State and discovers her family's Jewish roots and its history in the Nazi camps.

More than half a century after the war's end, we're learning not to forget those who died. But the act of survival should also be remembered, and honored.

Acknowledgements

There was much encouragement by friends and relatives for me to write my memoirs. It bespeaks many concerns—a period of my life which bears remembering, retelling, and reminiscing. It is based on profound reflection and introspection, and it needs to be told if for no other reason than to learn a lesson from it.

It is offered as a message to those who are willing and eager to apply eternal vigilance, lest our freedoms be lost.

Hopefully, readers will be able to feel the pulse and heartbeat of that period of time when I lived life one day at a time; when the word "tomorrow" took on the meaning of uncertainty, at best, or a hope for survival at most; when at the end of the day I was alive, with only the hope that the next day would not be worse.

My special thanks to Michael Olesker, who instilled me with the impetus to write my story; to my wife Flo, who stood by me steadfastly and unstintingly; and to my daughter Edie for her diligent assistance.

L.B.

Introduction

All these years later, such secrets we discover.

On the winter morning Max Bretholz was buried, and took his life-time of various secrets with him, the family came to our tiny apartment to comfort my mother. Only, in my family, it was not enough to comfort. Grand drama was called for, such outbursts from the relatives who were amateur actors in the Yiddish theater, and who seemed to be playing to some unseen audience. Nearly seven decades later, this is the memory that stays with me most vividly.

That, and unheard words whispered into various ears but not mine.

It was February of 1930, eight years before Hitler's arrival in Vienna, so I was not quite nine years old. My Uncle David Fischmann, the *shvitzer*, the man who sweated the way others took a breath, leaned down to say a word to me.

"Your father," he started to say, but the rest of his message was drowned out by my Aunt Mina, carrying on like a scene from one of her theatrical plays.

"My brother!" she cried. "My brother!"

"Your father," Uncle David started to tell me again. He needed someone to talk to, because no one else in the family wanted to listen to him. "Your father..."

On his hospital deathbed the last time I saw him, Max Bretholz had a face like yellowed parchment, like the very Dead Sea scrolls themselves. He was thirty-nine and had bleeding ulcers. He made his living sitting at his sewing machine in our little kitchen in Vienna, crouched over his work deep into the evenings. Nearly six feet tall, he towered over my mother, who was practically a foot shorter. In their wedding photo, they were almost the same height. He was sitting, and she was standing.

"He has to learn modern Hebrew," he told my mother the last time I saw him.

He meant for the journey to Palestine that he assumed we would take one day. He was not a religious man, and he never took me to synagogue, but he saw the only safe Jewish future, even in 1930 before Hitler, was to reach the land of Israel. So he decreed, "Learn modern Hebrew." In this final visit with him, I imagined he was making small talk and not issuing some edict to be carried out after he was gone.

His voice had faded. I remember him in his last year bent in pain from

Wedding photograph of Dora and Max Bretholz, Vienna, 1920.

the ulcers. He lived on bland food. I remember him smoking cigarettes, and sending me out of the apartment to buy more for him. And I remember him in the coffeehouse where he played dominoes and cards after his work at the sewing machine. Like his sister Mina, he was an actor in the Jewish Dramatic Arts League.

"My brother," Aunt Mina sobbed again on his burial day.

Her husband, my Uncle Sam Goldstein, tried to calm her. Such hysteria was a little unbecoming. It left no space for the widow of the deceased, my mother, to let go of her own emotions. Uncle Sam was a man of reason and firm religious convictions and dignified strength. He first embraced me on the day he married Aunt Mina. He embraced me again, when the conflict arrived, when I escaped from the authorities. He would keep his head in calamitous circumstances, but on this day, on the day of his brother-in-law's funeral, as he tried to pacify Aunt Mina, Uncle Sam got nowhere at all.

"My brother!" Aunt Mina cried again.

I watched the others gathered that day in a circle of solicitousness around my mother. "Papa's gone," she said to my younger sisters, who understood death even less than I. A good man, the uncles and aunts solemnly declared. And then there was the whispering again, and my mother wondered how she would care for her children. With so little money, and so little education, people would take advantage of her. And, out of the weeping voices, there came traces of murmurs, the telling of adult secrets, obscured as Uncle David tried to talk to me about my father.

I remembered my father in the gentlest and most unsettling times. In Vienna in the late 1920s, hungry musicians milled about the streets, men who had sat in orchestra pits and played background music for silent films in the city's theaters. When talking pictures arrived, they all lost their livelihoods. Some of them stood in the courtyard outside our apartment building and played music. Tenants leaned out of their windows and threw coins down to them. My father said this was undignified. He went outside and said to a violin player, "I don't want to throw coins. Give my son lessons and I'll pay you." I took violin lessons until my father's death.

Once, on a Sunday morning streetcar ride to my Grandmother Sara's apartment, I knelt on the seat next to my father so I could see through a window. On the other side of the aisle, a man looked up from his newspaper and said, "Tell that Jew kid to sit down."

A few passengers looked our way but said nothing. Calmly, my father said, "Sit down." He waited for the man to reach his stop, and then the two of us followed him off of the streetcar by the Danube Canal.

"This is not Grandma's stop," I said.

"We are getting off," my father said. "Don't worry, come on."

My father walked with long strides. In his right hand, he carried a cane, and in his left hand he held my hand. We quickly caught up with the man, and as he reached the street crossing, my father lifted his cane and struck him vigorously on each shoulder. The man turned and saw my father, risen now from his streetcar seat, and from his little sewing machine, and from his scorned religion. He fled across the street.

"That was for the Jew kid!" my father hollered after him.

When we reached my grandmother's apartment, my father told her the story.

"How did he know you are Jews?" my grandmother asked.

The two of them laughed, but there was anxiety behind it. My grandmother was a seamstress and a great maker of gefilte fish and latkes and chicken soup. One day she went to market, and a couple of boys yelled after her, "Sara, Sara, Sara."

"How did they know my name?" she asked later.

She didn't yet understand. In scripture, Sara married Abraham, father of our faith. "Sara" became a name thrown sneeringly at Jewish women in Vienna, a name which would so enmesh itself in the culture that, by the time of the Nazi takeover, all Jewish women would have to add "Sara" to their given names as a mark of official identification. And now, on the day of her son's burial, my Grandmother Sara sat in our little apartment and wept copiously. Death, I did not yet understand; my grandmother's tears, I understood.

"It will be all right," said my Aunt Rosa, her daughter. Aunt Rosa, divorced, lived with Grandma Sara. On this day, she assured her that things would be all right, and then she commenced with her own terrible wailing. Aunt Rosa was my godmother. She was a milliner by trade, a lover of opera, a player of gin rummy. She had a sweet voice and loved to sing for company. She enjoyed hearing scary stories, but she was frightened of the dark.

Aunt Rosa would die in the dark at Auschwitz.

Grandma Sara would die at Auschwitz.

Aunt Toba, who was also Grandma Sara's daughter, would die at Auschwitz.

It will be all right, said Aunt Rosa to Grandma Sara.

In my ear, Uncle David told me the same thing. It will be all right. He should talk to somebody else, I thought. Uncle Moritz was nearby, but Uncle Moritz didn't talk to Uncle David. Uncle Leon was nearby, but Uncle Leon wouldn't talk to Uncle David. Nobody liked to talk to Uncle David.

Once, Uncle David said to my mother, "Dora, why don't you go to Leon and borrow money for me?" So she did. And when Uncle David didn't pay Uncle Leon back for months and months, Uncle Leon went to my mother and said, "Dora, why don't you ask David for my money back?" So she did.

This was my mother. She was a dear, valiant woman of soft heart and strong will. Born in Czestochowa, a small city in Poland, she was one of ten children born to Orthodox parents. She had several years of schooling, and then left to help run the family's food store, and spent the rest of her life feeling a little insecure about her lack of learning. She married Max Bretholz in 1920. Later she took in embroidery and made button holes for bridal shops. Many trousseaus passed through her fingers. All day, she sat at the kitchen table, singing Polish folk songs and operettas, humming when she forgot the words and whistling when the spirit moved her. She had dark curly hair and deep-set eyes, and she wept miserably that morning as the uncles and the aunts gathered to console her.

There was Uncle Leon Fischmann, a man of elegance in three-piece suits and Homburg hats, a successful sales representative, a man of intelligence and wit. Uncle Leon married a gentile woman who converted and became more Jewish than Uncle Leon, everybody said, but they divorced not long before the German intrusion into Austria.

On the morning of my father's funeral, no one yet imagined such a future. Uncle Leon fled to Paris, and later fled to Vichy-France, where police arrested him. He was sent to the internment camp at Gurs, where he lost his mind, believing his family blamed the war on him. He wrote a letter to the German authorities from his hospital room, asking them to please come for him. They did. They took him to the concentration camp at Buchenwald.

Such slender divisions between life and death arrived for all of us in the coming years. On my father's burial day, my mother talked about her sister, my Aunt Erna, the pretty seamstress who spent the war years hiding with friends in Paris. I found her there in my running, but by then her husband, my Uncle David Szerer, a French soldier who was captured and escaped, had already been recaptured and deported to Auschwitz, where he died.

Leo's uncle, Leon Fischmann, 1936.

There were Uncle Isidore and Aunt Charlotte Bretholz. Their apartment by the Mariahilferstrasse was near the German motorcade on the day Hitler entered Vienna eight years after Max Bretholz's death. I was there that day, a seventeen-year-old boy who saw my elders as strong, self-assured adults. But that day I saw them cringe in their room, with my cousins Anne and Judith.

Uncle Isidore was not a man who cringed. He managed a successful ladies' knitwear shop. He wore spats and carried a walking stick and took confident command of his world. Aunt Charlotte was a zaftig, joyous woman, a designer of leather goods who turned a simple declarative sentence into the sound of laughter. But Uncle Isidore quickly lost his job after Hitler came to Vienna. Aunt Charlotte then took in sewing work during the day. At night, she visited the homes of dying people and sat with them until daybreak, and then one day all of this stopped when Uncle Isidore announced that they must try to escape.

The way I had escaped.

"You go," said Aunt Charlotte. "I'll stay."

She remained behind with my cousin Judith, born with a hole in her heart and too frail to run. Aunt Charlotte hoped the two of them could come later. Uncle Isidore would try to cross the German border with my cousin Anne, who was fourteen. She wore six dresses under her coat to avoid incriminating suitcases, but police stopped them. Uncle Isidore spent a month in jail for trying to leave the country with no visa. A few nights after he returned home, word reached their apartment that the Gestapo was rounding up Jewish men. Uncle Isidore's name was on the list.

"You have to hide," said Aunt Charlotte.

"I'm not going to hide," said Uncle Isidore.

He packed a little suitcase, and he sat down in one of his immaculate suits, and he waited to be taken. The Gestapo arrived that night and sent Uncle Isidore to Buchenwald, where he wrote letters home urging everyone not to worry, that things would be all right.

Aunt Charlotte and Anne and Judith tried to take comfort. They had a live-in maid. In the weeks after Hitler's arrival, the maid began openly seeing a German SS officer. One day she announced to Aunt Charlotte, "This is my apartment now," and she and her SS officer took it over.

Then the family broke apart. Cousin Anne reached Palestine through a Jewish youth group, and survived the war there. Uncle Isidore went

7

from Buchenwald to Auschwitz, where he died. Aunt Charlotte, who turned simple sentences into laughter, died there, too, and so did cousin Judith with the hole in her heart.

And I ran.

On the morning of my father's funeral, I watched my family and understood almost nothing that was coming. My father was gone, but I was absorbed mostly by the reaction of the women, by the wailing of Aunt Mina and Grandma Sara and some of the others. Trying to comfort me, my Uncle Moritz sat me on his lap. He was a handsome, athletic, robust man who took regular steam baths and seemed to have an eternal tan. He kissed my cheek. His wife, my mother's sister Karola, stood over us and stroked my hair. I would come to their house for Sabbath dinner, she said. She would bake cookies for me. She was short with reddish-blonde hair and gold-capped teeth. She and Uncle Moritz were deported from France and disappeared.

They had three daughters: my cousins Helen, Martha, and Sonja. Helen, who wanted to be an actress, was a keeper of secrets. She kept them until I was seventy years old and she told me the things whispered on the day of my father's funeral. Martha was a political activist, whom the Germans tried to arrest in the pre-dawn hours on the morning after Hitler's arrival, when they ransacked Uncle Moritz's store and took him away. And Sonja was the one everyone said looked like my twin. Sonja was deported from France with her month-old daughter, Nicole, and they went to Auschwitz to be killed. Sonja's husband Poldi went to Auschwitz, too, where he clung to life until the war's end and witnessed the murder of my cousin Kurt.

In my family, there was also another cousin Sonja—Sonja Fischmann—who returned to Vienna after the German surrender. Sonja Fischmann was my Uncle Leon's daughter. When Uncle Leon was losing his mind at Gurs, cousin Sonja went to Birkenau and to Auschwitz and then kept silent. She said there were no words left to say about her life in the war, but there were.

8

Leo, his sister Ditta, cousin Sonja Topor, and his other sister Henny, 1935.

At Birkenau, there was no light and no water. There were no toilets. Sonja thought she had entered an insane asylum. There were worn-down skeletons who did not resemble human beings. At Auschwitz, a guard kicked her all the way across camp to the office where her arm was tattooed. On a dunghill, she found a rusty container that she used as a dish. At night, the rats crawled over her. When she went to get her portion of soup and a piece of bread, she was beaten and told she had already gotten her portion. She fell into a ditch and landed atop corpses thrown there the night before. She worked in a medical office where men and women were given treatments that made them violently nauseous. No one yet knew what was happening, that they had been sterilized.

"What can I contribute to the story that hasn't been said?" Sonja asked me one day on the telephone from Vienna to America. The two of us were grown old now. My father had been gone for sixty-seven years, and the war was fifty-two years behind us. "How does my little story make a difference?"

"Every story is a piece of the puzzle," I said.

Sonja is the last piece of the puzzle I knew about my mother. She was the last one in my family who saw my mother alive.

Leo's cousin Helen Topor, an aspiring actress, 1936.

"Leo, be careful of the water."

I heard my mother warning me about the Danube. I remembered when we picnicked along the Danube Canal—all of us, my mother and father, and my sisters Henny and Ditta. We spread a blanket along the grassy banks, spread food across the blanket, and I headed off toward the water to swim.

"Leo, be careful of the water."

I heard my mother's voice again, referring to the River Sauer in Germany, when there was no longer a choice about my going in because I was forced to abandon the city of my birth and the family I loved.

Sonja Fischmann, 1938.

We lived in the twentieth district of Vienna, known as Brigittenau, a

10

working class area that was perhaps forty percent Jewish in a city about ten percent Jewish. Years earlier, Hitler himself had lived in Brigittenau. My sisters and I attended elementary school near our apartment. I remember a sense of formality and respect, with one exception: when we were taught about religion, the Jews were openly referred to as "Christ killers." It was the way things were done, a routine part of the public school culture which was a routine part of the nation's culture.

I remember a week when there was no school. It was in February, 1934, and the Social-Democrat government was attacked by the Christian-Social Party of Engelbert Dollfuss. Reds and Blacks, the parties were called. There was fighting in the streets, thousands of underground militia members against government forces and army units. For days, there was no gas or electricity. Streetcars stopped in their tracks all over the city. The Christian-Social Blacks attacked the government housing projects, claiming its residents were socialist Reds. Dollfuss eliminated his opponents and established a dictatorship. Austria's Nazi party remained underground, but rumblings persisted until the assassination of Dollfuss, who was replaced by Kurt von Schuschnigg—who capitulated to Hitler.

At night, in all of this political fighting and confusion of 1934, people used candles for light. As I studied for my bar mitzvah, I took my Torah lessons by candlelight.

I was bar mitzvahed at the Klucky Temple in March, 1934, several weeks after the February political uprisings. I was blessed by my rabbi, Dr. Benjamin Murmelstein, who placed his hands on my head and invoked the memory of my late father.

"He would have been proud today..."

I began to cry. My mother, sitting nearby, said, "Leo, it will be all right."

Some days, my mother took my sisters and me to the nearby Hannover Market, with its outdoor stalls of fruits and vegetables and meat. There, she bought ingredients for the soups and dumplings and

11

goulash and gefilte fish she prepared at home. My Uncle David had a stall there—Fischmann's Fish Fry—where he, *shvitzing* profusely, would cry out, "Best fish fry, fish cooked on the premises!"

Uncle David and his son Kurt would sleep across from me at the holding camp at St. Cyprien, and then Cousin Kurt would die at Auschwitz.

Not far from the mar-
ket, my Uncle Moritz had a
clothing store where the
Nazis came for him. Uncle
Moritz always handed me a
few coins. For a little candy,
he would say. In the years
after my father's death,
Uncle Moritz increasingly
took me under his wing.
On Saturdays, I helped at
his clothing store. On

The day of Leo's bar mitzvah, March, 1934.
L-R: Henny, Uncle Sam, Aunt Mina, Ditta, Leo,
and Leo's mother Dora.

Sundays, he took me to soccer matches. On Friday nights, he and Aunt Karola invited me to Sabbath dinners at their apartment.

"Why don't you ever come with me?" I asked my mother.

"Aunt Karola and I don't talk," my mother would say. "You know this."

Aunt Olga and Uncle David Fischmann,
Vienna, 1920.

"Why not?"

"Why not?" she mimicked me. "So? Nobody at all talks to Uncle David."

Only I had to listen to him. He sat by me on the day of my father's burial. My mother sat with my sister Ditta on her lap. Ditta was twenty-one months old. My sister Henny, seven years old, stood nearby. Eight years later, I waved to Ditta for the last time as she stood at her hospital window, without knowing what would happen to her. Then I waved to my mother and my sister Henny as I climbed aboard a streetcar to begin my running, without knowing what would happen to them.

My cousin Sonja Fischmann saw them for the last time. In our old age, Sonja says there is nothing left to say about the war. She lives in a

Leo age 9, Henny age 7.

Vienna where the citizens now call themselves "victims." Hitler's "first victims," they have long since titled themselves, hoping to keep their secret from the rest of the world. I hear this title, and I remember standing on the Mariahilferstrasse with the German army arriving, and flowers of welcome were thrown by these joyous victimized Austrians. And on that same afternoon Austria's poor victimized soldiers happily donned German uniforms, and a day later humiliated and bloodied Jews stumbled through the streets and my Uncle Moritz was taken away past applauding, victimized Austrian citizens.

Instead of being bloodied in Austria, I ran. While I ran, my mother in Vienna was trapped. My cousin Sonja Fischmann was the last to see her, when it was 1942, when the deportations to the camps had already been running for some time, when my mother walked along a cold Vienna street with a Jewish star on her coat. Sonja said she gave my mother a package that day. Some clothing, some bedding. She said my

Ditta (Edith) in 1931.

13

mother was afraid to carry it because the large package might cover up her Jewish star and she and my sisters would be arrested for attempting to hide such a star. Sonja said she tried to see my mother one last time, but there were barricades and she wasn't allowed near my mother's apartment in the Jewish ghetto.

Such imagery haunts me in a dream that has visited me through the years. There are barriers in the street, controlled by the Nazis, and I want to go to my mother in our old apartment. They are tearing down the building. A wall comes down, and then another. As the last wall collapses, there is my mother, who has been living there in secret.

All these years, such secrets we keep.

Family and friends. L-R: (standing) Franz Novotny, Marie Novotny, Leon Fischmann, Max Bretholz; (seated) Karola Topor, Moritz Topor, Dora Bretholz (pregnant with Leo); (bottom row) Martha Topor, Sonja Topor, Lisl (maid), Helen Topor, Chaya Fischmann, Vienna, 1920.

14

On that February morning in 1930, my family gathered to comfort my mother and her children. I can still hear the shrieks of my Aunt Mina, who wept for my father, and maybe for all of the ruinous years to come. The uncles and the aunts gathered in little circles, and whispered to each other, and I tried to hear their words over my Uncle David's chatter.

It will be all right, I heard them say. It will be all right.

But they were keeping such secrets.

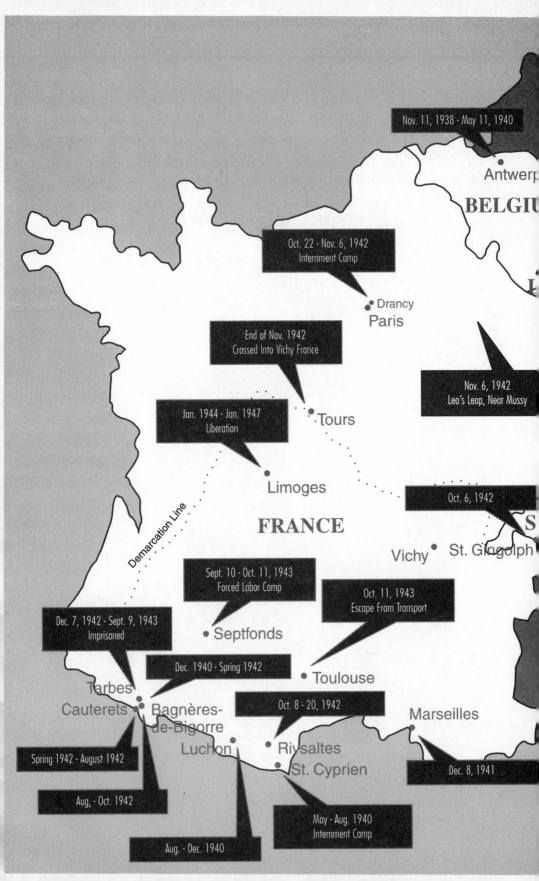

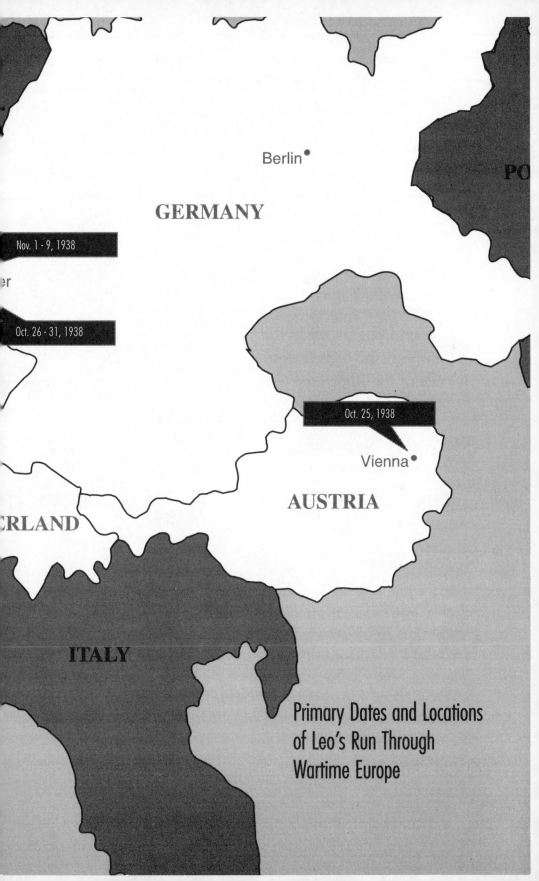

1

March – October 1938

 saw Adolf Hitler with my own eyes from a distance of perhaps twenty yards. I could have leaped on him and hit him with all my strength, or stabbed him with a kitchen knife if I had one, or strangled the life out of him, except we were separated by rows of cheering, rapturous people who would have torn my heart out before I could get near him.

It was March 16, 1938. Four days earlier, the German army entered Austria, and Austria ceased to exist. The world cringed for a moment, and then went about its own business, which it still imagined was separate from ours.

I took the streetcar that day to the apartment building where Uncle Isidore and Aunt Charlotte lived with my cousins Anne and Judith in their last hours of innocence, before Hitler, and before a place called Auschwitz where all of them but Anne would go to die.

The sidewalks outside their building were covered with celebrants dressed in suits and waving Nazi flags. The atmosphere felt like some grand civic carnival, with intimidating expressions of superiority. My uncle and aunt lived by the Mariahilferstrasse, the major business artery over which Hitler's motorcade would travel that day. But no one in my family was watching this, even from a distance.

When I reached their apartment, they were nervously huddled in a back room with neighbors. The sight shook me. Their neighbors' apartment directly overlooked the Mariahilferstrasse, but they'd been removed from it in order for Vienna to welcome Hitler more jubilantly. All Jews had been ordered away from windows overlooking the motorcade, and sympathetic gentiles of Vienna were thrust into the homes of these Jews. The gentiles stood at the windows waving Nazi flags that had been handed to them. The Jews like my uncle's neighbors were shoved into the apartments of other Jews, with their fear and outrage running hand in hand.

Uncle Isidore was trying to assure everyone that all would be well. My ebullient Aunt Charlotte was silent and stunned. My cousins, looking to their parents for reassurance, seemed confused at so much sudden commotion.

"Leo!" my uncle cried.

Uncle Isidore was a man who carefully choreographed his every move, who took two hours each day to dress himself impeccably. But now he was reaching for shreds of his customary calm, because the sanctity of his home had been violated and he had lost his sense of authority.

It was this way all along the Mariahilferstrasse, an endless river of swastikas and posters and banners flapping in the afternoon air. It was as if newsreels seen in cinemas over the past months had suddenly been transplanted to Vienna and painted vivid colors.

We had watched evening fade into darkness five days earlier with the Austrian red–white–red flags flying, and awoke on March 12 with all of them gone. I went to a Jewish youth group meeting that Friday evening, the 11th, where we talked about emigrating to Palestine. Modern Hebrew, my father had declared in his dying hours. We danced the horah and sang Hebrew songs. At about nine o'clock, I walked home with my friends Arnold Jussem and Robert Hochmann. They were strong, confident fellows. Arnold was a track and field man; Robert was an amateur boxer. But there was something intimidating in the night air, too many police moving quickly about, and I was rattled by my strong friends' worried looks. When I reached home, my mother was standing by the front door with a stricken look on her face.

"Where were you?" she asked.

"With my friends."

"Don't you know what is going on?" she asked. She'd been listening to the end of our world coming over the radio. "Come," she said, dragging me into the house. "Come."

The red-white-red Austrian flags were all gone the next morning. They were replaced by swastikas hanging aloft, and the German army goose-stepping through the streets. We were suitably intimidated; they seemed almost automated in their precision. Now, with the arrival of the *Anschluss,* Austrian police and soldiers took off their uniforms and put on German uniforms. Austria's army instantly disappeared; Germany's instantly swelled. Austrian Brownshirts, who had assassinated Dollfuss in 1934 and who had operated surreptitiously under Chancellor von Schuschnigg, now triumphantly strutted about with confident sneers on their faces and swastika armbands on their jackets.

"It will be all right," my mother said in the safety of our apartment.

"Yes," I said, wishing to give her the comfort she was trying to give me, and failing as she failed.

Von Schuschnigg had been broken a month earlier, in a humiliating meeting at Berchtesgaden at which Hitler had raged and fumed, telling von Schuschnigg that he would do as he pleased, and take his army where he pleased, and that von Schuschnigg was powerless to stop him. Safely back in Vienna, the Chancellor took to the radio airwaves as people gathered in homes all over Austria to listen to him.

"Austrians," he declared, "the time for decision has come."

He called for a March 13 plebiscite to decide whether Austria wanted to remain independent or become a part of Germany. An honest vote never occurred. By the time German troops began pouring across the border, von Schuschnigg was on the radio again, urging citizens not to resist the inevitable, that blood should not be spilled in a cause that was already lost.

"May God protect Austria," he declared in a heavy voice. But it was too late for such words to have meaning; besides, many Austrians had already ceased listening.

On March 12, when German troops began arriving, Nazis all over Austria were mobilized. They crammed into the halls of the Chancellery and took over offices in Vienna. Von Schuschnigg, understanding the tides of history, yielded power without a fight. That night, Heinrich Himmler arrived in Vienna to secure control of the secret police. Other SS officers were flown in, and arrests followed that totaled many thousands in Vienna alone. Among the first was von Schuschnigg, who was sent to Dachau.

"So I'll go outside," I said rather flippantly to my uncle and aunt on the day of the grand motorcade. "I want to see this Hitler."

"It's not safe out there," my aunt said.

But I went outside. I was seventeen, what did I know? I saw some shops with letters hand-painted across their doors: *Jude, verrecke!* Jew croak! But this was nothing new. "Christ killers," they called us in the religion classes of the public schools. After that, what were words scrawled on a door?

I stood in front of Beck's Shoes, in a crowd six or seven deep stretching as far as I could see. Church bells tolled. Voices boomed out orchestrated choruses of *"Sieg heil!"* The cries came from chests newly swollen with bravado. Tears of joy slipped down the scrubbed, beefy faces of loyal Germans of Vienna.

I sensed such longing for authority and power in the crowd, which would translate into acts of sadism within hours. But, standing on the sidewalk beneath my uncle's apartment, I felt more curiosity than fear. There were too many people here, too many of my own countrymen, to turn on one little Jew.

We still assumed that Hitler wouldn't last. He would go away if we simply minded our own business. We felt we knew him. We saw him as a type of lunatic bully, but also as one of Austria's own, an upstart born here, who had later nurtured his hatred here. But surely, he would be swallowed up in some act of modern civility that we imagined Europe still possessed.

As Hitler's motorcade approached, I had no sense of witnessing history. But I was surely watching splendid theater: the tolling church bells, the sporadic sound of martial music reverberating just below them, flowers tossing about. And then, as the crowd's roars reached a crescendo, Hitler appeared.

He stood in the back of an open Mercedes. He wore a brown uniform and lifted his right arm from the elbow until it reached the side of his cheek. Trumpets blared. The crowd roared and roared. Drums pounded. So much excitement for one man, so much belief in one idea, which was the eradication of people like me. But why? I had just turned seventeen. In my naiveté, I wondered: Had the Jews done something truly terrible, something that had been kept from me?

Hitler's car, traveling at perhaps fifteen miles per hour, headed toward the Hofburg, the erstwhile imperial residence in Vienna. I couldn't see the sky for all of the banners waving above my head. The crowd thrust its arms into the air and roared again, *"Heil Hitler!"* in precisely the manner they'd seen crowds behave in the movie theater newsreels. *"Ein Volk, ein Reich, ein Führer!"* they shouted en masse.

"First Victims" they will call themselves when the world loses its memory.

Hitler looked ahead at all times. His face was theatrically stern, his posture rigid, a man on a heroic mission, a figure out of grand opera too caught up in his crusade to openly notice the masses of humanity adoring him. But I saw his eyes darting from side to side, taking in some of the faces, trying to gauge the crowd's passion. He was human, and therefore uncertain: Could he get away with each new invasive move? Were

23

these Austrians embracing him wildly enough? In an instant he was gone, and already he had his exhilarating answer.

I went back upstairs to Uncle Isidore's apartment. His neighbors were leaving, shaken, and my uncle and aunt nervously attempted to make light of the intrusion, to say that it was over. Aunt Charlotte had her voice back, but its normal lilt was gone. This alone distressed me. My uncle and aunt wished not to appear upset in front of their little girls, but they wanted me to get back on the streetcar now and go carefully home to my mother. It was not a good time for Jews to be on the street.

On my way home, I saw words painted on the city's cobblestone avenues and its sidewalks, a slogan urging that Austria remain Austrian, that the anticipated nationwide plebiscite, now vanished, would affirm our independence from Germany. *"Rot-Weiss-Rot, Bis in den Tod,"* the words said.

Red–white–red.

Until dead.

The groundwork for the Holocaust was laid the day after Hitler's arrival. People who had imagined themselves part of Vienna's rich cosmopolitan tapestry found themselves, overnight, cast as pariahs. German stormtroopers went to Aunt Karola and Uncle Moritz's apartment, looking for my cousin Martha. She was twenty-five years old, tiny, an intellectual, and politically fervent. She believed that communism was Europe's salvation. The stormtroopers came for her at six o'clock in the morning, but Martha had outsmarted them. Sensing the dangers in the air, she was already gone, vanished. She left no note behind to serve as an explanation for sobbing Aunt Karola, or as a clue for the Nazis. She was the first in my family to disappear, one way or another.

So the stormtroopers left, and they went to Uncle Moritz's clothing store in the Hannovergasse. They knew Martha sometimes worked there as a bookkeeper, but she wasn't there. Uncle Moritz told the soldiers that he hadn't seen her. Where is she, they demanded. He said he didn't know. He was a strong, crewcut, athletic man not accustomed to being pushed

24

around. The Brownshirts shoved him aside, ransacked his store, and threw all of his merchandise into the street. When he protested, the Brownshirts took him away.

Uncle Moritz—who kissed my cheek on the day my father was buried—gone to Dachau on the morning of the second day of the *Anschluss*.

And cousin Martha—gone, too—ran all the way to Switzerland when there was still room for Jews there.

The Holocaust was still being invented on the morning after Hitler's arrival in Vienna. The Germans had not yet systematized the mechanics of genocide. Some Jews like cousin Martha could still slip through the cracks. In this same week, though, across Vienna, came the first roundups of Jewish men and women. Howling young people dragged university professors and doctors and lawyers into the street and forced them to the ground, along with women who had children at their sides. As the children looked on, their parents were handed toothbrushes and cold water and scrub brushes and ordered to wash the paint off the cobblestones. Red-white-red...until dead.

The deaths of the Jews would first arrive in little installments, in the debasement of those terrified people bullied into the streets while crowds taunted them. The white beards of rabbis were set afire and then doused with cold water thrown against their faces. Old people were forced to bend at the knee and shout *"Heil Hitler!"* in chorus.

I stood at the edge of one crowd, held back from interfering, yet knowing there was nothing I could do to stop the cruelty. I watched people on their hands and knees forced to scrub the street. They kept their eyes downcast in fear and humiliation. I glanced nervously about and wondered if some bullies might come for me. Those on their knees struggled for some sense of dignity; I watched them, because to turn away was to cease witnessing the overture to acts of murder.

But I felt all strength sapped from me. The world's rules of civility had been canceled, and I was terribly frightened and conflicted. To be singled

Hitler Youth and local residents look on as Jewish men and women are forced to get on their hands and knees and scrub the pavement, Vienna, 1938 (Yad Vashem Photo Archives, courtesy of USHMM Photo Archives).

out for our Jewishness made no sense, but we were being selected and punished at any random hour of the day for that simple fact alone. And yet, to see other Jews caught in the web, and to realize I myself had so far inexplicably escaped, was to suggest psychological deals to myself: Perhaps these victims were a different kind of a Jew; my kind of Jew, maybe they wouldn't come after. I must be a better kind of a Jew, a stronger Jew, a healthier and more productive Jew unlike these other Jews who were being punished. But such thinking was madness, a momentary safety valve for my fears. Ultimately, they would be coming for us all.

Slipping through the city's streets in the dark, I heard cries of small groups of people burst spontaneously with a raw joy that sent chills into my bones: "Germany awake! Jews perish!"

New atrocities happened in unpredictable outbursts across Vienna. Men were taken from hospitals, some of them fresh from surgery, and sent to Dachau. Some of our neighbors were arrested and never reappeared. We heard of ashes being sent to families. My friend Robert Hochmann had an uncle and a cousin whose ashes were delivered to their homes. Their families had to sign for the packages. Your husband was ill, the families were told. Your husband committed suicide, the story went. Your son was a prisoner and he tried to escape, others were told. Here were his ashen remains. And the families never knew for certain whose remains they really were.

As spring slipped into summer, we tried talking to non-Jewish neighbors, people we had known for many years. We had visited each other's homes, we'd helped them trim their Christmas trees. Never mind political explanations, we were searching for simple comfort, for words of solace. There were none.

Something had been stripped away to reveal an essential core of Austrian Jew-hatred wider than we had allowed ourselves to imagine. Our neighbors were simply too caught up in the moment, or too frightened, to offer comfort. They would not be seen conversing with us. Friendship with Jews was now a thing of the past. The organized cruelty in the streets eased off, but our sense of isolation deepened each day, and so did our fear of one day being cast into those streets.

Vienna was suffering from a housing shortage since the years of the great war. When the Germans entered Austria, they saw not only a shortage of about seventy thousand apartments, but an issue to be exploited. So they set up an Emigration Office in Vienna. Its chief officer was Adolf Eichmann, who forced Jewish leaders to assist him. Jews with money were ordered to finance the expulsion of Jews who had none. Soldiers descended on Jewish homes, forcing the evacuation of thirty-five thousand apartments. The Germans were doing whatever they pleased, and the bullied Jews who were forced from their homes had to find some new place to live, some relatives who would take them in. But now entire countries would be closing their doors. This being the case, something would have to be done to us within the confines of the German-occupied territories.

27

My mother talked urgently of my escaping Vienna. The very thought made me feel like a deserter. I was the man of the family. My father had beaten a man for calling me a name. *"That was for the Jew kid."* His son was now to take flight?

It was still possible to go on living in Vienna, and to walk through the streets each day, but the outbreaks of violence were unpredictable. People disappeared. In the months following Hitler's arrival, more than five hundred Jews, many of them elderly, frightened, and driven to despair, would take their own lives.

In our apartment one summer evening, I looked at my sister Henny. She was sixteen now. She was curly-haired, introspective, a lover of nature. She began to dream of emigration to Palestine. Modern Hebrew, my father had decreed eight years earlier. Across from Henny sat my sister Ditta, with her round face and curly brown hair. She was ten. She seemed bathed in her innocence: a chatterbox oblivious to politics who loved animals and possessed boundless enthusiasm for life.

She was a baby when my father died. When she was five, the Jewish Community Family Service arranged for her to live at an orphanage during the week. After my father's death, we were considered half-orphans, and Ditta's stay at the home helped my mother through difficult financial times. The orphanage was located in Doebling, on the other side of the Danube Canal. On Friday afternoons, my mother and Henny and I would pick up Ditta to come home for the weekend. Sometimes I went by myself, and Ditta and I would stop for ice cream.

"Vanilla," she would order with great enthusiasm.

"Lemon and raspberry," I would say. It pleased me to make her so happy so easily.

On Sunday evenings, we walked her back to the orphanage. It was a kind of mini-outing, going into the lovely area of Doebling with its elegant old buildings.

You must get away, my mother said as we sat at our little dinner table. I said this was impossible. But look at the Hochmanns, she said, with the

28

ashes arriving in the mail. Look at this neighbor bullied by Brownshirts, think of those people on their knees in the street. Maybe a knock will come on our door one night. Her arguments were ceaseless, and I began to feel the ground shifting beneath me.

Only days before Hitler's arrival, I had played soccer with friends. Now when they saw me, they spit at me and cried, *"Saujud!"* Jew-pig! I had left high school a year earlier to attend a trade school for apprentice electricians. On the first day of class, the instructor asked each student our name, and the name of the master electricians for whom we would work.

"Abraham Weinsaft," I responded.

The class erupted in laughter. Weinsaft was a Jewish name. The class's ridicule seemed instinctive, almost Pavlovian. I reddened in embarrassment and felt isolated. I waited for the teacher to admonish the class, but no words came from his mouth.

In the streets, I heard rhymes cried out by young people at their former friends who were Jewish: *"Jud, Jud, spuck in Hut; Sag der Mama das ist gut."* Jew, Jew, spit in your hat; Tell your mama it was good. Groups of Jewish children heard "Here comes the Jew-School" from the lips of other youngsters. And there were signs on lampposts and walls and kiosks: *"Juden nach Palästina."* Jews to Palestine.

The Nazis quickly instituted new rules for us, restrictions on shopping hours, places that were now off-limits to us. Where we were allowed, the supplies were minimal. New logistics had to be figured out: When was the best time of day to find necessities? When was the best time to avoid bullies in the street?

Park benches now carried stenciled warnings: No Dogs, No Jews. Movie theaters bore signs: No Jews Allowed. Public baths: Not for Jews. Restaurants: Jews Not Desired. We were now officially sanctioned lepers.

In elementary school the year my father died, I had a kindly third grade teacher, Robert Kadensky. He would pace the classroom absentmindedly, but then stop at my desk to tap gently on the top of my head. He smiled, exposing stained teeth. He knew about my father, and had come to our apartment one night to offer condolences to my mother. He had a son, Robert Jr., who was a year or two older than I. I'd gone to their apartment, and we'd played together.

But now, in the aftermath of Hitler's arrival, I saw the younger Kadensky in the street. He wore the brown uniform of the Hitler Youth. Good morning, Robert, I said. He stared straight ahead, not deigning even to acknowledge me. He was now a German, and I was still a Jew.

A few days later I saw his father on the Wallensteinstrasse. We shook hands, and I mentioned only that I had seen his son. My old teacher nodded wearily.

"Leo," he said, "don't be angry. Robert is young and foolhardy."

I sighed, and felt I'd been embraced. I remembered that, some years earlier, my teacher had worn in his lapel a three-arrow pin, the symbol of the Austrian Socialist Party.

"Herr Kadensky," I said, "my mother says that I must get away from Vienna. She is fearful for me. What do you think?"

"Deine Mutter hat Recht," he said softly. Your mother is right.

Each day, I made my way cautiously to my electrician's apprenticeship, steering my bicycle with one hand and carrying a ladder on my left shoulder between two rungs. Weinsaft was an excellent teacher. I learned quickly how to connect wires together without turning off the current. But I made mistakes, and sometimes found myself burned by 220-volt shocks.

"How are you doing?" my mother would ask me in the evenings.

"Oh, wonderful," I would laugh. "I can already make a short circuit."

One day Weinsaft and I installed wiring in a four-story building on the Währingerstrasse. It was several weeks after Hitler's motorcade, and Passover was approaching.

"I can't work on Pesach," I informed Weinsaft.

30

"We will work," he informed me right back. "When you're in Palestine, you won't have to work on Pesach."

April 20 was Hitler's birthday. "What do you say, we take that day off?" I asked Weinsaft.

"It's not our holiday," he said.

"When I'm in Palestine, should I celebrate it then?"

But we did take off on Hitler's birthday. The owners of the building were gentiles, and we didn't want to create controversy when the rest of the country would be celebrating. In barely a month, Hitler had become a figure of civic divinity.

The mood among Jews grew darker. A neighbor's son, Alfred Schochet, owned a motorcycle and was required to turn it in to authorities. He'd often taken me on a spin on it as a kid, but Jews were suddenly forbidden to own them. Schochet disappeared and was never seen again. Meanwhile, Uncle Moritz was languishing at Dachau, and his family was frantic.

"Have you heard from Aunt Karola?" I asked my mother.

But my mother never heard anything from Aunt Karola, her sister.

I tried to avoid crowds. Who knew when they might turn on you? I sensed which streets were dangerous, and knew which ones were forbidden. My mother, terrified I would leave the apartment one day and not return, pleaded with me, "Leo, don't go. You don't need it. Stay put."

I knew she was right, but I was young and still had some sense of invulnerability. Maybe I could outrun the bullies. In the streets now, they wore swastika armbands and greeted each other reflexively: *"Heil Hitler"* and *"Sieg heil,"* arms raised in the fascist salute. People gathered to listen to speeches that blared out of loudspeakers.

Every raised arm, every yell, every expression of this Nazi presence jangled my nerves. But in these adolescent days I was hungry to spend my energy, to have some sense of normalcy in my life. One day in late summer I rode my bike to The Prater, a recreational area where my friends and I could kick a soccer ball around.

31

"Don't go there," my mother cried. "What do you need this for?"

But this was the language of our entire lives now: Don't go here, don't do that. So half a dozen of us rode to the park, leaned our bikes against some nearby trees, and were kicking a ball when some hoodlums appeared—Brownshirts, fellows bigger than us and outnumbering us. They slammed our bikes to the ground. They stomped on them and broke the headlights and the spokes. They pulled out the seats and made them impossible to ride. Again, we had been made impotent.

Miserably, we made our way home with our bikes slung over our shoulders. But the hooligans reappeared and began to chase us. *"Jud! Jud!"* It was impossible to run and carry the bikes. We dropped them and ran off, and heard the taunts and laughter of the bullies. They didn't want to chase us, any more than a master wants to chase a dog. They were the new masters, and we were merely Jews. They wore belts that said, "Blood and Honor." We ran home and sought solace with our mothers.

Most of the time, the Brownshirts merely walked with disdain and an air of superiority. They'd been instructed to act like young gentlemen, fitting representatives of the new Germany. But they sang songs as they strutted about:

"When the blood of Jews spurts from the knife..."

"Hang the Jews, put the priests against the wall..."

"We are marching today until everything crumbles / For today Germany belongs to us / And tomorrow, the whole world..."

I returned home one afternoon, and my mother asked me about the mood in the streets.

"Mama," I said, "you're right, this is no longer a safe place for us."

The days were getting shorter now. Aunt Mina and Uncle Sam had managed to leave Vienna only weeks after the *Anschluss*. From Luxembourg, they exchanged a series of letters with my mother. She told them she wanted me to leave while I could. Let Leo come to us, they wrote back. I remembered Aunt Mina wailing on the day of my father's burial and imagined I could hear her cries all the way from Luxembourg now.

"It is only temporary," my mother assured me when I protested. "Leo, I'm afraid one day they'll come for you."

Inevitably, I wore down. Slowly, a plan began to emerge: I would slip out of Vienna before winter. I would leave on a Tuesday, because in Jewish folklore, Tuesday was good luck. I would take a streetcar, and then a train. I would deal with someone from the Ezra Committee. I would find a hiding place in the German town of Trier, which I could enter without a passport since Austria was now considered part of Germany. Then, under cover of darkness, with the chilly nights of November coming on, I would cross a river to safety.

"A river?" my mother wondered aloud when she heard this plan. She remembered the nervousness of picnics in calmer times. "Leo, be careful of the water."

"A shallow river," I told her. "What, I'm going to swim in such weather? It's not the Danube, you know, it's a little river. It's nothing, Mama."

Nothing...but a river. I would have to cross it, assuming I found shelter in Trier, assuming I was not pulled off the streets, assuming this Ezra Committee knew what it was doing.

The Ezra Committee was a Jewish aid organization trying to help refugees from Germany and Austria enter into Luxembourg. The landscape was now alive with such desperate people. Ezra could provide shelter and food, help to find documents to avoid arrest, help to move from one country to another without arrest and imprisonment. In other words, the Ezra people were smugglers, the type of underground organization beginning to crawl into life all over Europe.

We chose October 25, 1938, as my day of departure. I sensed I might not be returning home soon, so I visited my old friend Arnold Jussem. He lived around the corner in the Hannovergasse. I'd been with him the night before Hitler's arrival. I couldn't tell him my plans, because such things were forbidden. But I needed a sense of saying farewell.

"In a few days, I'll be leaving," I said. "What's new with Palestine?" He'd talked earnestly about going.

"I don't know anything yet," he said.

His widowed mother and younger sister stood nearby and listened. Mrs. Jussem was holding her chin, studying me. I felt her thinking, "Do what you have to do, Leo." She was another heartsick mother, worrying about what would become of her children. We said our goodbyes, pretending we might see each other again in some better time, but suspected we would not. Doors were beginning to close behind me.

As I walked home, I came across another fellow I knew from high school. He wore a white shirt and the ubiquitous Austrian lederhosen, the short pants with suspenders. As we passed each other, I nodded toward him.

"Wie geht's?" I said. "How are you?"

Without a word, he turned and spit in my face. Then he walked away hurriedly and faded into the night. I took a quick breath, and found myself crying. The Austria I had known—the civilized Old World Vienna of Schubert and Strauss, of Haydn and Beethoven, of Freud, Schnitzler, and Wittgenstein—this Vienna now gave us young men who spat in the faces of former classmates who dared say a simple hello. This was the Vienna now forcing me to desert the life I treasured.

On the evening of Friday, October 21, my sisters and my mother and I sat at our kitchen table for a final Sabbath dinner together. My mother had tears in her eyes. As she prepared to light the traditional Sabbath candles, she said, "This time, say the blessing together with me."

The lights of the candles flickered, and sadness consumed us. Normally, Friday evenings were warm and happy. My mother would tell us of her encounters during the day, of the happy brides whose dresses she was embroidering. My sister Ditta would tell us stories from her week at the orphanage. Now there was a silence, broken only when Henny said plaintively, "Why don't you say anything, Mama?"

"Do I have to explain?" my mother answered.

Two days earlier, we had gotten a letter from Luxembourg. Escape arrangements had been finalized. I looked at my mother and saw a woman aging before her time, and now I was adding to her burden. I thought of all the years of struggle since my father's death. My mother was the kindest of women. There was a painter around the corner from us, a Mr. Fried. When the apartment needed painting, she would call him. He was a terrible painter. Terrible, my mother agreed, but he had five children at home. So the newly painted room now had streaks on the walls. So the man left a mess behind him, but someone had looked after poor Mr. Fried and his family.

Now I wondered who would look after my mother. At forty-three, worn down by cares, her hair had turned gray and her eyes seemed ancient. I wanted to hear songs coming from her lips, the operettas she loved to hum. I wanted her to feel my father's embrace one last time. I wanted Uncle Moritz nearby, and Aunt Mina with her dramatics, and even Uncle David with his prodigious *shvitzing*. But that night there was only melancholia filling our little apartment, and the sense that a whole world was fading that had once seemed comfortable and safe.

On my last weekend at home, there was more trouble. My little sister Ditta was rushed by ambulance to the children's hospital in the Lazarettgasse. She had scarlet fever. She remained in the hospital for days, and when Tuesday afternoon came, and I was to leave Vienna, my mother and Henny and I went to see her. I had a sense of losing control, of too many loose ends in my life, of worrying about my family and feeling as if I were venturing into a vast, troubling, unknown world.

Ditta was my pet. She was not only my little sister, but the sweet-natured child who brought out every protective instinct in me.

"I can't go," I told my mother. "Not with Ditta like this."

"I'll take care of Ditta," said my mother, dismissing all debate.

My sister was quarantined in a ward for infectious patients. The ward was located on the mezzanine level of the hospital, with its windows facing a courtyard. We stood in a light rain and waited for her to come into view.

She looked frail. Her brown curly hair contrasted with her pale face. She looked tired. She held a small blackboard against the window, and showed us a piece of chalk in her other hand. This is the way we will communicate, she signaled. It felt like games we had played years earlier in our home.

From the courtyard, I looked up and signaled with my hands, "Tonight, I'll be leaving. I love you, Ditta."

Tears welled in my eyes, and I blinked so she wouldn't see them. I wanted to race through the hospital and hold her, and protect her against all of the world's endless troubles. But I stood there in the courtyard as she wrote something on the blackboard and held it against the window: *"Viel Glück, Leo,"* it said. "Good luck. Kisses for Aunt Mina. We'll be seeing each other soon."

I could see her eyes glistening, and I nodded my head lumpishly. She tried to look brave, and I felt like a cowardly deserter for leaving. Standing by the window, she looked like the last blameless angel on earth.

We stayed a few minutes longer, and then turned to leave the hospital grounds. Ditta waved her arm goodbye, and my mother and Henny and I cried as we walked through the rainy streets.

2

October – November 1938

When I reached home with my mother and Henny, we were emotionally spent. I was leaving in hours, but we had nothing left to say to each other. We had run out of all words. We were exhausted by our need to comfort each other, and our inability to do so. The whole family seemed to be breaking apart. No one had heard from my cousin Martha since she'd fled the stormtroopers after Hitler's arrival. Uncles and aunts talked of emigration, if only they could find openings in the blockades that seemed to be everywhere. And I was now sneaking away, with my little sister alone in a hospital ward.

My mother packed my things, while I stood dully nearby. Into a battered leather attaché case went toilet articles and some old photographs. Into a small valise went shirts and underwear and socks, and religious articles as well—a prayer book and tallis and tefillin, the leather-bound biblical scrolls worn by observant Jews during morning prayers.

We were not particularly observant Jews. We were deeply committed to our religion, but we weren't very observant of religious rituals. But this was about something else. It was my mother trying to keep a connection. She was reminding me, there are ancient things that bind us; don't forget who you are. Maybe it was superstition. Maybe she thought it would focus God's eyes on her son. It didn't occur to either of us that the articles might expose me as I went from Nazi-annexed Austria, through Germany itself, toward tiny Luxembourg.

Europe continued its spasms of self-destruction, and its relentless Jew-hate. Across Austria, Jews and half-Jews and those with Jewish relatives were dismissed from public posts. Jewish doctors and lawyers, honored professionals, were no longer allowed to practice. Jewish businesses were shut down and Aryanized. *"Entjudung,"* the Nazis called it. "De-Judaization." The German salute with the raised right hand was made compulsory in courts and other government offices, and was quickly finding its way into school rooms and other gathering places.

Within days after Hitler's arrival in Vienna, Adolf Eichmann shut down Jewish institutions and had Jewish leaders arrested. Those wishing to emigrate would lose their property and be left only with enough money to depart. But where could we go? And how could we seek papers when the mere asking was an admission of Jewishness, and to be a Jew was to be vulnerable. Then came a new regulation: Jews were forbidden to change their names, and were required to carry special identity cards. And there was one more: Jewish males had to add "Israel" to their names; females had to add "Sara."

"Sara, Sara, Sara," the schoolboys had taunted my grandmother in the marketplace.

For seven months, we huddled in our three-room, ground-floor apartment, wondering if the authorities would come for us. We ventured outside warily. On my final day, I looked through the apartment as though trying to commit its contents to memory, and looked for words to comfort my mother.

"Mama," I said, "don't worry. Everything will be all right."

She looked at me and smiled wanly. She said nothing. I was an immature seventeen-year-old boy trying to fool a care-worn woman with empty phrases. In a while, we put on our overcoats and walked to a nearby corner and waited for the No. 5 streetcar, which would take me to my grandmother's apartment in the Ottakring district. This would be goodbye to my mother. It was all too much for her now: the scene at the hospital, the menace in the city, the separation from her son. As I began my exodus from Austria, a trip across the city to the train station had become too much of a strain for her. It was too great a distance to carry so much sorrow.

Lights began to come on across Vienna. As my mother and Henny and I waited for my streetcar, I grew restless. I feared some kind of outburst from my mother, or words of my own misgivings that would embarrass me and make my mother feel even worse.

"Be very careful," she said as the streetcar came into view. A light mist hung in the air. I hugged my mother and Henny, and then I climbed aboard for the fifteen-minute streetcar ride to my grandmother's. "Take good care. Write as soon as possible."

I never saw my mother or my sisters again.

I was still a boy on my way to becoming a man. I'd had responsibility much of my life, but there always seemed to be understandable boundaries within which I felt secure. All those boundaries were now disappearing. I told myself this was the start of a fine adventure, a trip to Luxembourg to see an aunt and uncle. The separation was only for now.

There was more sadness when I reached my Grandmother Sara's apartment. Her daughter, my Aunt Rosa, was there, wringing her hands. Aunt Rosa, frightened of the dark, saw darkness descending all around us. A week earlier, she had taken me to the Vienna Opera House to see *La Traviata* as a parting gift, the two of us pretending there were still traces of culture in the world. My Uncle Isidore was also here. He looked nearly as distraught as the day of Hitler's arrival, when the strangers had forcibly entered Jewish apartments. My grandmother sat in a chair, immobilized, and wept openly.

I went to her and hugged her. She wept some more. It occurred to me, I was leaving a whole bunch of crying people behind me. Whatever visions I had of my family joining me in safety at some imagined hour in the distant future, I knew it was too late for my grandmother. She was too old, and this was to be our last time together, and even this could only last for a moment.

She was a treasure to me. When my father was alive, we'd visited her every Sunday. She made me feel loved. She was nearing seventy now, and the years had been difficult. As the mood in Vienna changed, she'd been taunted increasingly by young bullies looking for an easy mark. "Sara, Sara, Sara" had given way to harsher cries. And now she was losing her grandson, and it was clearly too much for her.

"Calm down," Aunt Rosa said to her, gently stroking her hand, not yet knowing what the two of them would one day face at Auschwitz. "Don't make it harder on him."

"Come," Uncle Isidore said quickly. "You don't want to miss your train."

I leaned down to kiss my grandmother, old and defeated, who whispered my name one last time.

A taxi took us through the drizzly Vienna streets to the same West Station where Hitler had entered the city months earlier. The station seemed more cavernous than usual. Uncle Isidore, fastidious as ever, was upset he'd forgotten his umbrella. Always, he strove for dignity. He never imagined the indignities awaiting him at Buchenwald and death at Auschwitz.

I'd always found railroads seductive. Who knew what might exist in the great unexplored beyond? Now there were soldiers milling about, and uniformed police, any of whom might turn on us on a whim. My uncle handed me my tickets, shook my hand, and said, *"Bleib gesund."* Stay well.

That was all. There had been too many goodbyes today, and we'd used up our inventory of farewell language. We walked along a platform to the train, my uncle carrying my valise and my aunt holding tightly to my left arm, as though I might fall without her. Inside the train, I slipped my head through a lowered window and found Aunt Rosa and Uncle Isidore on the platform.

"Thanks for everything," I said. My heart was caught between excitement and dread, but I smiled to give them encouragement that I was fine. Then they could tell my mother I was happy, and we could all participate in the same useful fiction.

"Say hello to Mina," they said simultaneously.

As the train began to move, they both reached up to the window to touch my hands. Rosa was crying. They walked along beside the train for a few seconds, then kept eye contact with me for several more. My uncle waved one last time, then turned away. I was still at the window, waving and waving as long as I could see their fading figures in the distance, for they were the final vestige of the life I had previously lived. I stood there until Aunt Rosa faded into the very darkness that terrified her.

Through the twenty-hour train ride that followed, I watched the Austrian countryside fade into Germany's. Vienna's drizzle became a downpour as we headed northwest. I shared my compartment with two nuns who sat silently. Could I take comfort in them? Surely no Brownshirts, no soldiers, would violate the sanctity of their very presence. But unpredictable outbursts were infecting the country.

When Hitler had reached Vienna in March, the Austrian Archdiocese greeted him with official words of approval, with references to "great historic events," to the Nazis' efforts to "ward off the peril of all-destructive godless Bolshevism." Within months, though, the official praise was muffled. Catholic schools were closed and church property began to be confiscated. At a service at St. Stephens Cathedral in Vienna, Cardinal Innitzer told thousands of young people, "Do not let yourselves be misled in any way." At St. Stephens Square, thousands of young people shouted, "We thank our bishop. We want our bishop." The chant became a kind of mockery, an echo of slogans previously reserved for Hitler.

The next evening, a Hitler Youth gang stormed the archbishop's residence. They smashed windows and destroyed furniture. On the oppo-

41

site side of the square, a curate was thrown out of a window. Police and fire marshals somehow did not arrive for an hour.

A few days later, Austrian officials derided "the clerics who dabble in politics, who try to stir up the public against the state." Then they went further. They blamed the Jews. They blamed the Czechs. The church fathers learned to hold their tongues.

Already, Czechoslovakia's Sudetendland had been swallowed by Hitler. On the last two days of September, in Munich, the leaders of Germany, France, Italy, and Britain met to decide the Czech future. No Czech voice was there. Hitler said this would be the last land he would need. Neville Chamberlain of Britain, in a vain attempt to keep his nation out of war, agreed to the bloodless takeover. "Peace in our time," he called it. Like Austria months earlier, Czechoslovakia would cease to exist. On March 15, 1939, Hitler dissolved the country, making Bohemia and Moravia a protectorate. Slovakia became a separate, collaborating country.

Across eastern Europe, a rope was tightening. As Czechoslovakia fell, Hungary shuddered. Thousands of Jews fled Poland, only to be sent back as immigration laws stiffened. The time had clearly come to flee. But how?

In my little compartment on the train, I looked at the nuns but said nothing. Even holy women were strangers, and all strangers were to be suspected. Were they Catholics who were infuriated over the Nazis' taking control of the schools, or had they been bullied into submission? The silence so far was overpowering.

In a few hours, lulled by the sound of the raindrops, rocked by the movement of the train, I fell asleep. I awoke as we pulled into the Frankfurt station. The nuns were leaving, and their exit made me anxious. We were still hours from daylight, still hundreds of miles from Trier, Germany. I pulled some notes from my pants pocket. They explained what I was to do when I left the train. I studied the words, as though preparing for some test to be given later when I might not be able to consult my instructions again.

I was to walk to the small office of the Trier Jewish Council to meet someone from Ezra. Ezra translates as "help." At this office, they would help me find safe haven for a few days while I awaited word from a Mr. Becker, who would try to lead me into Luxembourg.

I thought about Ditta, so small and so alone at the hospital. I thought about my mother and Henny, standing in the mist by the streetcar as I left. To my loved ones, goodbye and goodbye and goodbye. A madness had descended on the entire continent, and no one knew where to find sanctuary. Only a week earlier, Field Marshal Hermann Göring announced, "If the need arises, we will have to establish ghettos in the big cities." For the first time, he talked of Jewish work brigades. So what was I doing, heading out of newly annexed Germany into the old Germany, the very heart of the madness, and would I be able to slip out without papers?

Trier was not what I expected. When I walked out of the train station the following afternoon, the small city seemed quite peaceful. Vienna, by comparison, seemed a maelstrom, its citizens in a constant state of emotional arousal, as though convincing themselves that they were good Aryans, that they were true believers. The newness was still thrilling to them. But Germans had been living with Hitler for several years now, and their ardor was cooler. How can you keep any populace in a state of constant frenzy? In Trier, fewer soldiers walked the streets. No one seemed to strut. The city wasn't swarming with self-consciously overbearing people. I looked up and saw flower boxes in all of the windows. It felt like an oasis of grace.

Only the weather was threatening. Skies darkened, and it rained as I reached the Jewish Council. It was a small, time-worn office. Trier's Jewish population, never very large, had already dwindled to a few thousand.

"My name is Leo Bretholz," I said, introducing myself to a middle-aged man in the office.

"I thought so," he said. "How was your trip?"

I felt comforted that he'd expected me. I was just a young fellow on the run. The office had a couple of desks, a typewriter, a file cabinet. Our meeting was brief and businesslike, and left me a little edgy.

I was told where to go for a few days for room and board—No. 13 in the Peter Friedhofen Strasse. The number thirteen was bad luck, and so was the name Friedhof. In German, "Friedhof" means cemetery. Number thirteen at the cemetery; I kept my misgivings to myself.

"You do not have to give your full name," he said. "Just 'Leo.'"

"And who will be there?" I asked, pretending to be calm.

"Sie sind die barmherzigen Brüder," he smiled.

"Brüder?" I replied, quite astonished.

"Good luck," he said.

I would be depending on Franciscan friars in their monastery. Samaritan padres, he said. Good people, good gentiles. "We know each other very well," he added assuringly.

I found their stucco building behind a black fence on a cobblestone street, opened a creaky gate, and rang a bell. A door opened and a monk, clad in a brown robe, smiled and welcomed me. Brother Johannes, he said. As he closed the door behind me, I wondered: Am I safe in here? Outside was the persecution of the Jews; inside was the very heart of Christianity, which had learned to hold its tongue while Hitler moved from one outrage to another.

The monastery smelled of wax and incense. There were a few oil paintings of religious figures, but the general sense was austerity and a cleanliness I'd never experienced. We walked through a long, tiled foyer, up one flight of stairs, into a room with six or eight cots with white sheets showing at the top.

I tried to calm myself. Trust no one, my mother had warned me, not even nuns on a train. The world is full of dangers. I was to stay here until further instructions, but I had no idea when they might arrive.

"You must not be uneasy," Brother Johannes smiled at me.

As I lay on my bed before dinner, I saw friars in the halls. Some muttered prayers as they walked; others tended to chores. They kept to themselves. It was tacitly understood that I was not here to talk with them, but simply to wait until further notice.

That evening, there was a simple grace before dinner. I bowed my head but said nothing. We ate soup and vegetables, milk, a piece of bread. It tasted like manna from heaven. There was no conversation, and everyone quietly rose from the table after eating. It rained through the night, the drops sounding like music against a window pane near my bed, and I slept deeply until morning.

The rain continued into the next day. This was no good. The River Sauer was said to be shallow, possible to walk across with water below waist level in normal times. But now its banks might be swelling; it might need a few days to calm itself, or there could be difficulty. Did I dare wait extra days?

I wanted to go outside and buy a postcard to send to my mother. I felt comfortable, remembering the previous day's calm. As I walked out, I said hello to Brother Johannes, who opened the front door and greeted a visitor.

My heart stopped for a beat. Entering the monastery was a German soldier. I averted my eyes. He seemed nineteen or twenty, a few years older than I. I tried to seem preoccupied. He nodded hello. As Brother Johannes welcomed him, I walked outside to the rain-slicked streets, heart thumping, hoping the soldier would be gone when I returned.

I found a souvenir shop and bought a picture postcard. Trier seemed charming, a cathedral city that was a vestige of the Roman Empire, nestled in the Moselle Valley with scores of vineyards and wineries. Its streets were cobblestone. In Vienna, such cobblestones had been scrubbed by humiliated Jews. The rain continued to fall and fall.

I wrote a brief note home: "Everything went well. I am safe. Waiting to meet...," but I didn't mention Becker by name. As I mailed the card, I pictured my mother's relief when it reached her.

But my own relief vanished when I returned to the monastery. The German soldier was no longer standing at the front door, he was lying in the bed next to mine, shoes off, looking quite comfortable. He was now my roommate. I squelched an urge to run. I glanced beneath the bed and saw my valise hadn't been moved, nor its small lock disturbed. Take the tefillin, my mother had urged, take the tallis. If either were discovered, my true identity would be revealed.

But the soldier looked relaxed and benign, and the monks were so reassuring. Calm yourself, I thought. Why would they come here for one little Jew?

"I am Heinz," the soldier said, propping himself on his elbow and turning toward me. His face was scarred by acne. His accent seemed of south German provenance.

"I am Leo," I said, "and I am from Vienna."

We slipped past any questions of surnames. He said he'd come here to look up friends of his family. He had blond hair and a pointed chin. He was on leave from an army engineer work detail, and asked if I wanted to walk through the city with him. Splendid, I thought. Who would come after me, walking in the company of a German soldier?

"You are quite far from Vienna," he said.

As we walked through Trier's rainy streets, I remembered my mother's words about caution. I reached for a white lie wrapped in a half-truth.

"I have an aunt in Luxembourg who invited me to stay with her," I said. "I'm waiting for my uncle to come pick me up. He's coming here on business on Saturday or Sunday."

Heinz seemed to be a decent fellow. We walked to a local bookstore and found it packed with volumes about the Nazi regime and empty of almost everything else.

"Anything of interest here?" Heinz asked.

I shrugged, not wishing a discussion of Nazism, and we walked back to the monastery. Young schoolgirls who saw his uniform giggled flirtatiously; Heinz seemed barely to notice. At dinner, we sat next to each other. Again, there was silence as the monks dined. In the evening, Heinz and I lay on our cots, and when he fell asleep before me, he worried me. He muttered aloud in his sleep. His words were indecipherable, but I wondered about myself. What if I were to talk in my sleep? What if I said something revealing? Heinz seemed like a kindred soul, but who could imagine his reaction to a Jew?

In the morning there was mail for me downstairs: the anxiously anticipated postcard from Luxembourg. My hour was arriving.

"Leo," it said, "see you Monday evening, 9:30, in front of the monastery. No suitcase, please. Becker."

Becker: my guide to freedom, two days hence.

It was another rainy day. Becker's note was explicit: Bring no suitcase. It meant the river was too deep. The rains had been torrential, and a suitcase might make the crossing impossible. I would bring only my attaché case.

When Heinz returned that afternoon, I pondered asking him for help. He'd been to see a dentist and had a tooth filled. If he'd gone to the army dentist, he said cheerfully, he'd have simply pulled the tooth. The army had no inclination for the slightest subtleties: If there was a problem, get rid of it. He chuckled at such stupidity. The two of us laughed together. In the evening, as we lay on our cots and talked easily, I decided to trust him.

"I'm being picked up on Monday," I said, "so tomorrow will be my last night here. Might I ask you a favor?" I'd thought about asking Brother Johannes, but couldn't jeopardize this institution, which had

47

sheltered me in a time of need. "Could you possibly mail my suitcase to me?" I asked. "I'll give you postage for it."

I made up an explanation about my uncle driving a small car, about it being filled with belongings. I handed him a ten-mark bank note, more than enough for postage. Heinz was staying in Trier another two weeks, so I would simply send him my address.

On Saturday, the rain eased slightly. I still hoped to cross the river at waist level. Heinz and I walked through the city to an open-air market and lunched at a local tavern. We felt comfortable with each other. By the time we returned to the monastery, the rain was quite heavy again. I went to sleep that night and dreamed about swimming a river to another, safer place.

"Leo, be careful of the water."

My eyes opened to find another rainy day. Heinz was already up, and I heard water running in the bathroom at the far end of the dormitory. While he washed, I reached into my suitcase, took out my tallis and tefillin, and placed them in my attaché case. But I hesitated. If the River Sauer was too high, the religious items could be ruined. But, if I left them behind, might Heinz open the suitcase and send the authorities to find me?

Leave them behind, I told myself. Trust this young fellow. These German soldiers pride themselves on a sense of honor. But my mother had implored me to hold on to the tallis and tefillin, so I did, and only left the small prayer book behind, which was still incriminating enough if Heinz found it.

The day dragged on forever. My stomach felt raw. Would this Becker show up, would the rain ever stop, would the river be calm enough to cross? I checked my attaché case, and then again. I looked at Aunt Mina's instructions, and then again, and then destroyed them, as I'd been told to do. And then I remembered: Bring money for Becker, fifty marks in coins. The instructions had been specific about coins, because paper money could be damaged while crossing the river. I was to pay him once I had crossed the river and reached safety.

But I'd forgotten to get coins, and now it was too late. The banks were all closed. Well, too bad. By the time I would pay him, he could complain and it wouldn't matter. And anyway, I would put the money in my vest pocket, and surely it would stay dry so high up on my body.

"Take care of yourself, Leo," Heinz said when we parted. He took my valise, and I slipped out the front door.

In the darkness, I saw Becker waiting across the street. The rain had finally stopped. He drove a Peugeot with no back seat. Becker had removed it so I could lie down, after crossing the Sauer, for the drive into Luxembourg City.

"Your Aunt Mina is waiting on the other side," he said. His simple reference to her relaxed me as he drove through the streets of Trier.

"Do you swim?" he asked.

"Yes," I said. "Will it be necessary?" On this final night of October, I was dressed for the chilly night air.

"Perhaps not, but possibly yes," he said. He was cheerful and wore a cap with a visor pulled across his forehead. He told me to take off my socks when we reached the river and put them in my pockets, to keep them dry for the other side.

"Good, I'll do it," I said.

"Just be careful, don't get lost, go in the right direction."

He said he would drop me at the German border post. I would go through a brief inspection there, and questions would be asked. What kind of questions? Never mind. Answer briefly, and avoid details that might lead to further questions. Then I would get back in his car for a short drive to the river. He would drive himself through customs there. Since he was a Luxembourg resident, he would have no trouble; however, I had no visa, which meant nothing but trouble. I would be arrested for attempting to sneak into the country, and Becker would be charged with smuggling. The German customs officers had been bribed, but not the Luxembourg officers. Hence, my entrance into Luxembourg would have to come by the River Sauer.

"They know me," Becker said. He meant the German officers. "And they know what this is about. Don't be afraid."

But I was. He said to go straight across the river, and look for a sandbar in the middle if I needed to pause, and then go the rest of the way.

"There is a road alongside the Sauer," he said. "I'll be driving slowly, back and forth, blinking my headlights. When you come out of the water, lie in the ravine until I pass by. Then come out of the ravine when you see me coming back. Is that clear?"

I nodded, and felt my heart racing. We reached the border an hour before midnight. The air was chilly, and I felt myself shiver from something beyond the temperature. It was a moonless night with a cloudy sky. It was October 31—"All Saints Eve." Perhaps, I thought, the border police would display an appropriate saintly spirit.

"Break a leg," Becker said. My heart was thumping, and he was feeling puckish. He stopped his car as we reached the customs post, said good evening to the officers there, and then waited for me. The guards seemed smug and vaguely superior.

"Was tut dein Vater?" one of them asked. What does your father do?

"My father is dead. He was a tailor."

"Yes, that's what they all say, a tailor or a cobbler," one officer replied. Was I being challenged? I looked up and saw a photograph of Hitler. My body trembled. What about the arrangements that we'd made? I attempted to make myself look reasonable and harmless. The guards scarcely looked at me.

In a moment or two they waved me off disdainfully, and I made my way back to Becker. As we approached the side of the river, and I got out of the car carrying my attaché case, I could hear the water's thunderous roar.

"Don't forget to take off your socks," Becker said.

50

As he drove off, I walked down a slope to a soggy embankment. The Sauer seemed to be bellowing at me. It sounded horribly swollen. Normally calm and narrow, the week's rain had expanded its width to more than a hundred feet across, and its onrushing current carried large branches and various debris swiftly past me.

I wore a blue gabardine raincoat over a suit with knickers, and wondered nervously if my clothes would weigh me down too much once they got wet. My hands shook as I removed my socks and put them in my pocket. I put my shoes back on and felt my arms shaking against my sides. In the darkness it was impossible to judge the water's depth. I walked to the Sauer's edge with my entire body trembling.

I took one step into the water, holding my attaché case over my head, still figuring I might walk across. God, look after me. God, I am holding your holy items. I took my second step, but there was no bottom for my feet.

"Leo, be careful of the water."

The terribly cold River Sauer swirled around me, rushed through me, took my breath away. I started to swim and found myself carried by the current. I threw my attaché case slightly ahead of me with my right arm, held onto it, and then threw my left arm awkwardly forward. I wondered where Becker's sandbar might be, for I was already out of breath. I saw the attaché case bobbing in the water. My tefillin and my tallis would be soaked. God, are you watching me? I felt the weight of my overcoat and my shoes and struggled to keep my head above water. The Sauer spilled into my mouth. I gasped for air and tried to keep my head above water. The current pushed me down-river, but its strength also carried me across. Where was that sandbar of Becker's? My mother, I thought, should never see me in such a predicament.

Although it seemed like an eternity, the trip across took only a few minutes. Exhausted, I pushed against the muddy bank and struggled to my feet. I stepped out of the water drenched and sloshing in my shoes, pulling at the clothes stuck to my body but thrilled that I had made it.

51

I crouched in a dark ravine, too overwrought from my swim to feel the night's chill, and caught my breath. The soaked attaché case leaned against my knees, but I was too nervous to open it and check the condition of the tallis and tefillin. In a few minutes, Becker's blinking headlights signaled "all's clear."

"In the back," Becker said. I lay down and felt I'd found freedom. "The money," he added quickly. "You have the fifty marks?"

"Yes," I said sheepishly, "but not in coins. So sorry."

He was visibly unhappy. The money was soaked, and I hadn't followed instructions. Such a person wasn't to be trusted. He took the notes and put them between two pages of a newspaper on his front seat. I took off my topcoat. We drove for about fifteen minutes, as the River Sauer dripped from my clothing and formed a puddle in his car.

"If I knew you didn't have coins," Becker said, "I wouldn't have picked you up."

His tone was light, he was joking with me.

"Then you would have had to deal with my Aunt Mina," I said. "She's a pretty formidable woman." Aunt Mina had emotions out of grand opera. Becker nodded as though he understood.

"She's waiting for you down the road," Becker said. She was sitting in a little roadside tavern near the town of Echternach. Uncle Sam had stayed home. When I walked in, shivering in my wet clothes and trying to look as casual as I could under such ridiculous circumstances, she saw me and cried, "Leo, Leo!" Then she threw her arms around me and didn't let go as we lurched back to Becker's car for the drive to her apartment in Luxembourg City.

"So wet," she said, turning from her front seat next to Becker to look me over.

"Yes," I said, sitting in the back and happily pulling something out of my pocket. "Even my socks are wet."

I held them up and laughed aloud. Becker glanced back and held aloft the paper money I had given him. He held it between two delicate fingers, and laughed his own mordant laugh, and laid the money across the dashboard to dry. The very sound of our laughter made me feel safer than I had felt since Hitler's arrival in Vienna seven months earlier.

3

November 1938

Becker drove slowly into Luxembourg City, watching carefully for police patrols along the way. A cruiser passed us going the opposite way, and the officer and Becker waved to each other. I felt embraced by a man who seemed to have far-reaching connections across the entire continent, and imagined my life was now safe. Only a few hours ago, Becker had been a stranger. Only an hour ago, I'd been standing on the German side of a swollen river, about to plunge in. Now I was happily heading to Aunt Mina's apartment.

Aunt Mina, short and plump and always overly theatrical, had joined a Yiddish drama club as a young woman, but gave it up when she married Sam Goldstein and confined her acting to everyday life. Uncle Sam was handsome and educated, and made a steady living in the fur business. Now he was patiently waiting for us at their apartment. I could imagine him thinking: Let Mina go, let her have the stage, later I'll see Leo when it's calmer.

Sitting in the back of Becker's car, I remembered Aunt Mina's wedding to Uncle Sam. My mother made gefilte fish for the party, the best gefilte fish west of the Volga River, everyone declared. Henny held Aunt Mina's long wedding train. I was six years old then. Max Bretholz was still alive then. Sitting at his sewing machine, my father made a special outfit for me, since I was the ring bearer. A beautiful outfit, everyone said. This father of yours, they all declared, he's the best tailor west of the Volga River. Such a talented family, everyone agreed. Such beauty, and such gefilte fish and such tailoring, everyone declared, lifting their glasses happily. But now my father was gone nine years, and his son was running for his life and leaving loved ones behind. I wondered if my father was with me on this night, and wondered whether his benevolent spirit had helped me across the River Sauer.

I shifted uncomfortably in the back of the car, clammy and cold but feeling the tension lifting from my muscles. My aunt turned repeatedly to look at me. She beamed. She had done something not only to help me, but to honor her late brother's memory. It was a mitzvah! Though normally the most talkative of women, and given to the grandest hyperbole, she seemed overwhelmed by my arrival and didn't utter a syllable.

Wedding photograph of
Mina and Sam Goldstein, 1927.

"*Gut gemacht,*" Becker said when we arrived at Aunt Mina's apartment. "Good luck. Go upstairs, dry yourself, drink hot tea. Mina, it was a long day. Be proud of your nephew."

He hugged her, and her eyes filled up. He sounded like a member of the family. I'd known Becker only a few hours, but he'd saved my life. He disappeared as Aunt Mina and I turned and walked away.

Her apartment was located on the second floor above a bistro. A narrow door to the right of the café's entrance opened into a small, poorly lit vestibule behind which I saw a door slightly ajar. Uncle Sam opened it wide and burst through.

He rushed to me with arms outstretched from his stocky body. "Thank God, thank God," he cried. He hugged me for a moment. "Thank God, thank God," he said again. He was the calm one in the family. Then we hugged some more, and my uncle stepped back and looked at me.

"You're pretty wet, Leo."

I shrugged my shoulders. The river, I explained. The water was a little high.

It was well after midnight. I looked around and saw a modest flat, furnished plainly. No one was expecting to stay here forever. We were becoming a whole race of people on the run. There was a bedroom, a sitting room, a kitchen, and a small bathroom. I would sleep on a sofa. When I started to talk, Uncle Sam stopped me.

"First," he said, "out of this swim wear."

I took off my knickers and jacket, which had left a blue stain around my neck. My uncle handed me some of his dry underwear and pajamas; too large, but functional. My own clothing went into the bathroom to dry. My aunt sat in a chair and watched all of this, and I felt enveloped by their concern. This was now home.

Aunt Mina opened my attaché case and surveyed the damage. Everything was soaked, and she spread things

Leo's link with the past: photographs of Henny and Dora that were damaged during Leo's swim across the River Sauer.

on the kitchen table to dry. I looked at the photographs, the link with my quickly retreating past, that my mother packed. Some were stuck together and had to be separated delicately. I spread my socks and shoes over a radiator and felt its warmth run through me.

I felt I had re-entered a womb—part familial, part religious. My tallis was laid out to dry, though Uncle Sam said my tefillin had been badly damaged and, according to Jewish law, had been rendered impure. He would take them to a synagogue for ritual disposal. A synagogue, I thought. And the word did not have to be whispered.

They asked questions about the family and the mood in Vienna. The local papers were saying too little. What were the chances of the others slipping out? It was clear, they agreed, that my mother and my sisters could never escape the way I had. In my exhaustion, I sadly agreed, and in the early hours of the morning, Aunt Mina decreed it was time for all of us to sleep.

"We must be cautious," Uncle Sam warned, "because you're here illegally."

So were they. They were in Luxembourg on a temporary visa that had already expired. The trick was to avoid being stopped by police, so no one would know. The trick, also, was not to be linked with me, since I was here with no visa at all.

"And you'll write your mother an express letter in the morning," said Aunt Mina. I nodded. I drifted off to sleep, still feeling the strength of the River Sauer, still trying to keep my head above its onrushing current, wanting to send instant messages to my mother: I made it, I'm all right, sleep gently, Mama.

In the morning, there were new realities to face. I couldn't stay in this apartment for long because we were all here illegally. We mustn't endanger each other. But my aunt and uncle assured me that the Ezra Committee had contacted the Luxembourg government about refugee problems. Six months earlier, they had gotten their own temporary visas by showing proof of anticipated emigration to America. Luxembourg, they assured the authorities, was only a temporary stop, a matter of a few weeks. But six months was no longer considered "temporary," and

58

America was not spreading its welcoming arms so magnanimously. In a place called Baltimore, Maryland, my Aunt Sophie, who was Mina's sister, was trying to arrange visas for us all. So we waited.

By the time I woke, at 10:30 that morning, my aunt had pressed my wet clothes and hung them up, and prepared breakfast. All of my other clothes were still in Trier, in my suitcase with Heinz, waiting to be sent here.

"Isn't it something?" I said. "I'm having breakfast with my family today, and yesterday I had breakfast with monks at a monastery."

"This was Ezra's arrangement?"

"Of course. You didn't know?"

"The less talk, the better."

"And I roomed with a German soldier," I said.

"What, a German soldier?"

"Yes."

"Du bist doch meshugga," Aunt Mina cried. "You must be crazy. Don't you write this to Mama."

I told them I'd left my valise with the soldier, and they looked at each other worriedly. I was taking too many chances, the look said. After breakfast, I wrote a letter to my mother and said nothing about the German soldier. The three of us went for a walk, during which I was cautioned to stay half a block behind my aunt and uncle. Caution, they warned, always caution.

But I floated along with tremendous relief. I was alive on the other side of a river that had tried to swallow me whole. It felt safe in this Old World mini-state. Friendly Belgium and France were nearby, and the graceful Ardennes mountains were visible. Germany, too, was nearby, but that was behind me now. I sighed with relief each time I considered how far I'd come.

In the apartment that evening, we listened to Radio Luxembourg, which was known for its comprehensive news reports. I felt newly connected to the outside world. But the news was grim, and the radio reports only hinted at the depth of the troubles. Things were getting worse for the Jews in Poland. In Germany, the Nazis continued their "Aryanization" of Jewish property. In Vienna, there were still random outrages in the street. Would the bullies pick on my innocent sisters? We listened to classical music at evening's end, and then turned off the radio to sleep.

"In the morning," said Aunt Mina, "I have a doctor's appointment. You'll get breakfast downstairs at the café. We eat there sometimes, it's good."

"Just don't talk to anyone," said Uncle Sam.

When I awoke the next morning, I found some money they had left me for breakfast. Downstairs, I had a glass of cocoa and some hot buns. I wore my knickers, which still hadn't fully dried, and I scanned a newspaper, doing my best to look like a local fellow, an ordinary guy.

Maybe, I chuckled to myself, there will be a story in the newspaper: "Young Man Swims Across Raging River Sauer." I looked around the café and saw a middle-aged man looking at me. He smoked a pipe and wore a bow tie with a white half-apron. I took him to be the proprietor. He walked toward my table, and I murmured a polite, *"Bonjour."*

"Bonjour," he replied. "Be comfortable, sit here and read."

This, I figured, meant don't worry, your folks will be back soon. I assumed he knew my aunt and uncle. Perhaps he'd been told to look out for me. I felt reassured. A few other patrons sat at tables with checkered tablecloths, and seemed to take no notice.

The man in the apron walked behind a counter and disappeared behind a beaded curtain. I went back to my newspaper. When I looked up, there were two gendarmes striding briskly through the café door. They wore blue uniforms, flat-topped kepis, and they carried sidearms on their wide leather belts.

"Bonjour, tout le monde," one of them said loudly.

A few patrons responded. The police glanced about the room, and then began moving from table to table. *"Papiers?"* they asked. They wanted documents, identification. I had none. They stopped at each table, but I sensed they were looking for me. I looked for a nearby exit, but saw none. They seemed to be checking papers only perfunctorily, as though they had someone specific in mind. Perhaps, if I moved casually, I might simply walk past them as though I had other business and go through the very door they had entered. I felt breathless in my chair and looked down at my newspaper, as though indifferent to any police business, as though too busy with worldly affairs to concern myself with local matters.

"Papiers, bitte," one of the officers said, standing over me and mixing German with French. Oddly, it pleased me. The Nazis would never stoop to *"bitte*—please" when dealing with a Jew.

"Je n'ai pas des papiers," I replied. I don't have any papers.

"Alors venez avec nous," I was told. In that case, come with us.

In any language, it was clear that I was in trouble. I gestured, is there a problem? They asked if I had any belongings to take with me.

"No."

"You want to pay your bill before you leave, don't you?"

I tried to stay calm and ignore the dead silence in the room. I handed the man in the apron his money and waited for change. The officers glanced about lazily. I imagined my uncle and aunt's reaction to my arrest and wondered if the officers could hear my heart pounding beneath my chest. As the man in the apron returned my change, I wondered if he had called the gendarmes. Trust no one, my mother had warned.

We drove in silence to a nearby police post. But this isn't Nazi Germany, I told myself, this is Luxembourg. Would I be jailed? Was this how it started for others, now trapped behind the barbed wire at Dachau and Buchenwald?

The police led me into the Bureau de Gendarmerie to meet an examining officer. The foreboding stone and brick building was a combination prison/military barracks that looked like a castle out of a children's fairy tale. I wanted to go home. I wanted my mother and my father, and I wanted it to be 1920s Vienna all over again.

I sat before an examining officer's desk. Behind him was a picture of the ruling sovereign, the Grand Duchess Charlotte, wearing a glittering tiara. The officer frowned. He asked my name and age, but seemed almost not to notice my answers.

"How did you get across the border?" he asked.

"I swam across the Sauer," I said.

"But this was foolhardy," he said, seeming to take in my features for the first time. "It was at a high-water mark."

"Yes, you're right, sir," I said, hoping he might be touched by my plight, and by my honesty. "It was scary and strenuous, but the strong current carried me along. It was actually helpful to me."

"Of course, you are telling me the truth, aren't you?"

"Yes, sir," I said, "I swear. It was worth taking the chance to find freedom in your country. In Vienna, things were very bad for us. My mother sent me away."

I was telling the truth, and also reaching hungrily for his sympathy, feeling myself in more dangerous waters than the Sauer. The officer edged toward a smile. I looked up again at the portrait of the Grand Duchess. Her eyes seemed to convey kindness and compassion. I thought of Hitler, who was our common nemesis. Surely, there was room in Luxembourg for one harmless little Jew. How much room could I take up?

"Who helped you here, after you reached Luxembourg?" he asked.

"Nobody," I said quickly.

"Where are your wet clothes? You didn't swim in the nude, did you?"

"No, sir, here, touch my jacket, touch my trousers, if you don't mind." I stood up and took a step toward him. "Look at my shoes."

He touched my clothes and realized they were damp.

"You said you arrived here two days ago. How and when did you get to the city?"

"I arrived this morning," I lied. "An hour before my arrest in the café. I walked, and rested by the road, and yesterday I caught a ride here on a farmer's wagon."

To my own ears, it sounded plausible. The river was perhaps twenty miles from the city. Surely this policeman would have mercy and see that I was no criminal.

"And you swam that river?" he asked again, looking incredulous. I nodded earnestly.

"Do you have friends or relatives here?" he asked.

"No, sir," I said. "I wish I did, perhaps they could help me."

"No," he said, glancing at his desk and then back at me. "No one can help you." I felt myself sinking under the water. "You have broken our laws," he said. "You are here without a permit. You are an illegal."

"Yes," I admitted, trying to keep my voice from breaking. "What will happen to me?" I was a mere boy again. I was silly to have swum the river. I was at the mercy of strong men who would punish me for trying to take control of my own puny life. I would end up like Uncle Moritz at Dachau with my poor mother weeping for me.

He pulled a printed form out of his desk and began to write on it. Calm yourself, I thought. The officer seemed to be a reasonable man. The grand duchy would surely open its arms to such a harmless soul. When he finished writing, the officer leaned his elbows on his desk and looked at me.

"What will happen now," he said, "is in your hands."

He said I had three options. I could go back to Germany—clearly unthinkable. I could be escorted to the French or Belgian border and take my chances from there. Or I could face trial for illegally crossing into Luxembourg, and probably be found guilty and sent to prison.

"If you want to think it over," he said, "we will give you until tomorrow morning."

"And in the meantime?" I asked.

"In the meantime, we have a cell for you."

"A cell? May I give you the answer sooner?" I asked.

"Certainly," he said.

I glanced at a nearby clock. It was half past noon. "I have an aunt in Paris," I said. "Would it be possible to go there?"

He said yes. He said the closest French town to the Luxembourg border was Thionville. From there, it was about one hundred and fifty kilometers—about one hundred miles—to Paris.

"That's far," I said, "and I have no money for train fare." He had been very civil with me, so I felt relaxed enough to ask, somewhat rhetorically, "How will I get to Paris?"

He smiled. "If you managed to get across that swollen river, you'll have no trouble on dry land."

I sighed with relief. At least I wasn't going to jail. At least I wasn't being sent back to Germany. At least I might contact Aunt Mina and Uncle Sam at some point to let them know I was all right, so I wouldn't make anyone cry.

The officer suggested I walk to a collective farm, about five hundred meters over the border in France. The farm was used by a group of young Jews who were preparing to emigrate to Palestine. They would surely be hospitable, he said. That sounds likely, I said, and prepared to be on my way.

I was mistaken. I would be held overnight in a cell, he said, and released in the morning. I would be fingerprinted, and various information about my life would be placed into their files. I would now have an official police dossier in Luxembourg. Bureaucracy and protocol must be observed.

My cell was small and clean, with whitewashed walls, a cot and chair, and a small barred window opened to a courtyard three floors below. It wasn't so bad. In some ways, it felt safer being a prisoner in Luxembourg than a civilian in Germany. A guard brought me a reasonably digestible lunch, and I relaxed, knowing I had hours to pass before departure. I looked outside to see an overcast sky. But it was lunch time for my aunt and uncle, too, and I worried about them. I could hear

Aunt Mina now: "I brought him here to be arrested! From the frying pan into the fire!"

I began to pace the cell, nervous energy spilling out of me, wondering how to communicate with them. Could I reach them from that collective farm just over the border in France? Had the officer steered me honestly? Lying on the cot, I thought of Heinz at the monastery. How would I contact him about my valise?

It took a long time to fall asleep that night, and when I did, I dreamed of my mother and Heinz. They were my remembrances of what now seemed a safer time.

I awoke early the next morning to the sudden clang of military music coming through my cell window from the courtyard outside. Standing on my chair, looking down, I saw perhaps fifty soldiers in formation wearing colorful parade uniforms: the Luxembourg army. It seemed like a scene out of a sunlit fairyland, "The Parade of the Wooden Soldiers," marching across the courtyard with big cannons at each end while music filled the air. Hitler had an army for killing, but Luxembourg's troops were for making music. I felt like marching across my cell in step with the band. In a few minutes, breakfast arrived: coffee, rolls, cheese, jam. I dined to the strains of a military band playing songs that would delight a child.

I was taken back to the interrogation room at ten o'clock. Three officers waited, one of them the fellow from the previous day. The atmosphere was convivial. They wanted me to fill out papers saying I agreed to my expulsion to France and had no complaints about treatment during my incarceration. Were they kidding? I was ready to sign papers saying, "I recommend this jail highly."

The two new officers escorted me to a small commuter rail station where about a dozen people waited for a train. They gave me a voucher for my ticket. And then I spotted Uncle Sam. He walked slowly along the platform, outwardly calm, wishing to attract no attention. As he passed me, he muttered, barely loud enough for me to hear, *"Dreh iber dem dashik.*" In Yiddish, it meant, "Turn the visor around." Literally, he meant the visor on my cap. Figuratively, he meant: Try to come back. He continued to stroll along the platform, and he did not return.

I took the electric train to Mondorf-les-Bains, a therapeutic spa town of about three thousand people, which was about twenty kilometers from Luxembourg. The police accompanied me, each of them smoking cigarettes.

"I watched the soldiers marching in the courtyard this morning," I said, looking for common conversational ground.

A dress rehearsal, they explained, for Armistice Day ceremonies coming in a week commemorating the end of the great war.

"Those cannons," I said. "Are they real?"

"Oh, yes," one officer laughed, "they are real. But they can never fire them, you know. Even during military maneuvers."

"Why not?"

"Because," he laughed again, "whatever direction they fire, it lands in some other country."

"Luxembourg is very small," the other officer chuckled.

"Naturally," I said, "when I saw the band, I assumed they were there to welcome me."

The banter continued until we reached the station at Mondorf. There were no markers designating a change in countries. Customs posts existed only on main roads, and France and Luxembourg were historic friends. As my escorts walked me to a nearby wooded area, and we walked across a footbridge spanning a trickling rivulet, I noticed a nearby tavern.

"Here you go across," one said, "and you are in France."

"And good luck getting to Paris," the other said.

I thanked them and took a few steps into France. I stopped to look back toward the station. The gendarmes were already walking toward the nearby tavern, no doubt biding their time until the train back to Luxembourg City departed. I walked down a narrow lane, and moments later came to a cluster of farm buildings—the enclave for Jewish youths.

It happened so quickly, I didn't even have time to feel lost. I had no luggage, almost no money, just the clothes on my back.

"Shalom," I said. "Hello." There were several young men and women standing about.

"You're Jewish?" one fellow responded.

"Yes."

"How do you know about us?"

"I fled Germany for Luxembourg," I said. "I was expelled to France just minutes ago. They told me about your farm."

I felt clumsy with my French, and pressured by their questions, but comfortable that I was with Jews. I told them my plans to reach Paris, how my mother's sister, my aunt Erna, lived there. Politely, I asked if I might spend the night on their farm to stay out of trouble.

"No, this is not possible," came a chorus of voices.

One fellow, a German Jew who seemed to be their leader, said it would bring trouble on them all. They were doing *hachshara*, preparatory agricultural work for emigrating to Palestine. They only had temporary visas. The authorities visited from time to time, often at surprising hours, to check on the premises. They were here only by the grace of the French government and must adhere to the law. I was illegal. Jew or no Jew, I could not stay and jeopardize them.

I felt slapped in the face, but had no argument to offer. Chased by the Germans, expelled by Luxembourg, I was now rejected by my own people.

"An inspector could come even now," someone said.

"We would be vulnerable," someone else said.

"Yes, of course," I said, hoping they would find me so agreeable that they would change their minds. I thanked them for their courtesy and said I'd find another place to spend the night. It was now late afternoon.

"Are you hungry?"

As I turned to leave, I heard a young woman's voice, and nodded. I hadn't eaten since my breakfast in jail. She looked about twenty, with dark hair in a page-boy cut. She entered the farmhouse and returned a few minutes later with a paper bag containing bread and cheese, an apple, a chocolate bar, and a small container of milk.

"I am Leo," I said. "What's your name?"

"Edith."

"Edith? My sister's name, too." Edith was Ditta. Ditta was in Vienna, where they were pushing Jews into the street. This Edith was living on a peaceful farm, on her way to Palestine, and letting these Jews turn away one of their own.

The others stood silently. This small talk was getting me nowhere. I shook a few hands and started to walk back to the gravel path and the border. I waited for someone to say, "Wait a minute, stay a while, spend the night." I heard nothing. I remembered my uncle: Try to get back, he said. Turn the visor around. All right, so I would try that. I retraced my steps to the little footbridge, on the French side of the border, and watched the train station for the gendarmes who had brought me here.

It was a dry day, but the grass was damp. I sat beneath a tall tree behind some protective bushes, peering across the border. If necessary, I would walk all the way back to my aunt and uncle. I would simply wait until the gendarmes took their train back and left me alone.

One day at a time, I thought. Get through one day at a time. The sun peeked between clouds, and ducked behind them again. Dusk arrived. I drank some milk and ate the chocolate bar for energy. Imagine this, I thought: one day I'm dining with monks, then I'm picnicking at twilight on the French border. A train sat at the station. I hoped it would not rain, since my knickers were finally beginning to dry.

Nervously, I came out from behind the bush and crouched my way toward the footbridge. The rivulet below gurgled soothingly. I reached a ravine on the other side, and hoped I hadn't been noticed. The evening was growing darker. I carried the bag of food in one hand, but realized I'd left the milk container behind. Leo, Leo, I thought sardonically, you've littered France.

I walked a few hundred feet along the ravine to a utility box near a roadside. In the distance I saw houses, where the lights were beginning to go on. Families were gathering at dinner tables. I missed my sisters. I edged my way closer to the train station and sat in the dark. I heard a whistle: the station master's signal for a train's departure. I lifted my head above the edge of the shallow trench and peered from behind the utility box. The train was moving slowly, and would pass directly in front of me. There were lights on in the train, and there, also directly in front of me, were the two gendarmes. Fortunately, they did not spot me and, finally, they left.

I relaxed for a moment, and tried to sort things out. Luxembourg City was twenty kilometers from here—a long trek. My mouth was dry and sour. I hadn't brushed my teeth since the previous day. I felt dirty. I started to walk along the edge of the ravine. It would be easy to duck into it in an emergency. The sun had set on my left. The road looked familiar, since it ran parallel with the train tracks. Darkness has the tendency to distort distance and direction, but this seemed pretty easy. I thought of the officer's words the day before: If I could make it across that river, I could make it on land.

I walked for about two hours. When headlights approached, I slipped into the ravine. When they passed, I climbed to the dry upper edge. I grew tired and stopped to rest by a cluster of bushes near a picnic ground. There was a table and two benches, as well as a toilet facility, although it was locked. I found a wooden crate, and propped it against the rear bathroom wall and leaned against it. The November night air was chilly. I moved my arms across my chest to stimulate my bloodflow, and realized my clothes still hadn't fully dried.

The bread and cheese became a small banquet. I thought of picnics in Vienna with my sisters and ice cream cones with Ditta as I walked her home from the orphanage. I longed for something warm to drink. I listened for approaching traffic. I thought about Aunt Mina and Uncle Sam, fretting in their apartment and not knowing if my arrest had

69

endangered them. The sooner I reached them, the sooner I could ease their worries. I would only rest here for a little while, and then make my way back to them. And then I fell into an exhausted sleep.

I awoke past dawn, with no memory of going to sleep. With the daylight, I knew I would have to move more carefully. Walk slowly, I told myself. Turn sideways as traffic approaches, avoid encounters, walk away from the road without infringing on anyone's property. I was still six to eight miles from the city.

I walked for about an hour on a dirt path parallel to the main road when I heard hoofbeats behind me—a farmer's wagon. I raised my arm and saw the farmer, a man in his fifties, face craggy and unshaven. He slowed and stopped.

"How far to the city?"

"Half an hour," he said. I found this news stunning, and determined that his sense of time and direction were skewed. But he said he was heading there, and I delightedly accepted a ride and hopped onto his wagon, sitting on the front bench next to him.

We reached town in about an hour, exchanging few words, with the horse moving at its own pace. The farmer was headed to a market in town, and when we arrived it was almost half past seven. We weren't far from my uncle and aunt's.

When I reached the apartment, I found the door open. Uncle Sam, anticipating my return and never doubting it for a moment, had left it unlocked. I walked in and there he was, stout as ever, handsome face looking tired. Strong arms quickly wrapped around me.

"I told you so," he exclaimed to Aunt Mina. "I knew it!"

Aunt Mina lay in her bed with a compress on her forehead. The smell of vinegar permeated the apartment. The compress had been soaked in water and vinegar, an old folk remedy for curing strong headaches. Mina looked stricken. She scarcely had strength to talk. I remembered her flair for the dramatic, and tried to maintain perspective. She managed a brave smile, nodding and blinking with one uncovered eye. As I got close to her bed, she reached for my hand and kissed it.

"I told you," Uncle Sam declared. "If he could swim that river, dry land was no problem."

I held Aunt Mina's hands and bent over to put my lips to them. Then, as I turned to walk from her bed, she muttered softly, "You did it. You did it. Your uncle was right."

She drifted back to sleep, and Uncle Sam and I went to the kitchen for coffee. I wanted to know how he'd traced me to the train station, how he knew I'd been arrested.

"Never mind that," he said. "How did you like my signal with the hat?"

"You see, it worked," I said. The two of us felt quite proud of ourselves. The arrest was probably just a spot check, my uncle said. The café owner knew the two officers who had taken me in, and said they were both benign fellows. It was easy to learn the place of my confinement, and my uncle knew I would be taken to the French border. So he'd decided to go to the train station early, and simply wait for my arrival.

There was one drawback to our delight: A friend had told Ezra Committee officials of my arrest. Now that I was back, these officials were unsettled. My presence could endanger my relatives. I would have to be moved without delay.

That night I was taken to a local Jewish family sheltering other transients. The police had no reason to look for me there. In their eyes, I had crossed into France. Meanwhile, the Committee would try to arrange for my transfer into Belgium.

I learned no names at this new home, nor did I give my own. I took a hot bath in a large tub, and couldn't remember the last time I'd enjoyed such a luxury. At breakfast the next morning, I found a small group of people who'd simply been tossed together. We were Jews trying to outrun our fate, about ten of us, two of whom were children, and two who were Orthodox men.

The house had a large, veranda-like porch and overstuffed armchairs in a comfortable living room. People gathered in a foyer. There was a fireplace and a large den. I had no idea how long I would be allowed to stay. I was given strict orders: Do not venture outside.

One day Uncle Sam came to visit and brought some clothing for me. He wanted to know if I needed shoes. No, I said, I have another pair in my suitcase with Heinz, who was awaiting my instructions in Trier.

Later that day, another woman joined our group. She was German, middle-aged, heavy, and gray-haired. When she talked, it was clear her dentures were ill-fitting. They clicked as she spoke. We had a Sabbath meal that evening with tasty food. In Vienna, my mother made Sabbath dinners. She and Henny would be lighting candles now. I had no idea who cooked this dinner. But, I thought, I will have to write to my mother and tell her about the food. It would please her that I'm eating so well.

On Sunday, November 6, my uncle and aunt surprised me with a pair of brown laced shoes, not new but in good condition. I took mine off, hoping the air would finally allow them to dry. The River Sauer was still clinging to them. I felt restless and confined.

On Monday, we were told of moving plans. On the night of Wednesday, November 9, we would be moved to Belgium. Details would follow. Border crossings had to be arranged confidentially, and without too many involvements.

In the afternoon, Uncle Sam came by, and I told him the news. A good country, he said, very receptive to refugees. He said he would write to my mother and tell her I would contact her from my next stop, without mentioning where it was. Meanwhile, we had gotten no response to the postcard I'd sent her a week earlier. I imagined all sorts of dark possibilities.

I spent the next day in the sitting room, chatting with other residents: Where are you from? How did you get here? The stories were similar: Nazis, fleeing, trepidation, the fear for children, everyone fighting for time. You could play a record, and then replay it, substituting only names and faces.

For a while, I read a newspaper. In just a few days here, the outside world seemed to have grown distant and far more troubled. The Polish government had tightened the screws on the Jews. Early in October, they'd declared that citizenship would be denied to those whose passports were not renewed by October 29. It sounded like an excuse for a roundup. On October 26, the German Foreign Office told the Gestapo to deport as many Polish Jews living in Germany as possible. Over the next two days, special trains carrying nearly eighteen thousand Jews were sent to the Polish border, but they were denied entrance. Where to go? Some were forced across the border illegally by the Nazis. About five thousand were forced to a camp in a tiny Polish frontier village, Zbazsyn. It was just the beginning of a nightmare.

In Paris, unbeknownst to us, a seventeen-year-old student named Hershel Grynszpan received a letter from his father, one of those who'd been forced into Zbazsyn. Grynszpan was appalled at what his father had written. He went to the German embassy in Paris, intending to kill the ambassador. Instead, he shot a third secretary of the embassy, Ernst vom Rath. It was November 7. Vom Rath would die two days later, just hours before we were to leave Luxembourg for Belgium. His death would give the Nazis an excuse for outrage on the night of November 9, outrage that would make the sky itself bleed.

Late that very afternoon, Aunt Mina and Uncle Sam came to say good-bye. Aunt Mina was calm, for Aunt Mina. Write soon, be careful. They told me no mail had arrived from Vienna. I felt myself slipping irretrievably from the lives of my mother and sisters, and tried to hide my sadness. Mina's eyes welled, but tears did not spill. We hugged goodbye.

After dinner, we were told that six of us would be leaving at 11:30 p.m. Ezra's plans were falling into place, we were told. But we weren't told what those plans were. My companions would be a man in his sixties, who wore glasses and spoke only Yiddish, and four women, including the German with loose dentures.

We waited out the hours, thrown together by destiny and birth. We were given sandwiches and fruit to take with us. At 11:30, the doorbell rang, and the man who was to drive us to Belgium entered.

It was Becker. My heart leaped: Becker! He wore his leather visor cap and held his car keys in one hand. I raised my hand and waved to him. He seemed pleased to see me. I felt familiarity, I felt trust. I felt an old friend had arrived, my old partner in crime.

One of the women turned and asked me my name. After days in this house, we were still careful about questioning each other. My name is Leo, I said.

"Tell me, Leo," she said, "you know this man?"

"Yes, I met him last week."

"Seems very nice," she said. It sounded more like a question than a declaration. She wanted assurance.

"Yes," I said "very amiable. You are right."

He was the stranger in whose hands she was putting her life. As if confirming this news, she added, "Ezra knows what they are doing."

Becker led us to his car, the same Peugeot I knew from a week earlier. The back seat was now back in place, and the six of us were assigned cramped places according to body build. Becker tried to be funny about it, to relieve the tension in the air.

"You'll sit next to me," he said to a slender woman in her forties. I would sit on the other side of her. "You don't take up much space." To the plump German woman with the clacking dentures, he asked, "Is your lap large enough to hold someone?"

The woman did not laugh, but the air seemed a little less nervous. Into the back seat went the slender man in eyeglasses, a woman of medium build, the German woman, and a petite teenaged girl who tried to squeeze between the two other women but could not. So the German woman offered her lap. The girl seemed slightly offended, as if she were being treated like a child. Reluctantly, she said she would try to sit there for a while. We were trying to save our lives, and still figuring out a seating plan.

We left near midnight. The distance to Brussels was about one hundred thirty miles as the crow flies, but Becker would travel secondary roads to avoid police patrols. As we got into the car, he placed a flood light over his rear license tag. If we were pursued, he explained, he would turn on the light and hope it would shine in the pursuers' eyes.

We reached the frontier in less than an hour, but with seven of us, and luggage in the trunk, Becker's car seemed in no mood to speed. Arriving at the border crossing, he slowed to see if the post was manned. It was not. At this hour of the night, with minimal traffic on a secondary road, no guards were deemed necessary, particularly between Luxembourg and Belgium, two friendly neighbors. We sighed with relief. Becker knew his business. The sign at the crossing read: "Belgique—België."

We traveled along a wider, two-lane road headed northwest to Brussels. We passed through the Ardennes, whose beauty was not discernible in the dark. We saw forests along the road. None of us attempted to sleep. We were driving near the Bastogne region, not conceiving of the bloody fighting to come six years hence between the Americans and the Germans. All we knew was the fear in our own little lives.

Becker began driving faster and faster, and some of us grew anxious. From the back seat, unexpectedly, the petite girl, who'd been nervous all night, coughed and gagged, and then she vomited.

"What happened?" Becker asked.

"The little one threw up," the German woman answered, dentures clacking.

"Good," Becker laughed, "now I know I'm driving at the right speed."

He was trying to make light of our anxiety. It helped, but the vomit made the car smell horrible. As we drove through the chilly Belgian countryside, we threw open the windows.

"Is my driving bothering you?" Becker asked, turning to me.

"No."

"You know," he said, winking, "I can also drive slowly." He meant our little drive from the River Sauer. "I hope you won't leave a puddle on the floor this time."

He told the slender woman next to him she should try to sleep for a while. She wanted to watch, she said. A moment later, Becker took his hands off the steering wheel to light a cigarette.

"Don't do that," the woman cried. "Hold on to the wheel."

"I thought you were going to watch," said Becker.

He was trying hard to keep us calm, but our concerns mounted. Again, we were heading into a foreign country, with no idea what awaited us and no idea how close any pursuers might be.

In a while, the land seemed to open up. All trees vanished, and we saw a starry sky. I was staring ahead when I heard the man in the glasses, sitting directly behind me, cry in startled Yiddish, "Look, look to the right. Can you see what I'm seeing?"

It was the strangest night sky I'd ever seen in my life. Becker slowed down and tried to look across. He brought the car to a complete stop. All of us looked eastward. In the farthest perceptible distance, odd colorations streaked against a dark horizon. It could not have been a rainbow because it was still dark. We saw flashes of color, as if the sky were being finger-painted by some invisible giant.

We arrived in Brussels at about seven o'clock that morning, most of us sleepless through the hectic night. Becker dropped us at a small hotel. There were newspapers in the lobby. A headline declared, *Nuit de Terreur en Allemagne. Pogrom Contre Les Juifs.* Night of Terror in Germany. Pogrom Against the Jews.

Now we knew the answer to the strange colors on the horizon. We had seen the Nazis' response to the murder of the man at their embassy. We had seen Kristallnacht, the night of the broken glass.

4

November – December 1938

Kristallnacht unleashed Hitler's long night of barbarism. He'd been given a final, pathetic excuse by the actions of the young Hershel Grynszpan, who heard of his father's travails and wished to avenge them by marching on the German embassy in Paris. His killing of Ernst vom Rath was first mourned at a hero's burial service in Duesseldorf, attended by Hitler and his top henchmen, only hours after vom Rath's death on November 9. Then, at 11:55 that night, a message was issued from Gestapo headquarters in Berlin to all officers:

"At very short notice, action against Jews, especially at their synagogues, will take place throughout the whole of Germany. They are not to be hindered.... Preparations are to be made for the arrest of about twenty to thirty thousand Jews in the Reich. Wealthy Jews in particular are to be selected.... Should Jews be found in possession of weapons, the most severe measures are to be taken."

It was signed "Gestapo II Müller," whose signature was followed by these words: "This teleprinter message is secret."

It was a secret as easy to find as the sky itself.

As the seven of us paused on the road to Belgium that night, and watched the eerie horizon in the distance, we saw the catastrophic response to that Gestapo message. Germans in cities and towns and villages awoke to the sounds of shattering glass and the flashing of incendiary lights and the smell of burning synagogues, while police and fire crews did nothing to intervene. Gestapo officers led the assault, joined by crowds of civilian thugs wrecking businesses and smashing storefronts. And there was one more sound: the cries of helpless Jews, who were savagely beaten by their own countrymen and then paraded by the thousands before howling mobs.

By the time we reached our hotel in Brussels, and glimpsed headlines in the morning newspaper, we could only guess at the dimensions of the terror. Austria was now part of Germany; was my mother among the night's casualties? Thousands of Jews were pulled from their homes and arrested. Were my sisters among them? While Germans stood by and cheered, nearly three hundred synagogues were plundered and then turned to rubble. Was my own? Was my own rabbi, who'd blessed me at my bar mitzvah just four years earlier, among the doomed? Who was blessing him? On this night, nearly seven thousand Jewish stores and businesses were destroyed. In these few hours, as the streets sparkled with shards of glass, both the Jews and the Nazis learned a lesson. The Jews learned that the Nazis would stop at nothing; the Nazis learned that the world would permit almost anything.

Standing in the hotel lobby, exhausted from the long sleepless night, I remembered the day Hitler arrived in Vienna. So this is where we had come. I remembered when the Brownshirts came for my cousin Martha and destroyed Uncle Moritz's store while our entire family cringed, and wondered why no one came to help. Now there was a nation of such families, and thousands transported to places like Dachau, where my uncle was taken. Would they survive? No one knew, and we were haunted by fears newly roused by the fires of Kristallnacht.

In the little lobby of our hotel, strangers milled around a few upholstered chairs and settees with their morning papers, and tried to understand the implications of the stories they were reading.

"Stay together here," Becker told us.

He went to a nearby desk and showed a clerk some papers. Becker was a joker, he was playful, but such mannerisms were a ruse to avoid dwelling on the real dangers around us. Behind the clowning was a sense of authority, from which we took strength.

The six of us huddled together, trying to catch a word here, a phrase there, from the newspapers in people's hands. What kind of pogrom? What kind of terror? After our sleepless night on the road, the stories seemed unreal.

This was now my fourth foreign country in ten days. Belgium was an oasis, but Europe was erupting all around us. Becker gestured for calm. We were dependent on the good will of strangers to tell us where to go, what to do, how to stay alive. Belgium was now the place to call home. But for how long? Until the whole world returned to sanity? Becker glanced at me and sensed that my nerves were jangled. In ten days, he'd become an old friend whose features were familiar: his brown leather cap with the visor, his open smile, his impish demeanor.

"Leo," he smiled, "last night was rather dry."

"Yes," I said, "even the money in my purse is dry."

"You had to remind me of that money?" he laughed.

A young woman entered through the lobby's turnstile doors, spotted Becker, and smiled delightedly. Was there no one in all of Europe who did not know Becker? The woman's name was Miriam. She wore a tailored suit and carried an attaché case. She was friendly but businesslike. She strode to the registration desk, and Becker turned to us. Without warning, it was time for him to leave.

"When you are rich in America," he said, "you'll send me a ticket there."

Becker said the words flippantly, but he also meant: "Think of me."

I knew we would never see each other again, and I didn't know suitable words to thank him. We shook hands, and he said, "Chin up. I'll talk with Mina and Sam. I'll tell them everything."

I was too emotional to say anything. It was best not to think too much about the past, about Aunt Mina and Uncle Sam, about all those left behind. The man who had sat behind me in the car reached for Becker and gripped him with two trembling hands.

"*A dank' eich,*" he said simply, thanking Becker while wiping a tear from behind his glasses.

When Becker left, Miriam assumed control. We were told to stay in the hotel for the next twenty-four hours since we had no documents. There were vouchers for meals; the Ezra Committee had seen to the smallest details. In the morning, we would be taken to the local Ezra office for further instructions about "regularizing" our situations. We had no idea what this meant.

I brought a newspaper to my room. I had never been in a hotel room before. Behind my locked door I felt safe, and then guilty for feeling safe. My mother was prescient to send me away, but staying behind made her vulnerable. I struggled to decipher the newspaper. It was written in French, but I translated a sentence here, a paragraph there until a picture began to form of enormous devastation and cruelty, which the Germans were calling retaliation for the killing of their embassy secretary. A pattern was being established: You kill one of ours, we kill many of yours; don't even try to strike back.

I pulled at lacy curtains and glanced through my third-floor window. Below was a busy city street where people went to work, met with friends, shopped for groceries, walked with their children. Cars and buses drove about, and no one seemed to hide from police. It was a normal day...for peacetime. But we were only hours from a country where they were burning down houses of God. Was this the whole world's reaction? If the Germans burned God's home, might they also burn hospitals where children stood by windows and waved brave little farewells to their families?

I napped fitfully through much of that first day and night, and the next morning had breakfast and asked about news from Germany.

Sketchy, I was told, sketchy. It was already being sloughed off by nations with problems of their own. The Jews were protesting—those whose voices could still be heard—but who was listening to the Jews?

Joseph Goebbels, Hitler's minister of propaganda, boasted, "We can do with our Jews as we please." Then he placed a word into the war's vocabulary: Kristallnacht. He intended to describe glitter, to symbolize a festive mood caused by the billions of pieces of glass reflecting the synagogues burning through the night.

We met Miriam in the hotel lobby. She wore an overcoat and a dark beret and took us into the street. No synagogues were burning here, and no broken glass littered the sidewalks. Within minutes, we reached the Ezra office where a brass plaque was engraved "Ezra—Comité d'aide Juif." That the words did not have to be hidden seemed like an exclamation shouted to the hills. Inside, a few office workers busied themselves with chores while Miriam gathered my five companions. They would remain in Brussels; I would be moved to Antwerp within hours. I did not ask why. Antwerp, I knew, was a port city, a gateway to faraway places. I imagined the safety of great distances.

Miriam handed me a sheet of paper with an official stamp on it, authorization as a temporary alien to travel to Antwerp, about thirty miles away. I was handed a train ticket and two Belgian ten-franc notes. It was late morning. The trains to Antwerp ran every twenty minutes.

"When you get there," Miriam said, "you will present yourself at the Ezra office. They close at six."

I decided not to linger in Brussels. The city was immaculate, the mood was genial, but I wanted a place where I could sit down and not feel I would soon be running to some new destination.

I found the Ezra office at Pelikaan Straat near Mercator Straat in Antwerp, and a young man named Hirschfeld asked for my credentials. We were both from Vienna. From which district, he asked. Zwanzigster, Brigittenau, I said. Erster, he said. It was an idiosyncrasy not uncommon among the Viennese: Learn the backgrounds, establish the status symbols.

I came from a blue-collar district with a heavy Jewish population; he, from the center district with government buildings, the opera, and museums and the tourist sites. He'd arrived from a world of position, and was already a minor authority figure in a small office in a new country. I was the product of a poor widow from a working class community, now reduced to telling how I'd sneaked my way here.

"Ah," he said, "many here tell the same thing. You'll see, you're not alone." When I looked around, I saw others going through the same interview process.

"You are very busy here," I said.

"I believe we're going to get busier," he said simply. "Because of the events."

More word of Kristallnacht was reaching Belgium, including news from Vienna: All but one of its synagogues were now gone, scores of them burned to the ground. My own, where I'd gone to youth services, where I'd been bar mitzvahed, where I'd met with young friends before Hitler's arrival and talked of one day going to Palestine, was only ashes now. An entire world had gone up in smoke behind me, and I had no idea if my family had disappeared inside of it.

I imagined them crying my name from burning buildings. Hirschfeld handed me a lunch voucher. I saw my grandmother, too old to run for safety. Hirschfeld mentioned a nearby soup kitchen. I remembered the River Sauer, and thought crazily of swimming back and miraculously saving my family. Hirschfeld told me to go eat lunch and then we would talk about lodging for the night. The world might be tearing itself to shreds, but each day's necessities still had to be met.

Inside a spacious hall a few blocks away, I found people eating lunch at rows of tables. They talked animatedly. I stood in a short food line when I heard a familiar voice a few paces behind me. I turned and saw my Uncle David: Uncle David the *shvitzer*, my mother's oldest brother. Uncle David, the Fish Fry King of the Hannover Market in Vienna, and here he was in a soup kitchen in Antwerp!

84

A voice shouted, "Don't hold up the works," and someone handed me a tray. I called my uncle's name. "Uncle David! David Fischmann!" He looked my way, seemed momentarily startled, and cried to the man next to him, "Look, this is my nephew!"

"Uncle David, my God!" I shouted.

He had left Vienna days before me, trying unsuccessfully to get to Switzerland. He'd never known my day of departure, nor I his. We'd kept things secret from our own family members. Plans often too easily reached the wrong ears. Only Uncle David's wife, Olga, and his children, Hilde and Kurt, knew of his departure. They waited to join him. I marveled at the sight of him. Uncle David was an overwhelmer. I remembered the flamboyant way he hawked Fischmann's fish fry, wearing an oversized white cook's hat. He was a short, stocky bull of a man given to bursts of exaggeration. And, of course, there was the *shvitzing*, the exuberance always expressed in huge amounts of perspiration.

At the end of his workdays selling fish at the market, he made home deliveries on a tricycle hitched with a wagon. One day at the market, in the middle of a sale, a man approached Uncle David and said he was late on his monthly payment for the tricycle. Uncle David picked up the bike and threw it at the man. He was immovably difficult and temperamental. He was meticulous, which seemed odd for a man who carried the smell of fish with him. And he was often insulting. I remembered my father's burial day, and the secrets whispered all around me. The others ignored Uncle David that day, so he sat by me for company. But I put all such things aside now, utterly thrilled to find him here in this strange new city where I knew no one at all.

"Leo, what are you doing here?" Uncle David asked incredulously.

Your mother, he asked. Your sisters, he asked. The words were rapid-fire, so that I barely answered one question when he moved to the next. But, when I asked of his own experiences, he was quieter and more reflective. He'd tried to cross into Switzerland with his sister's son Herbert. Herbert had succeeded, but Uncle David hadn't. He'd been directed back to Belgium. His family in Vienna? Who knew? Uncle David shrugged and changed the subject. Where was I sleeping tonight, he asked.

"I have to go back to the Ezra office," I said. "A young man..."

"Hirschfeld, the Viennese?"

"Yes, you know him?"

"A nice young man," said Uncle David. "But I have a place for you." He was always the go-getter, a man who instantly fit into his surroundings. In Antwerp only two weeks, he was already connected.

He'd found some distant cousins from his hometown of Czestochowa, in Poland, and wanted to introduce me to them. I'd never met them, and I was only dimly conscious of ever having heard their names.

"After all," he said, "they are also your mother's cousins."

I began to feel more comfortable, and put myself into my uncle's strong embrace. He said he had befriended the owner of a fish store who knew a woman with a spare room above a bistro. He must let her know soon. Such facilities were in demand, and Ezra was always on the lookout for such places. The Committee would provide financial help for a while. We walked back to see Hirschfeld, who remembered Uncle David from a few weeks earlier.

"My nephew," said Uncle David, putting an arm around me.

"One of your jokes, Mr. Fischmann?"

"No, no, I am not joking."

Hirschfeld shrugged. Such things will happen more and more, he said, with Europe in flux, with families uprooted and displaced, with people fleeing and looking for the same safe havens.

"I have a room for my nephew," Uncle David said. "If it is agreeable to Ezra. On Lamorinière Straat."

Hirschfeld scanned a sheet of paper listing addresses.

"Number 68," he said.

"How do you know this?" Uncle David asked, *shvitzing* through his clothes.

"It's the only listing on Lamorinière. It's all right with us. Any address on our list is acceptable. I probably would have sent your nephew there anyway. Only..."

"Only, what?"

"Only," said Hirschfeld, "you have to fill out a voucher."

Always, there were vouchers. Forms had to be completed to eat, to sleep, to travel, to get the necessary monetary support, to survive. I was enormously grateful, but also impatient. I was safe, my belly was full, but my life was now controlled by events beyond my influence.

"Thank you for all your help," I told Hirschfeld as we left, hoping he understood my sincerity.

"Don't lose your kitchen voucher," he replied, and turned reflexively back to his work.

Uncle David and I went to 68 Lamorinière Straat and walked into the bistro there. The landlady had a Flemish name and spoke to my uncle in broken German.

"Your son?" she asked.

"My nephew."

"How old?"

"Seventeen."

"No girls," she admonished.

They were the last thing on my mind, but it pleased me that she imagined such a possibility. I started to say, "Not tonight, I'm tired. Perhaps tomorrow." But such a remark might get lost in translation, and she looked quite businesslike and not given to levity.

We climbed steep steps that felt like an oversized ladder and reached a second-floor room with a double bed, a night stand with an alarm clock, a chest of drawers with a mirror, a chair, and a sink with a mirror. Jalousies covered a window that opened to a courtyard behind the bistro.

"The toilet?" I asked.

"Down the hall," she said.

"With a bath?"

"For the bath," she said, "you go down the street. A public bath house."

I nodded, because there was nothing else to do but nod. In Germany, they were burning synagogues to the ground. In Antwerp, I felt blessed to have a bath only a few blocks away.

The room would be my home until the spring of 1940, when German bombs would begin to fall and I would be expelled from Belgium, losing my adoptive family and a girl named Anny who I was beginning to love.

5

December 1938 – May 1940

In our isolation, Uncle David and I turned to each other. It was not easy bonding because my uncle's abrasiveness was legendary. But he was my mother's brother, so I sought refuge in our blood ties, and imagined they counted for something.

At dinner in the community kitchen that first evening, we analyzed the news from Germany and worried over those left behind. Walking the chilly Antwerp streets later that night, we fantasized about liberating our entire families, and tried not to slip too miserably into depression at such dim likelihood. The others, the others: this was the focus of our conversation. I tried not to think how alone I was, or how long it might be until I was not.

"I have plans," Uncle David said.

But he avoided any specific talk and let his voice drift away. I presumed that, like me, he imagined scenes of great reunions full of laughter and weeping without actually having worked out any particular schemes.

"These plans," I said. "Would they work for my family?"

"We'll see later," he said, brushing me off. "One has to be cautious. And be prepared for the worst."

It was a change from his normal swagger. We were crushed by the news from Germany: a second night of fire and destruction, and more rounding up of Jews to be taken to camps. We worried that our letters home would disappear without a trace.

In my little room on Lamorinière Straat that night, I put my few things away but sensed something missing: my prayer book. I thought I'd switched it from my valise to my attaché case at the Trier monastery, but now remembered that I hadn't. It reminded me to contact Heinz; I wondered if he'd opened the valise and gone through its contents. How would he react to a Jewish book of prayer? In Germany they were burning such books. Would he toss it onto the flames, or allow our brief friendship to transcend politics? He was a good-hearted soul, I told myself, and would surely come through for me.

I lay in bed and struggled for sleep. The bistro was open until ten, and through my courtyard window came the din of loud voices, cheerful souls who lived here, who had friends to share laughter across the evenings. My own friends were in Vienna, dreaming of Palestine. My sister Henny dreamed of Palestine. I wondered if my sisters had a safe place to rest tonight. Soon singing joined the laughter from below. My mother sang Polish melodies. She sang as she embroidered young brides' wedding dresses. Would my sisters ever become brides? Downstairs, the singing grew louder and more rollicking. I imagined a crush of bullies on the darkened streets of Vienna, preying on my family. I suspected a long, wide-awake night ahead of me, but escaped into sleep as if jumping off a cliff, and did not awaken until the next morning.

I went to the post office and found a stunning revelation: all signs were printed in Flemish, French, and Yiddish. I was thrilled at the sight. In Germany and Austria, those who spoke this dialect were being pulled from their homes. Here, in a nation with a small Jewish population, Yiddish was part of the official discourse. This, I thought, I will immediately report to my mother.

The post office was located on Pelikaan Straat, across from the rail-road station. I walked beneath its elevated tracks through a mild November morning and took in my surroundings. It was a sizeable, wealthy city showing few signs that a war was grinding into gear. There were jewelry stores everywhere with diamonds gleaming in their win-dows. I passed a gothic cathedral and a museum devoted fully to the master Peter Paul Rubens. A sign pointed to a nearby zoo. I walked onto the Meir, the main artery of the city, and found cafés and flower beds along the sidewalks. I remembered the café in Luxembourg, and instinctively felt in my pocket for the identity papers I received at the Ezra office.

I went back to my room and wrote a letter home to my family, telling them that Antwerp felt like Jerusalem. Such was the impact of seeing the post office signs in Yiddish and having my own room. It was a little room, but it was my place of sanctuary. I could stop running for a while.

I lay back on my bed and imagined my family's happiness at hearing of my great luck in arriving here. But I wanted them with me, and the thought gnawed at me. I picked up another piece of paper, and did the only productive thing I could do at that moment: I sent a letter to Heinz asking him to forward my valise.

That afternoon, Uncle David and I took a streetcar ride to Berchem, a suburb of Antwerp with playgrounds and parks and open fields, to meet our distant relations. The head of the family was Nachum Rosenblum, a cousin of my mother's mother, who owned a grocery store in a section of Antwerp where the Jewish population was steadily growing. Many Jews settled here after being chased from their home-lands. Nachum and his wife had a daughter and a son who lived at home, and another daughter, Rachel, who lived with her own family in Berchem. Rachel Frajermauer and her husband, Joseph, lived on Dixmuide Laan with their two daughters. She was a friendly, full-figured woman in her early forties with chestnut hair and a smile that spread across her face when Uncle David introduced me.

"The nephew," he declared grandly, while sweating heavily from our walk up the steps. "Dora's son. You know, Deworah in Czestochowa."

I felt authenticated. He was presenting not only me, but my blood ties. Into the room walked Rachel's husband Joseph—tall, stout, broad-shouldered, with a few strands of hair pulled across his head. He puffed with great relish on a pipe and had the handshake of a truck driver, though he worked in the manufacturing of women's blouses.

Sitting in their kitchen, they asked about my adventures. I unburdended myself. "It's lucky that you're both here," Rachel said, turning to Uncle David.

"The others, also, we'll get out," he replied. I looked at him expectantly, waiting for details to lift my spirits. If there were specific plans, I wanted to know about them. But Uncle David turned away, and I let myself be comforted by Rachel and Joseph's concern for me.

Soon the Frajermauers' daughters arrived home, their chattering, happy voices preceding them as they ran up the steps to the second floor apartment. Anny, sixteen, the quieter of the two, blushed slightly, but smiled and showed perfect teeth. Netty, eleven, reached up unselfconsciously and planted a peck on my cheek. The smell of cinnamon and apples drifted through the apartment, and a tea kettle whistled. We gathered at the table and ate hot noodle kugel.

"Like my mother's," I said, relishing the touch of home. "The highest compliment I can give."

"Have another piece," Rachel said. Again, like my mother.

"Leo," said Joseph, between puffs on his pipe, "we want you to feel at home with us."

The words touched my heart, but left me at loose ends. I was still figuring out the geographical logistics of my confusing existence, as well as the mingled emotions that accompanied that existence.

"You have sisters," said Anny, the older daughter.

"Yes," I said. "My sister Henny is about your age. She was sixteen on the 18th of October."

"I was sixteen on the 25th of October," Anny said.

"That was the day I left Vienna," I said. "Three weeks ago on Tuesday."

The girls asked about my adventures. I was comforted by their interest. In a while Uncle David rose to leave, and I moved to join him. Then two lovely things happened: Rachel echoed Joseph's words that I should feel at home with them, and Anny asked me to join her the following weekend to meet some of her friends. It felt like more than a gesture of friendship. After so many changes in so many different places, to make plans for seven days away felt like a long-term commitment. I was thrilled to say yes, and thrilled to imagine I would stay in one place for so long.

On Monday, Uncle David and I walked to Antwerp's City Hall—a large, ornate building with a gilded facade. The city was filled with busy people, and I paused repeatedly to look into store windows. Move on, Uncle David prodded me. At City Hall, a bespectacled clerk with a green visor welcomed me to Belgium. He sat near another sign printed in Yiddish. The clerk seemed empathetic, as though understanding the effort it had taken to get here. He asked about my schooling, my religion, my reasons for leaving Germany. I told him of my family left behind. Yes, yes, he nodded. He knew such stories.

"And the future?" he asked. "Do you have plans to emigrate?"

Tiny Belgium, wedged between France and Germany, had been absorbing refugees since 1933, the numbers growing with each new act of German aggression, each new gesture of appeasement by the West, each new antagonism toward the Jews. Belgian officials wanted assurances that stays would only be temporary.

"I have an aunt, my Aunt Sophie, living in the United States," I said. "I would like to go there. But I don't know how long it will take to obtain a visa."

He nodded again. America sent mixed signals on Europe's troubles. President Roosevelt shuffled his political cards, and Jewish faces seemed to carry little value. Aunt Sophie was waiting in America, arms extended, but others also waited for her embrace, including a sister, my Aunt Mina, and a sister-in-law, who was my mother, and other family members. In the meantime, in Vienna and in Luxembourg and now in Antwerp, we all waited and waited.

The clerk gave me a temporary permit of residency, and then two identity photos were taken, more confirmation that I'd arrived in a welcoming place. And I tried to welcome Antwerp into my own life, quickly studying Flemish, the Dutch-rooted language spoken in northern Belgium. My knowledge of German was helpful, and so were my two years of high school French when all else failed.

The world was stumbling toward another great war, but life was still comprised of the small details of getting through each day. The weather soon turned colder, and the closest public shower was several blocks away. I avoided it on Friday afternoons, when many Jews lined up to bathe before the Sabbath. My landlady told me of a portable tin tub in a hallway utility closet, where I could sponge bathe myself. It was suitable sometimes, but when I went to the public bath, a shower became such a luxury that it took much pounding on the door from those still in line to rouse me from my reveries.

As the weather worsened, my blue gabardine raincoat, having survived the River Sauer, breathed its last. But a connection was made: Joseph Frajermauer knew someone in the business. A deal was struck— a *metziah*, a bargain—and a new, belted tan raincoat appeared.

I met with Anny Frajermauer again. She took me to a boy's house in the suburbs, near her parents' apartment, where about a dozen of her friends gathered. Some were Jewish, some not. I'd almost forgotten how it felt to talk with people my own age. We overcame language difficulties easily enough. There was also the universal language of music to help overcome our differences. A Victrola played pop tunes of the era, almost all of them from America.

"Jeepers, creepers; Where'd you get those peepers?"

"A tisket, a tasket; A green and yellow basket..."

"Bet mir Bist du Schein..."

In Germany, this kind of music was forbidden, officially declared decadent by Aryan standards. Here, it was a gentle connection for adolescent sensibilities. In Germany, the Hitler Youth strode through the streets. Here, we happily sang along with little snatches of verse, and then played games of musical chairs and charades. Being too unfamiliar with the language, I watched from the sidelines during charades, and found Anny next to me.

"Are you having fun?" she asked shyly.

"Surely," I said. "I'm happier than I've been in months."

She beamed. I didn't know how much she knew of me, apart from my brief account of reaching Antwerp from Vienna.

Leo strolling on the streets of Antwerp in 1940.

"Your friends are very nice," I said. "I like them. And I like you."

I meant it in a friendly way, but I felt something else stirring. Anny was lovely, but we were related. She was a second cousin, twice removed, so how "related" were we? I only wanted to show my appreciation for meeting her friends, but I noticed that Anny was blushing a little. We fell silent. Searching for safe emotional ground, I looked around the room and asked about her friends.

"That boy," I said, pointing to a fellow who seemed slightly more mature than the others. He had dark eyes and an aquiline nose. He wore a necktie and jacket, and his hair was immaculately pomaded.

"Leon Oesterreicher," said Anny. "A very nice fellow."

It felt nice to be among people my own age, but I felt isolated as well. These young people all seemed comfortable with each other. I was a stranger. It hadn't yet occurred to me: we were becoming an entire world of migrants, each of us out of place, each searching for a sense of belonging. I walked Anny home after the party.

"This way, I can tell your parents hello," I said. But I wanted to walk her home just to walk with her. And when I left her and went back to my own room, I felt the first vague stirrings of what might have been romance, or maybe the simple need for companionship.

In a few weeks, good news arrived from the authorities: my official papers registering me as an alien, which granted me permission to stay in Belgium until May 30, 1940. It was eighteen months of breathing room, official word that I could stop running and hiding. I wanted to sing praises to the heavens. I was now a normal refugee, and not merely an international fugitive. I went quickly to the soup kitchen to look for Uncle David. He had his own good news, which he related without making eye contact.

Leon Oesterreicher

"A letter," he said. I looked at him, and wondered vaguely why he wasn't looking at me. "From Olga and the children. They're coming here to Belgium. It's in the letter."

"*Mazel tov*," I muttered, covering my anger and shock. His family was coming here, but what about my family? Was their value any less than his family's? Was there no way to have brought them here? Uncle David had been evasive with me. Always, he had plans. Never did he offer details, never did he suggest help for my mother. I'd assumed he'd been day-dreaming of escapes, fantasizing miracles of reunion the way I had. Instead, he'd formulated a method to save his loved ones, but not mine. I felt they'd been abandoned, left to languish in Vienna, and I struggled to hide my anger toward my uncle. After all, he was an elder. He'd helped me find a room in Antwerp. But I remembered how others had called him the maverick of the family. I remembered when my father died, and Uncle David borrowed money from my mother, which she'd gotten as a small insurance payment. She never got the money back from him. The money, she would say. Have some fish, he would say. It was a family joke, but it enraged me now, and my fears for my mother and sisters intensified.

A letter arrived that afternoon from Aunt Mina and Uncle Sam in Luxembourg, thrilled that I was safe. They'd heard from Becker, who told them I was not only in Antwerp but "also dry." Good old Becker, still playing that scene to the hilt. And then the best news: They'd heard from my grandmother in Vienna. The family was all right. They'd gotten through the worst nights unscathed. But why hadn't I heard from my mother? Had the German authorities spot-checked the mail? Were they censoring letters?

A few days later came a letter in Henny's handwriting. My heart leaped. They were well, and life went on, she wrote. There was no direct reference to the events of Kristallnacht, only this: "Everything is back to normal." But what was normal? The Austria that predated Hitler's arrival, or the Vienna where thugs forced old people onto their knees in the streets? Henny said Aunt Olga and the children were preparing to join Uncle David, but there was no explanation of how they had arranged to leave.

I was happy for my family's safety, but furious with Uncle David. The world had new rules about secrecy, I understood. No one could be trusted. But, surely, Uncle David could have trusted me. Was he not my mother's own brother? I wanted to confront him, but held back. He was an adult, and I merely a youth. He was a tough, abrasive fellow. I was a seventeen-year-old boy who'd been taught to be respectful. Was money the hidden connection? Uncle David was not wealthy, but I had no money at all, save for small assistance from the Ezra Committee. Did he have well-placed connections? He never said, and I never found a way to make him explain.

Then the world got a little colder. A letter arrived from Heinz, who had left the monastery to return to his army unit, declaring the following: "Because of some difficulties, I must let you know that a continuation of correspondence is not possible. Sorry. Much luck. Heinz."

What had happened? Had he been caught with my prayer book? Had there been official interrogations? Or had he simply found the book, discovered I was a Jew, and expressed his disgust with this well-mannered, but cryptic, letter? I never found out; I never had further contact, nor saw my possessions again.

In December, Aunt Olga and the children arrived in Belgium. They brought general news of Vienna, but no personal word from my mother. A wall came down between Uncle David and me, which his daughter, my cousin Hilde, sensed immediately.

"You're upset," she said, embracing me when we were alone.

"My mother was left behind," I said. "My sisters, too. Don't their lives count for something?"

"Yes," Hilde said. "And my own grandmother? We have abandoned her, too."

Matilda Fischer, Aunt Olga's mother, had been left in Vienna. Hilde sobbed openly. She was sixteen, and close to her grandmother.

"And your mother?" I asked. "She would let this happen to her own mother?"

Hilde shrugged. "My mother leaves such decisions to my father," she said.

She expressed her own anger by distancing herself from her father. In Antwerp, Hilde became my companion. The two of us often joined Anny and her friends.

One rainy day in February of 1939, I stopped by the Ezra offices. I knew my family could never escape the way I had, but surely Ezra must have other connections. Germany was increasing its threats toward Poland. Hitler declared to the Czech foreign minister, Frantisek Chvalkovsky, "Our Jews will be destroyed." In Hungary, Premier Imredy was forced to resign because of his Jewish ancestry.

"Is there anything that can be done for my family?" I asked Hirschfeld at the Ezra office. He shook his head and asked if Uncle David had connections. He knew about my uncle's family, and said their migration here was not the work of Ezra. I said nothing. The subject still infuriated me.

"Would you be interested," Hirschfeld suddenly asked, "in going to school here?"

He explained that the government wanted to take young refugees off the street, fearing they had too much free time on their hands and might cause troubles. I liked the idea, and enrolled at the Public Trade School for Boys, on the Mei Straat near Market Square not far from Antwerp's port. The classes were taught in Flemish, but I'd been in Antwerp more than three months now and the language had sunk in. Anny and her sister Netty were speaking strictly Flemish with me. I was seeing them a lot. Invitations to dinner came frequently, and Anny and I strolled off by ourselves afterwards. Take your sister along, Rachel Frajermauer would call after Anny as we walked out the door.

In school, I took the standard high school academic courses, plus electrical shop. My studies went well. At dinner one night at Anny's, her father told me, "You don't have anything to worry about. Anyone who can master this guttural language"—he grimaced comically as he said it—"can learn anything."

On weekends, Anny and I were increasingly inseparable, to the clear delight of her parents and giggly outbursts from Netty. Saturday night dances were held in a social hall on the Lange Kievit Straat, near the De Beukelaar cookie factory. Nearby was Gotteiner's Bakery, a mecca of Jewish breads and rolls and challahs. The loveliest aromas filled the evening air. Many of the Gotteiners perished later in Auschwitz.

For the moment, it seemed an almost idyllic existence—except that I worried constantly about my family. In March, German troops marched into Prague. Weeks later, Hungary enacted newly restrictive anti-Jewish laws, including the planned expulsion of all Jews within five years. From Vienna, my mother said the mood had calmed, I shouldn't worry too much about them. Her words failed to register; it was just my mother trying not to alarm me, covering her feelings in a code that the Germans might not figure out. At Passover, I sent a package with matzo and other food items as a little remembrance of holidays past.

I avoided Uncle David. When we met, everyone was tense. Aunt Olga said little, not wishing to set off her husband's temper, and I wanted to control my own emotions. Distance became best for all of us.

In school, I passed all courses with high marks. Joseph Frajermauer took fatherly pride in my accomplishments, and boasted to anyone who entered his home what a fine student I was. He became my greatest booster, and a father figure I hadn't known since I was a small boy, when Uncle Moritz took me under his wing after my father died.

That August, the Frajermauers went to the coastal resort of Blankenberge, about fifty-five miles from Antwerp, and they invited me to join them later for a few days. During the interim, I missed Anny very much. One Sunday morning, I borrowed a bicycle from the owner of a bistro near my apartment, and pedaled my way to the North Sea coast, with the sun and a fresh breeze providing a dazzling setting. I reached Blankenberge by mid-afternoon, and was embraced with great warmth. What delight to have found this second family; what torment, when I thought of Vienna, and accused myself of abandoning my mother and sisters.

"Why don't you go for a walk?" Rachel said, gesturing to Anny and me. "And take Netty." So we did, and comfortably held hands when Netty wasn't looking. I began to think of Joseph and Rachel as prospective in-laws. I'd turned eighteen in March, and yearned for Anny. We walked on the beach and our feet sank into the sand. We were light-hearted and romantic. The blue-green North Sea stretched before us, and waves crashed about. Anny and I walked into the surf, and let it splash about us, and drew closer for warmth.

One evening, Rachel and Joseph took us all to a café talent show, where we went to hear a singer named Albert Hershkowitz, a chubby fellow with a voice that soared. "We're related," Joseph

Leo and the Frajermauers—Netty, Rachel, Joseph, and Anny—in Blankenberge, August, 1939.

101

announced proudly. "He is my sister's brother-in-law." He had a wonderful tenor voice and a lively stage presence. I had no idea we would one day share a freight train to Auschwitz.

This August week in 1939, such things were still off in the distance. The North Sea was enchanting. My mother had sent me reassuring notes. The notes said nothing about Uncle Isidore or his whereabouts. The sea breezes were soothing. The notes said nothing about Uncle Moritz, wherever he might be. I was infatuated with Anny. The notes said nothing of my mother's fears for my sisters.

In a few days, I said farewell to Anny and her family and pedaled my bicycle back to Antwerp. I awoke the next morning with intense pain in my right groin. It was swollen and tender, and I knew it was a hernia. The Ezra Committee sent me to a doctor, who said the cycling had probably caused it. He prescribed a truss, and I went home, imagining the pain would go away.

On September 1, everything changed. At dawn, the German armies swarmed across the Polish border, and World War II began. England and France issued an ultimatum to Germany to immediately cease all operations. Hitler refused to comply. On September 3, 1939, the two nations declared war on Germany. Then German troops converged on Warsaw, wreaking terror and destruction never before seen, and adding a new word to the world's vocabulary: *blitzkrieg*. And the terror was quickly personalized. Some of the trains transporting German soldiers across the border carried slogans: "We're going to Poland to thrash the Jews." There were more than three million Jews in Poland, many steeped in learning, many representing the wellsprings of creativity. They were singled out for special torment. At the Reich Security Office, Reinhard Heydrich issued instructions: Those Jews living in towns and villages were to be transferred to ghettos which would be established in large cities. It was merely a transitional stage before the final solution.

Then came new decrees for Poland's Jews: forced labor, the wearing of special Jewish badges, prohibiting Jews from conducting business, thus denying them the right to earn a living. Jewish property was looted. Thousands were sent to labor camps, overcrowded and filthy places where they were barely fed enough to live. In the ghettos, there was more overcrowding, more starvation, more disease. Rations were meager. Infectious diseases broke out.

In Belgium, we wondered when the war would reach us. School started, and I went back to class. When the Jewish high holidays arrived, I went to synagogue services and wondered if God was protecting my family. One day a letter arrived from Ditta, offering the standard assurances: everyone was getting along, surely the troubles would blow over. She enclosed a photograph of my old friend Kurt Steinbach, whose family had lived in our building. On the back of the photograph, Kurt wrote these lines:

"While you are in a foreign land
Think of Vienna and your friend
The good times shared, far in the past
Help these memories to last."

I sat on my bed and wept over a world that now seemed gone beyond recall. I tried to get on with my life. There was school on weekdays, and visits with Anny on weekends.

Late in December, my hernia bothered me again. The doctor blamed the weather, and told me to stay warm. He suggested surgery. I resisted. He mentioned the possibility of a strangulated hernia. We scheduled surgery for the spring.

Before the new year, there was an unanticipated arrival in Belgium: Aunt Mina and Uncle Sam. In America, Aunt Sophie had triumphantly secured affidavits for them, and they would leave for Baltimore, from the port of Antwerp. We embraced at the railroad station in Antwerp, Aunt Mina quite emotional, Uncle Sam smiling and attempting to keep Aunt Mina at least relatively calm.

Four months later, on an April morning not long after my nineteenth birthday, I stood on a pier at the port of Antwerp, and watched as their ship, the Dutch vessel *SS Volendam*, sailed for the port of New York. Aunt Mina and Uncle Sam waved to me from the deck, and I fought off a crushing lonelinesss and tried not to let them see that I was crying. You'll come soon, they said. Of course, I said.

Aunt Mina and Uncle Sam Goldstein walking through Antwerp, 1939.

I entered Berchem General Hospital a few weeks later—on the afternoon of Thursday, May 9, 1940—for hernia surgery. It was scheduled for the next morning. I went to sleep in peacetime, and awoke to the wail of sirens all around me. It was six in the morning, not quite light. The beds on both sides of me were empty, and the whole hospital seemed to tremble. In a courtyard outside my window, there was a violent explosion and flashing lights. Flames rose around the windows, and then glass crashed into the room.

The lowlands—Holland, Belgium, and Luxembourg—had been attacked by the Luftwaffe's low-flying bombers. They were skimming over Antwerp's rooftops, nearly touching them, discharging bombs on innocent civilians. There was havoc on the grounds of the hospital, and on a loudspeaker a voice declared: "We are under attack. Be calm. If you are bedridden, stay where you are. If you are ambulatory, please proceed calmly to the administration office to collect your documents and receive instructions."

I dressed as quickly as I could and went to the admissions office. Hospital staffers were visibly shaken, but braced themselves for the arrival of bombing victims. Civil defense workers raced in, wearing white helmets and issuing instructions to leave the premises, walk close to houses, and not to venture near the middle of streets.

I walked outside and tried to calm myself. The ferocious noise quieted for a moment, then turned thunderous again. Anny and her parents lived fifteen minutes from the hospital. Crossing an open area, I crouched low to the ground. Around me, people scurried in all directions, frightened and grim, seeking temporary shelter as ambulance sirens wailed around us and bombs fell near the center of Antwerp. They fell on all those innocent people, on the animals at the zoo, on shops with diamonds in their windows whose value was now worth nothing at all.

New pain pierced my groin. I'd left my truss back at my room, thinking I would no longer need it after surgery. The bending and crouching caused new discomfort. War erupted all around me, and I was bothered by an absurd hernia!

When I reached the Frajermauers, out of breath, they were already listening to reports on the radio and trying to stay calm in a world gone utterly mad. Should we report to some safe place? Should we stay where we were? Had the German troops already crossed our borders? Within hours, orders were given for male enemy aliens to present themselves at district police stations. I was from Vienna, which now was part of Germany. Was I considered an enemy? The order was clear: come to the police, bring enough provisions for two days, a change of underwear, a blanket, and other necessities. Joseph suggested that I bring my Polish passport.

My father was a Pole who never changed his citizenship. Since Poland had been plundered by Germany, Joseph suggested I explain my status as a refugee from religious persecution. Surely this would show where my sympathies stood. I said a quick goodbye. I was confident I would be back within hours, and thus no emotional farewells were needed. But, just in case, I took provisions.

"See you soon," I said confidently.

Outside, the bombing seemed to have stopped. At the police station, an officer examined my papers. I thought about the ridiculousness of a hernia at the outbreak of a war, and waited to be sent back home.

105

"Pursuant to the laws of the kingdom, and in the interest of national security," the officer declared in a monotone, "you are under arrest."

I felt I had been run over by a German tank.

"Sir," I said, speaking in Flemish and trying to keep my composure, "I am not an enemy, I am a friend."

"Flemish?" he said.

"Yes, I learned it at the trade school. I have lived here for eighteen months. I came here," I said, speaking rapidly and trying not to trip over the words, "because I am a Jew. Long before this attack, I arrived. We have the same enemy. We're on the same side. I am young, I can fight. But don't lock me up. Do you understand?"

"Yes," he said slowly.

Around me, others were making the same case: German nationals working for corporations, members of embassy staffs, travel agents, all pleading with police officials.

"But the law is the law," the officer said, looking at me sadly.

All words counted for nothing now. The Belgians didn't know who among us might be foreign agents, and who was a friend. They could not take any chances. We were to be held, and there was the possibility we might be sent back to our countries of origin, exchanged for Belgians living in Germany. We were assembled and taken to austere military barracks, where we remained until the next afternoon, May 11, 1940. Then we were taken to the train station where I had arrived exactly eighteen months earlier, November 11, 1938.

This time, we were being taken to parts unknown.

6

May – August 1940

At the railroad station, we saw a world fracturing all about us. Soldiers said goodbye to their families and left for faraway battle areas. Legions of police moved with new urgency. We filed into a long passenger train, untold hundreds of men headed toward a destination utterly unknown to any of us.

"Southern Belgium," some conjectured. "An internment camp."

"France," others were certain.

But no one knew the truth, and no one knew how long our journey might take. France, southern Belgium, what difference did it make to us? Our lives were in someone else's hands, and all of our conjecture was merely an attempt to vent our anxieties and fears.

Around us, Europe was on fire. Germany, seizing more opportunities to make war, had invaded Belgium, The Netherlands, and Luxembourg despite repeated declarations of neutrality from all three. Hitler called such statements a lie, claiming the countries were staging areas for a planned British and French invasion of Germany. The Belgians issued official protests. "Premeditated aggression," the government called it. But such language counted for nothing; the time for words was over. France, in a virtual, albeit inactive, state of war with Germany for eight months, had now been invaded by Germany.

In fact, we would learn, the German invasion was aimed primarily at France and a quick knockout blow at Allies in the west. Within hours, German troops advanced across the four countries. Belgian forces, outmanned and tragically unprepared for war, retreated so desperately that they failed to demolish important bridges, and German troops thus found the going astonishingly easy.

As our train pulled out of the Antwerp station and rolled through Berchem, I wondered if the Frajermauers were safe, and wondered if Anny would think about me. Goodbye and goodbye once again. In my train compartment were Uncle David and his son Kurt, in the same predicament as my own. I still nursed grievances toward my uncle, and took no comfort in his nearness. As for poor Kurt, he was submissive to his overbearing father, and withdrawn.

I imagined my mother and my sisters cringing in their little apartment, or being dragged through the streets by squadrons of Nazi thugs. I imagined them calling for me, and I was too far away to hear them, and too swept up in my own miserable troubles to call back to them.

We came to Brussels and stopped in the city's train station. Railroad officials conferred with soldiers outside our windows, and then they were gone. Daylight began to fade. Officials moved through our car and asked for identification papers. More officials followed—customs officers, French gendarmes, military types.

We stopped for more than an hour. No one knew where we were. In the darkness, we could only offer guesses. More Belgian and French officers boarded. Several passengers were taken from the train. They were German nationals, to be exchanged for French and Belgian citizens stranded in Germany.

"Maybe," someone in our compartment said, "we're being taken away to safety from the Nazis. Maybe the Belgians are taking care of us."

"We are Jews," Uncle David replied morosely. "Who worries about us?"

His words lingered in the air while we waited in the darkness. France was blacked out. Our train was waiting for radio instructions based on troop movements, based on air attack possibilities, based on a thousand scenarios changing by the minute. We moved; we stopped again. Somewhere in the French countryside, we heard the sound of sirens. Were we near a big city? We heard the sound of aircraft overhead, and explosions moments later. How close, we had no idea. Should we sit calmly or throw ourselves to the floor? Even the flashes of light outside our windows gave little clue of distance. Were the planes friend or foe? No one knew. How long might the attacks last? No one even ventured a guess.

After half an hour, sirens faded, explosions ceased. The silence was eerie. Then, we heard a shrill engine whistle and the bumping of train couplings. We were on our way again, snaking through the dark countryside. Some slept. I drifted off and awoke when we reached a small depot in the morning. On a platform outside, civilians looked in at us. They seemed angry. One man moved his hand across his throat in a cutting motion.

"What does that mean?" someone in our compartment asked.

"Jew haters everywhere," another fellow said. "Let there be one Jew, and someone will hate him."

"How do they know we're Jewish?" someone else wondered.

"Maybe they think we're Germans."

We headed farther south, traveling faster through a sunny countryside. The train was hot and the windows were sealed. We pulled into a rural depot in southwest France, and found more civilians lined along the tracks. Many appeared to be farmers and working class people. Shouldn't they be on our side? But they were holding up signs:

A bas les Boches—Down with the Krauts

Mort aux Traîtres—Death to Traitors

"They think we're the enemy," I said.

"Somebody must have said we're German prisoners," another fellow said.

We traveled another night, another morning. For several hours we stopped at a small depot, marked Agen, southeast of Bordeaux, and then came a mid-afternoon directive: Everyone off the train.

I carried a backpack with items the Belgian authorities had told us to take: a change of clothes, a blanket. Standing in line, I turned back to glance at the outside of the train and saw words painted in white on the side: Fifth Column.

A light went on in my head: so that's what all that anger was about. "Fifth Column" described people who aided an enemy from within their own country. We'd been billed as spies, as traitors. A rage boiled through me, which turned to fear. I knew what happened to traitors in wartime. Were they planning to kill all of us? I was no spy, just a harmless Jew from Vienna, a victim of the Germans, a friend and ally of the French and the Belgians. To whom could I explain who I was?

But there was no one assigned for listening, and we would only learn the truth later. At the Franco-Belgian border, where the German nationals had been taken from the train, negotiations were held for the rest of us. The French had already taken thousands of refugees since 1933, many of whom were now living in internment camps, unable to stabilize their legal status. The Belgians were in a state of emergency, about to be swallowed up by the German invaders. As Jews, we might be thrown to the wolves again.

So the French found a solution. Our convoy would proceed if we were given the designation of subversives, a threat to the security of the state. It would get us into France, after which they would deal with us. We would suffer the sneers of the mobs until then.

We marched from the train to a nearby rail yard cluttered with old cars. A handful of unarmed guards kept us in line. No weapons; a good sign. We were civilian internees, nothing to fear from us. Where would we go? How far could we go? A continent at war, and we were refugees from everywhere.

In an hour, we were all assigned various railroad cars. Some had bunks, others only straw spread across the floor. Uncle David and Kurt and I shared a car with a few others. A military field kitchen, a giant boiler on a cart, was rolled into the compound to cook our food.

For the moment, it seemed almost serene. In northeast France, German paratroopers were landing, and General Rommel was crossing the Meuse River and driving a wedge into the French Ninth Army. In The Netherlands, German Stuka bombers attacked Rotterdam and destroyed twenty thousand buildings. The government of The Netherlands fled to Britain. All Dutch resistance ceased. In Luxembourg, where I'd once found brief refuge, the Germans confiscated Jewish property, transferring stores and factories and farms to Aryan ownership. Then, within months, came the announcement that the Jews of Luxembourg had three weeks to leave or be deported to forced labor camps. The day of deportation was set for October 12—Yom Kippur, the Jewish Day of Atonement.

In our tiny corner of the world, we sat and waited. In the evening we ate a stew made of beans, potatoes, and cubes of beef. In the morning, after sweating through a warm and balmy night, we were given bread and cheese. After eating, we lined up for registration. The lines moved slowly. Papers had to be examined, questions asked: nationality, date and place of birth, names of parents, religion, profession or trade.

"Have you ever been in France before?" they asked to facilitate another search of records.

"Have you ever had a communicable disease?" they asked for some unknown reason.

I ventured a question of my own: Would we stay here, or move? But there was no answer.

Registration lasted until evening. We remained at Agen for a few nights and days, getting hotter and dirtier, wanting to shower, hoping to

111

move on. My hernia bothered me off and on. If I avoided kneeling and bending, it behaved itself.

At daybreak on May 20, loudspeakers told us to line up near our quarters. Soon we were back on the train which had brought us here from Antwerp. The "Fifth Column" words had been scrubbed off, leaving behind white smears. The train went farther south, picking up speed. By late afternoon we reached our destination: the beach at St. Cyprien, in southern France, with its internment camp first established during the Spanish Civil War a few years earlier, now sitting parched in the sun.

We marched into the camp and saw sand stretching toward the Mediterranean Sea. Unlike Blankenberge, the resort where my heart lifted in Anny's presence, the beach and water at St. Cyprien were not for our enjoyment. The camp was divided into two sections, and these were separated by barbed wire. Detainees waved from their side of the wire, but said nothing. There was barbed wire near the water's edge, and barbed wire hemmed us in from all other directions. To the southwest was Spain, where the beach touched the Pyrénées Mountains. The blue sea against the backdrop of rugged mountains, bathed by the setting sun, provided a glimpse at nature's awesome beauty.

Such beauty eluded our immediate surroundings and our living quarters, a line of wooden barracks with corrugated metal roofs that ran parallel with the coastline. There were no floors, only the sandy beach itself covered with straw. The metal roofs radiated heat, and a foul odor rose from the straw. The air was stale and stifling. I reached for a light switch near the entrance. There was none. I looked at the ceiling, and saw no lights. I looked for water faucets, and found none. I looked for toilets, and learned they were lined along the barbed wire at the edge of the sea. They were elevated on stilts, with steps leading up. During high tide, the incoming Mediterranean washed over the steps.

A small pile of dry straw became my bed.

"Horses, they treat better than this," someone said. "At least they get their straw changed."

"Yes, but horses are beasts of labor," I said. "They are useful. Of what use are we?"

"We are Jews," said Uncle David, sweating madly in the heat. "Who cares about us?"

He and Kurt slept across from me, but we kept our distance. In the evenings, I stood outside and enjoyed the breezes blowing in from the sea. I thought of sleeping outside, but the wind shifted the sand around. It was better to stay inside, with all of its odors and all of its prickly straw. As darkness arrived, I could see flickering lights from seagoing vessels and fishing boats, and I imagined sailing great distances from this place. Aunt Mina and Uncle Sam were in America now. They had gotten me to Luxembourg, but America was too far away, even farther than my imagination.

There were about forty men in our barracks. Many passed the night without sleep, unable to cope with the new surroundings and the uncomfortable floor. When I dropped off, I was awakened: someone sneezing, someone talking. Some would walk outside for fresh air. Every shuffling step through the straw stirred the dust, and the sneezes.

At dawn, I walked barefoot on the beach, stepping on sand that had cooled overnight. It felt dewy and refreshing. Anny and I had walked on such sand. Now she seemed one more person to add to my vanished past.

In the barracks that morning, I watched Uncle David and Kurt busily straightening their sleeping area. Despite his grand perspiring, my uncle was a fanatic about neatness. These conditions clearly irritated him, and Kurt was paying a price for it.

"Put this over there," Uncle David said.

He was directing Kurt where to move pieces of straw. This piece should go here, and that piece there, Uncle David ordered while under the delusion that the straw would then stay in one place.

"Uncle David," I said haltingly, "this can't help much. You're only moving dirt from one place to another."

113

"Who asked you?" he snapped.

I joined others in cleaning the barracks—not the straw, but the vestiges of previous occupants: old socks, hairbrushes, a belt, a bent can that once contained *pâté de foie gras*, a handkerchief stained with dried blood and a torn strip of used gauze, some crumpled paper bags. These were not trash, but treasures, precious commodities when there was no toilet paper. I put them in my backpack for safekeeping. Later, men would fight over scraps of paper. With no tissues in the latrine, some were using straw, and then they rinsed their hands at the edge of the sea.

I walked listlessly along the beach in a pair of shorts, barefoot and shirtless, absorbing the breeze and the sun, and found many others doing the same. We were a colony of wanderers, beachcombers without destinations, killers of time. At one end of the camp was a barracks building with a sign: Commandature. The sign was more impressive than the men inside, who were merely a handful of guards, weary and worn out by the sun, leftovers from the previous war—Moroccans, Senegalese, and other French Colonials. Now, with their country in peril, gasping for salvation, they watched over people who didn't need to be watched, wretched displaced Jews who were not the enemy.

Each hour passed slowly. As June approached, the days grew hotter and the barracks' interior became stifling by mid-day. A dry wind, which the French called the "mistral," blew across the campsite occasionally, bringing cooler air, but not for long. Many of us were perpetually on the edge of nausea.

It was an isolated, maddening little world, in which we had no notion of the turmoil outside. An avalanche of civilians, frightened by the invasions and rumors, had taken to the roads. Relief facilities were overwhelmed. Officials had no idea what to do, and so internment camps became the simplest solution.

One morning in the camp the skeletal remains of some animal were discovered. It seemed to be a jawbone, from a lamb or a goat judging by the size. Great discussions ensued, experts sought. Anything, to take us out of the sameness of our unchanging little world.

We approached a guard and held up the animal remains, asking, "Where does this come from?"

"You'll find a lot of those bones if you look for them," he said lazily. "The Spaniards, it is they who abandoned this garbage."

The guards' boredom was matched by our own. There was nothing to do. The sun was relentless, and the only shade was inside the barracks, which were impossible during the day. So we searched for more bones, seeking distraction from each day's ennui, looking like children digging for seashells. We found a piece of a fossil that looked like part of a steer's horn. Near one of the latrines, I found part of a small animal's ribcage, still connected. The guard had been right: Look for it, and you'll find it.

We shared the chore of bringing meals to the barracks from the kitchen, which was several hundred yards away. It took two men to do this. We used long sticks to carry the canteens, their handles suspended from them. One man on each side held the sticks, trotting carefully on the hot sand to prevent the canteens from swinging and spilling over. On windy days, sand blew into the food.

The man who ran the kitchen was a refugee from Germany named Rothschild. He was a short, rotund butcher, proud that he served relatively palatable food. Once, he handed me a bone with some meat still on it and said, "Here, take this. Something to gnaw on." It was a man giving a bone to a dog, but I reached for it and lingered over the unexpected treat.

One day a delivery of beef arrived. Rothschild refused to accept it. "A bad smell," he said. The delivery man was reluctant to take it back, but Rothschild was insistent.

"I don't want to poison these people," he said. "They are hungry, but not this hungry. If I want to smell something this bad, I'll go to my barracks."

115

By now, many of the barracks were infested with vermin. Lice and fleas were abundant. What had seemed a barn was now a privy. Men chosen to represent the internees reported the situation to the commandant, and soon workers appeared, dressed in protective garb, who sprayed disinfectant in all the barracks. We evacuated the premises. Doors were closed, leaving the barracks sealed for two hours. The old, putrid odors were gone, replaced by a new, foul chemical odor.

My skin turned dark and leathery by mid-June. I could walk on the sand now without noticing its heat, and lost track of much time. Here and there, rumors arrived that the Germans had broken through on all fronts, that Belgium and Holland had been defeated, and the French were fighting, but not well.

"How goes it with France?" I asked a French guard. "These rumors are troubling."

"Ah, good God," he replied lazily. "France will never surrender."

On June 22, 1940, Marshal Henri-Philippe Pétain signed the French armistice with the Germans at Compiègne. One of the guards passed us the news. With France suffering humiliating defeat, what would happen to us? As a nation, France would survive. As a people, the Jews were far less assured.

Early one morning I stood on the brick patio by the water faucets, waiting in line to wash. A man behind me tapped me on the shoulder and pointed to the soap I held in my hand.

"Where does this come from?" he asked.

I'd brought it when the Belgian government first advised us to bring provisions to the police districts. By now, it was one of the last pieces of soap in the camp.

"You're lucky to have it," he said.

"Would you like to use it?"

He looked at it, as though finding a treasure.

"Yes," he said, almost apologetically, "but only for my face."

The soap lasted a few more days, and then vanished.

Food, meanwhile, was plentiful enough that we could keep bread overnight in our barracks. But it had to be protected from marauding rats. So we hung the bread from overhead traverse bars running just below the ceiling. Sometimes this helped, but sometimes the rats got to it.

Then came a new calamity: simultaneous flooding and an outbreak of dysentery. The Mediterranean rose to the top steps leading to the elevated latrines. As we stood in line to use them, we had to wade through water. Men grew sick and short-tempered, banging on the latrine doors and snapping at those who took too long in the toilets. Soon there was pushing and shoving, and then fights. Many leaving the latrines to make room for those in line quickly returned to the line, awaiting a new sitting. Scraps of paper took on great new value. Soon there was nothing left but straw. Between June and September, a dozen inmates died. Hundreds more lingered in their barracks, sick with fever, attended by fellow inmates. The scent of death began to mix with the overwhelming heat.

By August, I took fate into my own hands. A messenger from the camp office came for me in my barracks and handed me a visitor's permit with a name on it: Leon Oesterreicher, Anny's friend from Antwerp, who I had met just just briefly in Berchem where we played records on a little Victrola.

"What are you doing here?"

"Intending to get you out," he whispered. I was flabbergasted. I hoped for a miracle, but never anticipated it from the passers-by in my life.

"I've been watching the guards," he said. "They're disgusted with their jobs. You think they care who stays and who goes?"

"What are you proposing?"

I could hardly believe Leon's mere presence, much less absorb the details of an escape, which still seemed preposterous.

"I could bribe one of them," Leon said. "I could have them look the other way at the right moment. But this might be risky."

"Yes, risky," I agreed. "You'll wind up in here, with me."

"Leo," he said, "in Toulouse, I heard of escapes from here. And I've seen a spot where you could get out. No one will miss you."

I stood there for a moment, dumbstruck, when he added, "By the way, I have news of the Frajermauers. I know where Anny is staying."

He took me to a spot near the kitchen delivery entrance and showed me a gap between the wire and the sand. He lifted the barbed wire a few inches and gestured as if to say, "You see? You could crawl beneath it." He said he would stand a few meters away and be my lookout. He didn't have to ask me twice. What punishment could they give me worse than this?

I went back to my barracks to fetch my few belongings. It was late in the afternoon. I put on my shirt and shoes, the first time I'd worn them in weeks. Uncle David peered at me through the gloomy barracks light.

"I have a friend who's here," I said. I was torn between memories of my uncle's callousness, and the simple desire to tell him of escape plans he himself might attempt. "He says I should get away from here. He says it is possible."

"A friend," said Uncle David, waving disgustedly. "What does he know? Don't get involved in such a thing."

I nodded my head, finished gathering my things and turned to go.

"You are mad," Uncle David said. As I reached the door, he said, "Do as you wish."

I said goodbye to my cousin Kurt, who would never leave without his father, and walked back to the kitchen, trying not to look conspicuous. Leon was waiting on the outside of the barbed wire. No guards seemed to be watching the area. Was the hole in the sand deep enough? I dug one heel into it, trying to make it deeper. Was I small enough to fit through? My heart pounded. Would the guards see me?

I slid the backpack through the opening, and Leon lifted the wire several inches. I slid down, feet first, blocking all sights and sounds around me, as though this tiny piece of geography were the only world that existed and I merely had to slide through to find salvation.

And there I was, climbing out of the other side of the fence, with Leon brushing sand off my clothes. We stood there for a second or two, as though not quite believing it.

"Stay calm if anyone approaches," Leon said. "Walk normally."

We began to walk, and not a soul seemed to notice, or to care. Neither of us said a word for perhaps two minutes. I was lighthearted and wanted to run.

Finally, Leon declared, exuberantly, *"Ça y est."* That's it.

We quickened our steps and in an hour came to a narrow road leading to Perpignan. Occasionally, cyclists rode past and waved to us. We saw no one else.

"How did you know how to find me?" I asked.

"I learned that the Belgian transports were brought here," he said. "I knew you'd be here."

He said Anny and her family had fled Antwerp soon after Belgium's capitulation. They'd gone south by train and by truck. When he looked through the Red Cross lists of refugees in the Toulouse office, he found the name Frajermauer. They were in Luchon, in the mountains near the Spanish border.

"I can put you on a train," Leon said.

"I have no money."

"I'll take care of it," he said. "My gift to you."

A day later, still scarcely believing my freedom, I was in Luchon.

7

August 1940 – December 1941

Luchon was a vacation town usually visited by lighthearted revelers. Now it was filled with the uprooted and anxious citizens of Europe who were like me. They were on the run, and they were trying to figure out each step of the journey in the midst of their running.

The great breadth of upheaval had been lost on me in the isolation of St. Cyprien. As the Germans advanced across Europe, millions forced from their homes gathered up whatever belongings they could carry and boarded trains and trucks and wagons, or simply walked the continent's roads in search of some safe haven. The routes into southern France were filled with columns of fleeing refugees who were sometimes driven off the roads when low-flying German planes strafed them. When the French government capitulated, and signed its armistice with Germany, the strafing ceased. But where would people hide now that the Germans could move about at will?

Luchon was one of those places where the uprooted paused to catch their breath, and hide for a while, and hope that the Germans found it too insignificant to invade. When I reached the train station there, town council representatives were giving directions to a local Red Cross office where they kept the names of refugees and information on lodging. On the main street in town I found an information office, which had been set up hurriedly. Sheets of paper were spread across wooden tables, and anxious people examined their contents.

I found lists and lists: names of people running with no destinations while their native countries collapsed behind them. Many of the names were Jewish. In the aftermath of the German invasions, the massive exodus to the south overwhelmed towns and villages. Luchon, trying its best to adjust, was an inexplicable resting place, a resort area in the rugged Pyrénées Mountains near the Spanish border known for its hot thermal spas and its skiing. People came here to play. But now it was overrun by those with the simple wish to stay alive, people who'd once led reputable lives, who'd built families and done honest work, who'd contributed to their communities, who'd imagined themselves safe in their homes because they were a part of something. Now they were just names on lists and more lists, trying to get through each unpredictable day.

On one of the lists, I found the Frajermauers. I wanted to jump miles into the air. A Red Cross official gave me the address, 7 Rue Hortense, and I found their apartment a few blocks away, hoping they would be there to welcome me and not find me a burden.

Joseph Frajermauer opened the door. His pipe nearly fell from his mouth. His muscular arms wrapped around me, and he cried, "Rachel, Anneke, Netty, come see who it is!"

He was flabbergasted as I'd never seen him before, and in seconds I was embraced by everyone. Rachel's eyes filled up, and Anny kissed me on the cheek.

"You're so dark," Netty said.

"Yes, three months on the beach, at the sea," I laughed.

"We had no idea where the train from Antwerp had taken you," Joseph said.

Rachel wiped a tear from her eyes and said, "Man thinks, but God guides."

It was decided quickly: I would stay with them. Such relief to hear the words! I would sleep on a sofa. They asked, will this be all right? My God, after the straw bed at St. Cyprien, this was a monarch's luxury. We talked as though we'd been parted years instead of months. They'd arrived here several weeks after Germany's bombing of Belgium, joined by Joseph's brothers and sisters and their spouses. I told them how I'd escaped from St. Cyprien.

"Leon?" they said.

"Out of the blue," I said.

"Typical," said Anny. And, just as suddenly as Leon Oesterreicher entered my life, he'd exited again and was gone forever, caught up in his own unpredictable version of the war.

Anny and I walked through the town later in the day. There were elegant sidewalk cafés and a casino set in a park. In the distance, all around us, was a breathtaking mountainous paradise. I held Anny's hand, and wondered if I would still hold it tomorrow.

In the morning, her father and I went to the town hall to register me as a "refugee from the north." My Belgian identification papers were enough; no questions were asked. I was just another straggler who'd managed to escape a war zone. Registration meant I was now a legal, temporary resident of Luchon, just like all the others.

Joseph and I walked slowly through the town and found a sign that advertised: "Buy one chicken, get one dozen eggs free." Remarkable, I thought. In Vienna, we'd had a saying about people living so sumptuously: He lives like God in France. Here was confirmation of it, a cornucopia with no rations, no restrictions, plenty of meat and vegetables, luscious fruit, delicious breads. The Pyrénées was a land of plenty.

It was wonderful while it lasted. By controlling the occupied areas of France, the Germans also affected the unoccupied areas. Within weeks, food was scarce and had to be rationed. Even salt ran out. The Germans occupied the salt mines in the southwest and requisitioned salt for the production of ammunition. Soon it was impossible to find soap in the

123

Leo's Belgian identification papers, which helped him register as a temporary resident in Luchon.

stores. People hoarded. Joseph had no inclination to stand in line for a bar of soap. He remembered that, during the last war, his father had made soap in Poland.

"I even helped him with it," he said happily.

One day he came home with a container filled with suet that he'd gotten from a friendly butcher. From a druggist, he bought lye. Voilà! He was ready to produce soap for the whole family.

As the days went by, the Vichy government, under Marshal Pétain, became an eager participant in Hitler's new Europe. Jews were barred from holding official positions in the French government, and were forbidden to practice law, to teach, or to join the military. Jobs of all sorts were now closed. Then, in the first week of October, thousands of Jews who'd fled Nazi persecution were arrested and taken to the internment camp of Gurs, in the lower Pyrénées. Many died of starvation there. Many froze. All suffered from malnutrition.

In Luchon, in the autumn of 1940, we suffered mainly from anxiety and restlessness, wondering where we could run if the Germans approached. As Jews in Luchon, we were clearly outsiders. The town's

inhabitants had never seen Jews before, and now they were about to witness something else that was new to them: the Jewish high holidays. The
town council authorized use of a hall— the municipal casino—for high
holiday services. The man conducting the services was a cantor from
Vienna named Kreitstein, in whose choir I had sung for a short time as
a boy alto, at the Kaschlgasse Synagogue. He and his family fled Austria
after the *Anschluss.*

On Rosh Hashanah, God seemed to smile. The weather in Luchon
was glorious, with southern France in all of her autumn radiance. The
casino grounds were awash in sunlight, and mountain breezes wafted
through the open doors. More than a hundred people gathered and
recited the ancient prayers, and we told ourselves that the new year
would bring better times. Though the cantor chanted emotionally, the
music took on incongruous tones. Mixed with the ancient Judaic
melodies, we could hear the strains of Catalan music emanating from a
nearby bistro.

We were startled as we left the service. Outside the casino, a large
crowd gathered some yards from the entrance, studying us, eyeing our
religious articles, as though looking at visitors from another galaxy.
Many of us associated crowds with menace, but this one seemed
merely curious.

Wearing a Basque beret, and my face still deeply tanned from the
camp at St. Cyprien, I looked more "Mediterranean" than Viennese. A
local man approached me as I left the service.

"Why were you inside with the others?" he asked.

"The others?"

"The Jews."

"I'm Jewish," I explained.

"Oh, you are Jewish," he said. "You look like one of us."

I walked away and wondered: What do Jews look like? Could it not
be an easy progression from this man's benign questioning to Hitler's
Aryan stereotyping? Ten days later, there were services for Yom Kippur,

the solemn Day of Atonement. I sat in our makeshift synagogue and wondered: Atone for what?

"I have sinned," the holiday's liturgy reminds us incessantly. "I have sinned, I have sinned."

I wondered: Have I sinned? And the answer came to me in the faces of my mother and my sisters. They were hiding in their apartment, and I was living in a mountain resort. I have sinned, I have sinned. In Vienna, the synagogues had been burned; I was praying in a synagogue converted from a casino. I have sinned, I have sinned. Should I leave this place now, and reach across the war zones for a rescue miracle to save my sisters?

"*Al cheit,*" the cantor Kreitstein intoned, "*al cheit, al cheit.*" I have sinned, I have sinned.

And the others, I thought: Were those who harmed innocent people ready for their own day of atonement? Was there anyone in all of France who would enter a confessional and declare, "I have sinned against my fellow man because he is a Jew, as was Jesus"?

With France fallen to Germany, the nation suddenly found itself in a crisis regarding one of its cherished industries. With so many involved in military affairs, who would harvest grapes for wine? The southern vineyards were satiated after a long summer. Grapes couldn't be allowed to remain on the vine once they had ripened. The Vichy government, realizing that Jewish refugees were living in towns and villages across the south, where we were eager to ingratiate ourselves, issued an appeal: Work in the vineyards, help us harvest the grapes. In Luchon, about fifty of us signed up. There were no cash payments, but we were given poultry and eggs, cheese and butter and vegetables, and wine. With so many foods now hard to find, such payment was as valuable as gold coins.

Five of us in the family took a train to the walled city of Carcassonne, located on the banks of the river Aude, where we slept next to a farmhouse and were awakened at 4:30 the next morning, when the air was still frosty. Breakfast was a hearty, well-stocked vegetable soup, prepared by the farmer's wife, who held a skillet the size of a manhole cover with both hands over a large fireplace and prepared marvelous mushroom and onion omelets served with red wine and fresh bread. At such moments, I seemed to be having a fortunate war.

In an hour, we went to a vineyard and were handed pruning shears to cut grapes from vines. The autumn air was chilly, and there were braziers spread around the work area to warm our hands. The morning dew on the vines was cold, and numbed our fingers. But the day grew warmer toward late morning, and we fell into routines. Hod carriers came by every fifteen or twenty minutes to empty the baskets of grapes. They were dumped into a contraption above a vat sitting on a flatbed truck, and three female farm hands stood barefoot and stomped the grapes into pulp, the juice flowing into the vat below through sieve-like openings.

The farm seemed a place out of another time. Neither politics nor religion was discussed. The war had its place, and the wine had its place. The farmer's concerns, and the war's, did not mix. At week's end, we returned to Luchon with enough food for several days' bountiful eating. And then the realities of war began to creep back into our lives.

Orders arrived: We had to leave Luchon within days. We were stunned. We'd just helped the French with their precious wine, and imagined they might feign gratitude for at least a little longer. We were assigned to Bagnères-de-Bigorre, as Luchon was emptied of all new-comers. We were in the hands of a bureaucratic system that did not issue explanations.

"Winter is coming," Joseph said cynically. "Luchon must be made ready for the ski season."

Time was essential. The land was heavy with refugees now, and living quarters were difficult to find, particularly for our extended family of more than a dozen people. Bagnères was about forty miles northwest of Luchon, and Joseph rented an old truck, which we drove for two hours down steep, winding roads, wondering what mysteries this new town held for us.

127

Bagnères was located in a basin encircled by lush and verdant foothills. Behind them were the snowcapped Pyrénées. It was late November now, and we crowded into a farmhouse with a thatched roof, several bedrooms, and a kitchen. I shared a room with two of Anny's cousins, Joseph and Willy Gischlider. Joseph was twenty-one, a college student in Brussels when the Germans attacked. Willy, twenty-four, was a chemist. They were happy fellows, exuding life and enthusiasm until March 4, 1943, when they were deported to Auschwitz to die.

But now, Bagnères continued to swell with refugees. The townspeople had never seen Jews before, and now we were everywhere. At breakfast one day, Rachel laughed, "A kosher butcher could get rich here."

But there was hardly any meat at all. Rationing was a way of life. That winter, it was difficult finding most commodities. All over France, the Germans requisitioned everything they could get their hands on. The Vichy regime cooperated fully. Butter was rationed at a few ounces per week. Joseph Frajermauer, always thinking, noticed a farmer on a wagon delivering milk to a dairy store, which was itself almost devoid of dairy items.

"We are refugees," he told the farmer. "We are living at an old farmhouse. We have old people and young children. If you could deliver milk to us, we would pay you more than the going rate."

The farmer understood that this exchange was to be done out of sight. Black markets operated everywhere. You did what you had to in order to feed your family. The farmer agreed to deliver milk once a week. To Joseph, though, the milk was only a means to an end. The farmer delivered ten liters of milk in green bottles each week. From the milk, Joseph made butter. Milk was reasonably accessible in stores; butter was not.

Joseph showed us how the milk bottles were to be held by the neck and shaken steadily up and down, like a bartender mixing drinks, until tiny particles of sediment began to show against the green glass and joined to form bigger lumps. This took half an hour and exhausted our

128

arms. Then we would uncork the bottle, pour the milk into a pot and release the thick remainder into a container by hitting the bottle solidly at the bottom. In Bagnères, we never ran out of butter.

Nor did we run out of news. Early in 1941, the German general policy was to expel Jews from the occupied areas. But there were differences in approach. While the government talked of banning all Jewish influence in every area of public life, the military authorities still worried about international law, and about antagonizing French public opinion. They wanted more overt cooperation from the French people themselves. In Bagnères, we held our breath.

In March, as I turned twenty, I brooded increasingly over the fate of my mother and my sisters. We'd had no contact since my days in Belgium, and my mother knew I would attempt to write to ease her fears about me. But postal service between Germany and France had ceased, so I needed a device. My cousin Herbert Fischmann was in Switzerland, at a labor camp. Mail between France and Switzerland, and between Switzerland and Germany, still flowed. So Herbie became the middle man between my mother and me, shuffling letters back and forth. Within weeks, he received a letter and photograph from my sister Henny. I was elated. The letter said they were well. It felt as if a wall had been torn down, and a vision of life once thought to be gone might yet return.

In April, we resettled in a brick and stucco cottage near the edge of town. There was room for all of us and a serene view of the surrounding foothills. Meanwhile, I wrote letters: to Vienna, but also to America. Aunt Mina and Uncle Sam were in Baltimore with Aunt Sophie, who prepared an affidavit of support for me, hoping to obtain a visa of immigration to the United States. The thought of going to America supplied me with hope, but also confusion. Could I leave my family on the other side of an ocean? Could I leave Anny? My feelings for her were strong, but the war muddled all of our emotions.

One day—while queuing up at the covered market, ration coupons in hand—I met a man named Mendel Spira, who came from Paris with

129

his wife and two teenaged daughters. He had a radio. At night, we sat in his apartment and listened to the BBC's transmission of Radio Free France, with the set turned to the lowest audible volume. The Vichy government had decreed that no one was to listen. Those caught were punished severely.

The radio was difficult to hear because the Germans inflicted static interference. Shh, Spira would say. One night in June, there was stunning news on the BBC. Germany had launched a massive attack against the Russians. The next day, Germany ordered the arrest of White Russian expatriates in France, most of whom were Jews. Vichy complied. The internment camps now received new inmates.

Quickly, Jews were purged from professions, from business, from crafts and industry. From June to December came decrees that limited Jewish participation in the practice of medicine, law, architecture,

The Spira family—Susie, Recha, Recha's husband, Helene, and Mendel.

theater, dentistry. The amount of Jewish students was also controlled.

Elsewhere, the stories were worse. In June, the BBC reported, there were nearly four thousand deaths at a Jewish pogrom in Kaunas, Lithuania. In July, the Germans moved into Lwow, Poland, and murdered seven thousand Jews. A week later, all Jews in the Baltic states were ordered to wear the Star of David on their shirts. In August, Vichy France cracked down heavily on all anti-Nazi activity. In September, a German officer was shot and killed in Paris, setting off mass reprisal executions. In America, Charles Lindbergh, the greatest hero of his age, accused the

British, the Jewish, and the Roosevelt administration of pressing the United States toward war. In October, Gestapo troops began destroying the synagogues of Paris.

Through all of this, I felt personal grand luck and consuming guilt. Each day, I awaited word from my mother through Herbie in Switzerland. Letters arrived about once a month, but the words were guarded. There was nothing about the situation at home, just general news about family. The fear that censors would alert authorities was too strong to allow any frank and open correspondence. At best, an amateur code developed: "Uncle Heini is never in a good mood. He gets worse every day." I had no Uncle Heini. Heini was Hitler; the situation was worse every day.

Obtaining the barest necessities became a chore. The Jews of Austria were given ration cards marked with a "J." They could shop only in certain stores and at given times. They received no ration cards for clothing and no special allotments. Eventually, they would no longer be sold meat, milk, fish, eggs, white flour, or fruit and vegetables.

Slowly life for me in southern France grew worse, too. When we first arrived in Bagnères, we had to register at the local police station. Now we had to register again simply as Jews. Our time here was clearly coming to an end. We fretted our way through the hours. I sat on the sloping banks of the Adour with Anny and wondered which would triumph—our feelings for each other, or the war. At the movie theater, we watched newsreels that were heavy-handed Nazi propaganda: German victories without end, Russians in retreat, France's niche in the new Europe, Vichy fighting the Maquis, the French resistance movement. We left the theater and wondered how humanity managed to stay alive, and held on to each other's hands.

Shhh, said Mendel Spira, as we listened to the radio news at night. We heard dreadful stories of the German killing squads called the Einsatzgruppen, who pillaged and burned towns from the Baltic to the Black Sea. It was nerve-wracking merely listening to the radio. The

131

Einsatzgruppen entered communities and gathered all Jews for "resettlement." The Jews had to hand over all of their valuables and take off their clothes. Then they were led to places of execution next to deeply dug ditches, into which their corpses were flung.

That autumn, deportations from Vienna to the east began. Aunt Charlotte and my cousin Judith were shipped to a Lodz ghetto *en route* to Auschwitz. Uncle Isidore was already there. I was in France, dreaming of America. Each day I went to the post office, hoping to find good news somewhere beyond so much awfulness. One day, my eyes fell on a red-white-and-blue bordered envelope from America.

"Enfin, ça y est," the postal clerk said. At last, it's here.

He knew. For weeks, I'd been sighing disappointingly when no mail arrived from America. Now, Aunt Sophie in Baltimore was writing to me. With the help of the Hebrew Immigration Aid Society, my affidavit was accepted by the U.S. Immigration and Naturalization Service. In the near future, she wrote, I should receive notification from a U.S. Consulate to appear at its office for my visa.

I was overjoyed, and then I was not. My mother wasn't in America; she was huddling with my sisters in Vienna. Anny wasn't in America; she was here in the mountains of France.

"So," Joseph Frajermauer said, when I told everyone the news, "you're going to America."

His voice trailed off, and there were no more words. In October, we harvested the grapes once more. In November, I received notification: Present yourself at the U.S. Consulate in Marseilles on December 8, 1941.

"When I come back," I told everyone, "I'll have my visa."

"Well, you've made up your mind," Joseph said. "But I always imagined you living in Belgium, getting into the diamond business."

Anny, who was never very loquacious, kept silent. Again, I thought, goodbye to my loved ones, goodbye and goodbye.

With my heart torn, I boarded a train for Marseilles to pick up my papers and then return to the Frajermauers long enough to book passage to America. On Sunday, December 7, I strolled the Canebière, the main artery of Marseilles. The evening was mild. The Château D'If, Marseilles' landmark, was silhouetted beneath an opaque sky. I slept in a small hotel room, feeling isolated but happy and liberated, feeling I would have a chance to live out my full life in America.

Early the next morning, I left the hotel and stopped at a newspaper kiosk on my way to the U.S. Consulate. I saw a headline: *Le Japon Attaque La Flotille Américaine A Pearl Harbor.*

I stood transfixed. Never had I heard of Pearl Harbor, and now it was the fulcrum of my entire life. At nine o'clock, I presented myself to a receptionist at the consulate, and saw more than a dozen other visa applicants.

"In view of the hostilities," we were told, "the consulate has been instructed to cease all visa-processing formalities until further notice."

A woman standing with her small children began to cry, so the children also cried. A dreadful wailing commenced. A mistake, we proclaimed. People are waiting for us, we moaned. Yes, yes, we were told placatingly, but this is war. We all must make sacrifices.

We waited for someone in authority to enter the room, to tell us our pleas would be answered, that an exception would be made for us. No one came. The train ride back to Bagnères seemed like a descent into doom.

8

December 1941 - October 1942

I rode the train back to Bagnères in a state of melancholia. America, goodbye. Once so vivid I'd practically held it in my hand, it had now disappeared beyond a vast ocean. When I returned to the Frajermauers, they saw the gloom into which I'd descended, and tried to comfort me. And I tried to let them.

Within days, a letter arrived from Vienna. My mother and Henny had been removed from their apartment to new surroundings, and my little sister Ditta was taken somewhere else. "Transfers," they said, the bland, operative word for the uprootings. My mother and Henny were in one place, and Ditta in another, and my grandmother and my Aunt Rosa and my Aunt Toba were each transferred to some other ghetto created for Vienna's Jews. My sense of dread deepened, and my helplessness, and I feared I would never see any of them again.

In the Christmas season, I walked the subdued streets of Bagnères. The holiday was a solemn occasion here, not given to great festivities, and this was no time for rejoicing. On Mendel Spira's radio, we heard reports of the German Einsatzgruppen committing atrocities beyond belief. Sshhh, Spira said, fine-tuning between bursts of static, as we struggled to hear the tally of daily killing. In Lithuania, Einsatzgruppen execution squads murdered thirty-two thousand Jews in a matter of days; in the Baltic states, more than a quarter-million Jews were murdered during the first six months of German occupation. People all over the world were being killed, but in our case, it was killing for the singular reason of being Jewish. Sshhh, Spira would say. It was important to know the mathematics of genocide.

In February came the twelfth anniversary of my father's death, and my mother wrote to remind me. Say *Kaddish* for him, she said. Remember him. Remember the dead, and hope the living will remember us when we're gone. I remembered that I was nine when my father died, and I wondered if his spirit could see his widow and his children separated across Europe, and if he suffered to see us so vulnerable.

In the iron cold of winter, a sense of dread hung in the air. In France, the Pétain regime was assigning Jews to specific towns, to register with officials at regular intervals. This way, they could keep track of us. The alternative was not to register, but without registering there was no access to ration cards for food. So you stayed in your place. Anyone trying to leave would be imprisoned. The death camps were just beginning to accomplish their fullest potential, and we were beginning to hear rumors that terrified us.

We were assigned to Cauterets, a small town about twenty miles southwest of Bagnères, near the Spanish border. It was a mecca for skiers. It had about a thousand residents, most of whom had rarely seen a Jew. Joseph Frajermauer and his brother found a house, and again we gathered our belongings. It seemed an exodus, and I thought about the coming holiday of Passover commemorating the Jewish exodus from Egypt. "Remember," the rabbis tell us, "that once, we were slaves in Egypt, and the Lord led us out of bondage." Where was that God now?

Another letter from Vienna arrived, via my cousin Herbie in Switzerland, with a present marking my twenty-first birthday: a photograph of my sister Ditta. The photograph warmed my heart, for it confirmed her very existence. Words counted for something, but faces showed life. There she was, eyes wide open, expression sensitive and lovely, almost as I'd remembered her. But the photo also confirmed the passage of time. It was already more than three years since I'd left, and my sister was now shrugging off the last vestiges of childhood for adolescence. The emptiness of those three years renewed the sense of distance in our lives.

As we left Bagnères for Cauterets, I packed my knapsack and we said goodbye to those staying behind:

The photograph of Ditta, age 13, Leo received for his birthday.

Mendel Spira and his radio broadcasts, and his wife and two daughters, and the singer Albert Hershkowitz.

In Cauterets, we moved into a house on a hilly street. Rationing was tighter, so Joseph Frajermauer planted a vegetable garden. The town's residents were friendly, and we passed the summer lazily. I hiked in the mountains with Joseph Gischlider and shot billiards with him in a local café. We talked of escape, but when we ventured far enough from the town we could see barbed wire separating France from Spain, and we knew that Franco's guards were watching. We were tucked away from a world in turmoil, but trapped from fleeing whatever troubles were surely approaching.

"Go for a walk," Rachel would tell Anny and me. "And take Netty," she would always add, as Anny and I shot quick glances at each other. So we strolled about, and pretended to be carefree young people, and told ourselves we would survive this madness.

But there were rumors, and there were news reports, and each arrived like a blow. There was a camp in Drancy, a suburb of Paris. From Drancy there were reports of freight trains carrying people. The trains were going east. There was talk of camps in the east where dreadful things were happening.

In July, Marshal Pétain declared a distinction among Jews. In France, there were now French Jews, and there were not-so-French Jews, and there were foreign Jews. For the moment, the French Jews could feel safe. And, from now on, the foreign Jews could not.

In August, roundups began. Arrests, detainment. The mechanisms of organized killing took on greater dimension. The camp at Drancy was filled, and then filled again as freight trains headed east with its former inhabitants. Late in August, the mayor of Cauterets, Monsieur Salle-Laffont, leaked word that a raid would be staged the following day. The warning spread through the Jewish community like an electric shock, and brought frenzied conjecture: Should we believe it? Could the mayor be trusted? The panic became a living thing. Within hours, life-and-death decisions had to be made. New rumors updated old: Yes, the raid was coming, but there were local people offering hiding places. Wonderful! But could the local people be trusted? Was this all part of a vast web of deceit? Trust no one, my mother had warned.

Netty, Leo, and Anny pose for a picture in Cauterets during one of their walks.

The mayor, we were told, was a trustworthy man, an old socialist who fought in the last war and hated the Germans. He wouldn't have issued the warning without good reason.

We gathered in our house and made quick decisions. Go our separate ways for now, hide where we could, wait out the raid and come back when the time seemed right.

I hid in the mountains with Joseph Gischlider and two other young fellows. We carried blankets and enough food for a day. The mountains were thick with trees and plants. We climbed uphill for half an hour and sat in a clearing surrounded by bushes, feeling safe and protected and lucky to have balmy weather. No one could see us, but we could see the town's red rooftops and the outline of a church steeple. It was a hazy August afternoon.

We slept on the ground that night, and I imagined spending the rest of the war in such a safe spot. Perhaps we could build a hut here, or an entire farm. When daylight arrived, we waited some more. Afternoon became evening, and we descended cautiously in the dark.

The town was calm. We breathed a little easier. The streets were empty, and we saw no gendarmes, and heard no voices, and soon we were back in our house—edgy, sweaty, hearts thumping, alive.

I slept on a cot in an attic storage room that night. The Frajermauers, Belgian nationals, had temporary reprieve. Those Jews rounded up were mostly Germans, Poles, Russians, or stateless people.

"We're locking you in," Joseph Frajermauer told me the next night.

He padlocked the wooden door leading to my hiding place. The door was made of three boards held together by a simple slat across them, but there was space between the boards through which it was possible to peek. I could see the staircase from my cot. I fell asleep, and awoke thinking of Anny.

Sweet Anny. She said she would bring me breakfast when everyone awakened. Sweet Anny, who held my hand as we walked the streets, who patted my arm when I sank to my lowest. She touched something tender in me, something sweetly romantic but also a protective instinct.

139

"After the war," her father would say, "you'll live in Belgium."

The rest was implicit, a wink between happy conspirators. I would live there as part of their family, and maybe take Anny as my wife, if we lived so long.

As I lay on my cot, I heard voices below me, and then footsteps coming up the stairs. It was Anny's voice, and a strange male voice speaking French. My body tightened. The Frajermauers always spoke Flemish or Yiddish among themselves. I heard Anny's voice, louder and more animated.

"He is not here," she said.

"We'll see," the male voice said.

I lifted myself slowly off the cot, careful not to make any noise that would betray me. A squeak, a crackle, and I was done. On hands and knees, I moved from the cot to the edge of the door and peeked between narrow slats near the floor. My heart thumped. I heard no voices, but I could see Anny. She stood on the landing just below the doorway, and a gendarme pressed her against the wall. The trembling in my body became a convulsion.

"You must have a key," the gendarme said. He spoke with a policeman's authority, but also with a certain lasciviousness.

"No, I don't," Anny said.

"How do you get into this room?" he asked. Was he really looking for me, or for an empty space to have his way with Anny? A sickness ran through my body.

"We don't go into this room," Anny said.

"You know, I can break down the door."

I glanced around, hoping for a hiding place within this hiding place.

"We never use it," Anny said. "This is the landlord's storage space. We only rent."

The gendarme approached the door. I remained crouched on my hands and knees, afraid to move a muscle and set off a chorus of creaky floorboards. The gendarme jiggled the padlock on the door, put his hands on the wooden panels, and pushed. I imagined him trying to peek inside and hoped he wouldn't notice me below him.

"Please, sir," Anny said imploringly. No response; the gendarme wasn't moving. Again: "Please, sir, can we go? He's not here. He ran away, we don't know where."

The gendarme moved a few feet back now, and I could see him standing next to Anny. He reached for her and wrapped his arm around her waist. I resisted an impulse to scream at him, to knock down the door and beat him with my fists. He pushed Anny against a wall and tried to kiss her. She turned her head to one side. He tried to reach her face. She turned the other way, trying to resist him without infuriating him. I remained crouched on the floor, helpless, emasculated, sickened.

"Please, don't," Anny said.

In Vienna, they had thrown Jews to their knees in the streets as I stood watching.

"Please, don't," she said again, as he pulled her closer.

In Vienna, standing at the edge of the crowd, I saw them scrubbing the street with toothbrushes and was helpless to rescue them, as I was now.

"A kiss," the gendarme said.

"Later," Anny said, "downstairs."

"If you kiss me," he said, "I won't come back."

I heard her mutter something inaudible as they walked back down the stairs, as she gently led him away, as she protected me when I should have protected her.

Breathing heavily, fighting back fear and nausea, I climbed onto my cot and lay motionless. Anny saved me, I thought. She drew on instincts and *savoir faire* beyond her years, and bravery beyond my own, and I knew the time had come to leave and put her in no more jeopardy on my account.

In a while Rachel Frajermauer removed the lock from my door. Anny was resting in her room, she said. I told her I'd heard commotion, but didn't let on any details.

When I saw Anny later, we embraced tightly. No words, no hint that I'd seen her on the edge of terrible compromise.

"Leo," she said after a long silence, "you know what this means. You can't stay in Cauterets any longer. They'll find you and arrest you. And us with you."

Arrests had been made in the previous day's raid, and transfers to Drancy. Anny's father concurred, the time had come to run. I went back to the attic and waited through the endless afternoon. The lock was back on the door. Go back to Bagnères, Joseph Frajermauer said, and look for Mendel Spira. The Spiras had temporary dispensation because of a paralyzed relative who lived with them.

"Spira," Joseph said admiringly, "always had connections."

I would have to walk back to Bagnères, because there were gendarmes at all the train stations. On foot, I could reach it in a day. But it meant farewell to the Frajermauers, and this time I sensed I would not return to them. We ate a final, subdued dinner together. In Antwerp, when I'd left for the police station, Joseph had given assurances I'd return within hours. This time, there were no assurances.

Over the past two years, we had become a family. Now: goodbye and goodbye and goodbye. The women wept, and Anny and I hugged, holding on to each other for a final moment with more fervor than ever before.

In the darkness, I walked down our hilly street and waved to them all a few times, and then we were gone from each other's sight. The road was dark and deserted. I had thirty-five miles ahead of me, and no one expecting me. I'll surprise the Spiras, I thought, if I'm not arrested. The darkness was an ally, cloaking me, but it also played tricks on me. Forms and distance were distorted. Tree branches became spidery arms reaching down at me. Could my father's ghost find me in such darkness? In the distance, a roadside bush became a person. The closer I came, the farther away it seemed. An eeriness descended.

When I passed the small town of Pierrefitte-Nastalas, I rested behind bushes. Once, I found a safe spot at the edge of a field behind a row of shrubs. I saw flickering lights in the distance: two gendarmes on bicycles, talking animatedly. I crouched breathlessly behind shrubs until their red tail lights faded in the distance. I dozed for a little while and moved on. I reached the edge of Lourdes near dawn, and decided to rest again when I found a large tree behind a roadside restaurant.

I was hungry and ate a sandwich Rachel had packed for me. At the bottom of the paper bag was a note from Anny. "My thoughts are with you," it read. The note wished me luck and expressed hope that we would see each other again. I thought of the previous morning, when Anny had risked herself for me. I was sick at heart and already trying to remember her face. I walked for an hour and stopped when I heard hoofbeats. A young farmer, driving his wagon, was heading for Bagnères.

"Where are you from?" he asked, as I climbed aboard. He had a beret on his head and a space where a front tooth had once been.

"Lourdes," I lied. Fortunately, he asked me no other questions during our ride to town.

I reached the Spira residence by late morning. A large iron gate with two concrete columns opened to a garden. I thought of all the nights I had listened to the radio broadcasts here, and wondered if I would be welcomed back for a little while.

The Spiras had an apartment on one side of the building, and Madame Leroy lived next door with her fourteen-year-old son. Her husband was a prisoner of war. She was a righteous French woman, an embracing Christian. I rang the Spiras' bell, hoping there would still be a friendly face behind the door.

Spira, standing with one of his daughters, yelled happily when he saw me, and moments later insisted I stay with them. Yes, I said. It was no time to be coy. Spira lived with his wife Helene and two daughters,

Recha and Susie. With them was Helene's sister, Bine, partially paralyzed since giving birth to her son Henri, who was now eighteen months old. She and her husband were interned in a holding camp when they received notice of an exit visa. But Bine, pregnant, had already suffered a stroke. She'd gone into a coma. The baby was delivered, but with her paralysis, Bine couldn't travel. She was allowed to live with the Spiras, and a decision had been made that her husband would go to America, and hope that his wife and child could join him later.

For now, I spent my nights in the attic of Madame Leroy's apartment and my days in the Spiras' apartment. Spira brought the newspapers home, and I read them every day. Sometimes there were books to read. Occasionally, we played gin rummy, and we ate dinner together and then listened to the radio in the evening. Bine received daily massages on her bad left arm from Recha and Susie. All of us grew impatient with waiting and waiting, and not knowing how long the waiting would last, or what we were waiting for.

"Don't even think about leaving the house," Spira said, glaring at me, sensing my restlessness. He was a tall man with thinning hair and black-rimmed glasses. When excited, his voice reached high pitch and his nose twitched nervously. What he said counted. His daughters knew it, and I learned to live with it.

The Spiras were a loving family. Susie, fourteen, was tomboyish and had a hearty laugh. Recha, seventeen, was thoughtful and studious. Their mother, a frail woman with gray hair, looked sad and distracted, but brightened when she held her sister's son Henri. I envied them their closeness, and wondered who was caring for my own family in Vienna, and then wondered if they were still in Vienna, or had been transferred where neither I nor the ghost of my father could ever find them.

It was September, and I hadn't heard from them since the previous February, when the photograph of Ditta arrived for my birthday. The radio continued to broadcast reports of deportations to the east. I looked at the photo and thought of her standing at the hospital window the last

The Spiras' house in Bagnères-de-Bigorre
(courtesy of Susie Spira-Pernitz.)

time I saw her. I thought of my mother, and wondered if they had put her on a train to the east.

One day, Spira talked about a friend who supplied identification cards. The Resistance movement produced them as quickly as they could, as news of the camp at Drancy worsened.

"And where would I go," I said, "if I got one of these cards?"

Spira shrugged. Where does anyone go in the midst of a war? They go one step beyond those pursuing them. Dangers were everywhere, but perhaps the Resistance would have ideas. Then he mentioned a familiar name: Albert Hershkowitz, the singer. He, too, was trying to get a card. For the first time, Spira mentioned Switzerland.

In a few days, I had a new identity card, and a new identity. Instead of Leo Bretholz, I was now Paul Meunier. Instead of Vienna, I was now born in Strasbourg. Instead of twenty-one, I was now magically eighteen years old. I always looked young for my age, and now I could prove it. As for Strasbourg, the forger asked Spira if I spoke French. Yes, he said, but with a German accent. Good enough, he was told. As for the name, Meunier was a common one. I would go to Switzerland with Albert Hershkowitz, who would also have a new identity.

And so, goodbye again. We said our farewells with tears.

145

"I hope you like the Swiss girls," Susie teased.

"Thank you for letting me use your attic," I told Madame Leroy.

"If you come back," she said, "you can use it again."

"Thank you," I said. "I hope it won't be necessary."

I put on my beret, and I walked into the street on Sunday, October 4, 1942. Spira walked with me to the train station, where Albert was waiting. He also wore his beret. The two of us wanted to look like ordinary Frenchmen. We wanted to look like anything but what we were: two Jews trying to sneak away with the remains of our ragged lives.

"Take good care of yourself," said Spira, grabbing me by my shoulders. Then he turned and walked away, and did not look back. As our train pulled out of the station, I turned to Albert and said, "This will end our running."

"We hope so," he said. He had the voice of an angel and the heart of a fatalist. Some of this, I understood. The underground network had made plans for us, but who knew if the plans would work? We were entering unknown territory again, leaving our loved ones farther behind and depending on strangers to keep us free.

We had an address in Evian-les-Bains, a spa resort on Lake Geneva. There, we were to contact a Frenchman by the name of Sceaux, who would arrange our crossing to Switzerland.

We arrived in Evian that evening and found Sceaux in a small house on a hillside. He looked about thirty. He was quiet but reassuring. We had the sense that he'd been through this before.

We were going to cross the Alps. I was familiar with mountainous terrain, and thus skittish. I enjoyed hiking, but I worried about my hernia. I'd devised a homemade truss, and hoped it would work. Albert was nervous and withdrawn.

"I'll be your guide," Sceaux said, "until we reach Swiss territory, at which point I'll accept payment. Fifty francs each. For bringing you there, only. In my house, you sleep as guests tonight."

146

In Germany and in Belgium, Becker was my guide. Bring coins, he had said, to keep the money dry. I smiled at the memory. But now we were going across mountains, and I hoped this Sceaux knew what he was doing. When we went to sleep that night, Albert seemed momentarily cheery. With the lights out, we lay in our beds and he hummed an Italian folk tune, and then another, and then the two of us drifted off.

We left at dawn the next day with food and a thermos of hot coffee in our backpacks. Evian is fourteen miles from the Swiss border traveling by road, just an hour's bicycle ride. However, we weren't traveling by bicycle or by road. Across the mountain, it would take us all day and the next night to hike.

We wore shoes that covered our ankles, and warm overcoats. Sceaux walked vigorously through wooded areas. The path narrowed as we ascended. The terrain reached four thousand feet at its apex. The paths wound through thick woods, and we crouched to avoid tree limbs. The scenery was breathtaking, but we took few glances at the sights around us and merely bent our heads, stooped our shoulders, and held up our hands to block branches aimed at our eyes.

At noon, slightly breathless and lightheaded, we sat in a clearing and ate lunch. My feet hurt. I needed thicker socks. My feet were cold, and beginning to blister. We sat for half an hour, and then climbed until dusk.

"The worst is over," Sceaux said. "From here, it will be downhill."

The view was magnificent now, with Lake Geneva shimmering beneath us. As dusk turned to night, the flickering lights on the Swiss shore of the lake reflected in its dark waters. The lights alone were remarkable. Across Europe, the continent was blacked out, but neutral Switzerland was a sea of lights which I imagined as a beacon of humanity, and an end to my wandering.

We walked for a few hours in the dark, then decided to rest. My feet were now hurting badly. In my eagerness to reach safety, I'd resisted the urge to stop and examine them, but they burned like fire. Albert, fifteen years older than I and heavy, was exhausted. He panted and perspired in the mountain chill.

Sceaux pulled two blankets off of his backpack, and the three of us lay in a thick grassy area on a slight incline near our path. I took off my shoes to ease the pressure, but left my socks on in the chilly air. By the time dawn arrived, a layer of frost covered our berets and our blankets, and penetrated my bones. The coffee was still hot in the thermos, and helped considerably, but when I tried to put on my shoes, my feet were swollen and the shoes grew tight. Each step sent sharp pains through me, and I hoped I could make it to the valley.

"Last leg," Sceaux said.

He meant for him. To the east, we saw Lake Geneva, the rising sun beaming off its waters. When we reached a narrow mountain brook, Sceaux declared rather grandly, *"C'est ça. C'est ici. La frontière."* The border. He would leave us now. With my anxiety rising, he instructed us to cross the brook, which was the Franco–Swiss border, and continue along the same path until the border village of St. Gingolph.

"Don't go into the village," he said. "Bypass it and make your way toward the northeast shore of the lake. In the direction of Montreux."

"We'll know when we reach Montreux?"

"There's a landmark," Sceaux said. "The Château de Chillon, which you will see when you look across the lakefront. Be very cautious."

He paused for his money. Then we said goodbye, and forded the brook, and thus found ourselves in Switzerland. I broke into a large grin, and Albert burst into song. Even the pain in my feet seemed momentarily to ease.

For thirty marvelous minutes, Switzerland was glorious and freedom was wonderful. Then a Swiss border guard with a German shepherd at his side suddenly appeared.

I was rattled, but tried not to show it. Sceaux had warned us of such a possibility. The guard wore a green uniform and a round, stiff hat. The dog was on a leash. The guard asked for identification, and declared in perfect French, "You must come with me. You are here in Switzerland without authorization."

We knew that. I also knew, in that instant, that I had set my hopes too high, but shouldn't despair. As refugees, we'd be processed. Probably, they would send us to some reception center, some mindless work detail, where we might wait out the war in peace and safety, the way my cousin Herbie had lived in his labor camp here since 1938.

The border guard was friendly, a Swiss version of the Luxembourg police four years earlier. Relax, I gestured to Albert, I've seen officials like this before. In a little while, we reached the police station in St. Gingolph. The village was half Swiss, half French, with the boundary running through the middle of town. We were left with the sergeant in charge of the border post, and the guard who had stopped us departed with a friendly wave.

And then the world changed again. The sergeant's name was Arretaz, and he wore a sadistic countenance like a badge of honor.

"False papers," he sneered. "I've seen these before."

"Sir," I admitted quickly, knowing when to capitulate, "these cards are false. They have served us only to reach the border."

"You can't enter Switzerland with these," Arretaz snapped.

Yes, sir, I said. I reached into my backpack to retrieve my Belgian identification card and handed it to him. Albert did the same. I sensed a cruelty in this man, and searched for words that would change everything about this nerve-wracking moment. I wanted to tell him about the Nazis who were rounding up the Jews for no other reason than our Jewishness, about our long hike through the cold Alps, about my throbbing feet, and how much we admired Switzerland for its history of civility. And I knew none of this would matter even slightly.

"My name is Bretholz, Leo Bretholz," I said.

"Mr. Bretholz," he said, "you are going back to France. You have no right to be in Switzerland."

I struggled to hold back a sob. "I was born in Vienna," I said. "I ran away from the Nazis. I left my mother and my sisters in Vienna."

I wanted to impress him with honest admissions. I wanted to pretend I hadn't heard him talking about France, so that maybe he would forget he'd ever said it. I heard Albert echoing my own cries.

"Sir, my name is Hershkowitz," he said. "I was born in Poland, in Lodz."

We might as well have pleaded with the hard and icy walls of Mont Blanc. Arretaz was rigid, immovable, heartless. False papers, he sneered again. We implored some more. He seemed to find satisfaction in our obsequiousness. I reached for his hand, asking for permission to explain my situation to a judge, begging to be interned in a work camp. He stared at me, gloating. I wondered if he had a family. I found myself on my knees. In Vienna, they were on their knees in the street. In my begging, I found myself kissing his hand. But he would not be moved.

Albert stood next to me, impassive and fatalistic. Already, he saw the futility. Arretaz pulled his hand from me and smugly turned us over to the Vichy police near the border post on the French side of St. Gingolph. I was ushered into one holding cell, and Albert into another.

I lay on a stiff cot and gently removed my shoes. My feet had swollen more since the previous night. I tried to remove my socks, and could not. They were stuck to my feet, which were caked with blood. The fabric of the socks seemed to have melted into my bloody skin, and dried, and become a part of me.

A gendarme brought me some food, and I asked for warm water for my feet. After Arretaz, this man seemed a model of civility. Slowly I peeled back the socks, and then bathed my bloody feet, and in a while restless sleep arrived.

In the morning, gendarmes escorted us to another train station. We were going to the internment camp at Rivesaltes, joined now by a young woman from Luxembourg named Milly Cahen. She, too, had been stopped at the border. Faced with the threat of deportation, she and

her family had fled Luxembourg in 1940. Her family was hiding somewhere in France. Milly didn't know where.

We arrived at Rivesaltes in late afternoon. It was about twenty miles
from the internment camp at St. Cyprien. Glumly, I realized the obvi-
ous: In months of struggle, I'd managed to move virtually nowhere. I'd
simply come full circle.

Rivesaltes was a sewer comparable to St. Cyprien. Built during the
last great war as a transit center for troops from Senegal and Morocco, it
was a huge encampment of wooden barracks spread over a few miles of
stony plain. The Mediterranean was nearby. Sometimes ferocious winds
blew through the camp. Quickly, we found there was little water for
drinking or bathing, and no soap. It was filthy.

The camp's inhabitants walked about with disheveled clothes and
dull stares. Many had been transferred from one camp to another. They
seemed weak from living under progressively worse conditions. Even the
sick had to walk nearly a quarter-mile from the infirmary to an outdoor
toilet. Food arrived cold after being carried long distances. Unlike St.
Cyprien, there were mattresses to sleep on, but they were merely cloth
coverings with a few bits of straw stuffed into them. Children were separated from their mothers, who could visit them only briefly.

And yet, the camp had undergone its small improvements by the time
we arrived. The previous winter, they'd gone virtually without fuel, and
internees walked about with insufficient clothing. Some had simply
worn blankets; some had no shoes. More than a hundred died.

Now, with winter still a few months off, our biggest obstacles were
boredom and uncertainty and hunger. I became friendlier with Milly
Cahen, and the two of us stood near the barbed wire that separated our
sections to talk about surviving the war. She had wavy auburn hair and
a sweet beaming smile. She wrote poetry and played the piano. We talked
about music. Albert, wandering past, would join us, humming idly, and
then drift away. I watched people move about aimlessly, and felt as if
some of them would surely never smile again.

I didn't wish to be among them. I thought almost unceasingly of escape, and imagined endless horizons in front of me. I looked for openings in the barbed wire fences around us, but found none. I glanced at the guards, and wondered if they cared as little as those at St. Cyprien.

"We have to escape," I told Milly through the barbed wire.

"Of course," she said placatingly. "But where?"

We had no papers and almost no money. We were allowed to keep our belongings at Rivesaltes, but they amounted to little.

"We could wait out the war in such a place as this," Albert said.

"This suits you?"

"No," he said, looking over his shoulder, "but we could wait out the war in such a place."

I wasn't ready for such a future. One day I lay on my bunk and stared at the ceiling above me. It was a drop-ceiling, and surely there would be a crawl space above it. The day was coming, I suspected, when they would gather us for deportation. Might I hide up there and, if so, for how long?

On October 20, twelve days after my arrival, we were advised of a transfer...to Drancy, where trains left for ominous camps in the east. I stood by the barbed wire on my last night and found Milly in the dark. They were keeping her here, she said. There was a brief deferment for Luxembourgers.

Milly Cahen, 1942, interned at Rivesaltes with Leo.

"We will see each other again one day?"

"Of course," she said gently.

But we both knew better. In the moonlight, we said goodbye and wept openly. I returned forlornly to my barracks and lay in bed for hours with dread rushing through me. In the morning, heart pounding, I watched the others assemble for deportation. Then, picking up my backpack, I climbed up wooden beams, horizontal posts nailed into the wall, pushed aside a piece of drop-ceiling and climbed into the crawl space.

In the dark, I struggled to remain quiet, to keep my body still, to avoid sneezing from the dust around me. Lying flat on my back, with my backpack as a pillow, I listened for sounds of movement. There were none, save for the thumping of my heart. Outside, guards counted those assigned to Drancy. The numbers had clearly come up short, for now there were voices below me.

"He must be here," one was saying.

I imagined the slightest move, the merest breath, would give me away, but there still seemed indecision in the guard's voice.

"Come out from where you're hiding," the second voice cried now, much more decisively. I knew they wouldn't leave without finding me, and dreaded what they would do if they did. I imagined beatings, humiliation, a firing squad. I heard a noise. The thin wood on which I was lying was breaking beneath me. My weight was too much for it. Now, more voices: "You, up there." The end of the world. "Come down fast." They would surely kill me. "We don't have an eternity."

I slipped a piece of drop-ceiling back and fell to the floor below. The impact jarred my hernia. My mind raced frantically for words of excuse.

"You really think you're special," a guard said.

"No, sir."

He led me to the barracks door. But there was no hitting, not even pushing. They were simply doing a job, and the job today was to deport one hundred and seven human beings to the camp at Drancy, the last stop before the end of the world.

9

October 1942

Drancy was the waiting room for Auschwitz, more than a thousand miles and four days away by lumbering freight train. Outside Drancy's gates was a dreary working class French suburb northeast of Paris. Inside, a vast, desolate, oval complex of unfinished apartment buildings with holes where windows and doors were meant to be, ringed entirely by barbed wire and guard towers. The condemned shuffled about miserably, defeated and dreamlike. Here, one instinctively thought of escape, or imagined the war's miraculous end in the next thirty seconds, or capitulated to the idea of death.

"Yes," I said to myself, "escape."

And a voice from within me answered back wearily, "Yes? And where will you go?"

We arrived October 22, 1942, when Drancy was already in full ruin. In Paris fifteen months earlier, the Germans ordered the seizure of all radio sets belonging to Jews. Then, all bicycles. Then, manhunts began. The busy eleventh *arrondissement* of Paris was sealed off by French police, so that German police and inspectors of the French Prefecture of police could make arrests. Four thousand Jews were taken to Drancy that August.

By the following May, Reinhard Heydrich arrived in Paris and, with the help of the head of French police, mapped plans for the deportation of stateless Jews. Those in Drancy filled the first trains east. Three weeks later, on May 29, 1942, a decree ordered all Jews—those of the Reich, and of France, Poland, Holland, Belgium, Czechoslovakia, and Romania—to wear yellow Jewish stars. Then, on the morning of July 16, three months before our arrival, the French rounded up thousands more Jews in the greater Paris region. There were lists of names, focusing initially on stateless and foreign Jews, making no exceptions for health. Children living with those arrested were also taken, and any pets were left behind. Arrestees could take enough food for two days. They joined the thousands of Jews who had been brought to Drancy since the previous August.

The manhunt was staged by nine thousand French police officials. It lasted two days. That week, there were reports of a hundred Jewish suicides. The Germans, hoping for twenty-eight thousand arrests, settled for about thirteen thousand. A few days earlier, some sympathetic police slipped word about the manhunt to come. An underground paper advised Jews to flee. Some Parisians were sympathetic, especially to children. And some police made preliminary visits to homes, and announced they would return in an hour or two. The Jews understood. It was a graveside warning cry.

But some never heard it. Nearly seven thousand people were taken to a Parisian stadium, the Velodrôme d'Hiver. Families remained there for days without food or water or sanitary facilities. Some people died; others went insane.

Those taken to Drancy found their own misery awaiting them. There were only twelve hundred beds for the initial four thousand detainees. Forty or fifty people were packed into each room. One month after their arrival, when requests were made for toilet paper and straw to lie on, they were told such shipments would arrive, but not for another month.

People began to die. Dysentery made the inmates look like skeletons. When we arrived on October 22, we were stunned at what we saw. There were one hundred and seven of us brought there by train, wearing the same rancid clothing we'd worn every day at Rivesaltes for the previous two weeks. I felt lonely and tired. I saw poor elderly souls carried into the camp on stretchers, and lonely children, and doomed couples who could do nothing to save each other.

We'd heard rumors about Drancy for six months: deportations from here to the east, labor camps, deaths. After a busy September, the last transport had left Drancy in early October. But who knew where the trains had gone? Gloomy speculation ran rampant, though none of us yet knew the full truth—Drancy was the last stop before Auschwitz's gas chambers.

I imagined the worst, even as I heard the others trying to talk themselves out of it. The Germans are a practical people, they said, they can use us wisely. This was said by those it suited most, the doctors who imagined the Germans would need their skills, or the barbers, the tailors, the teachers who would nurture the German children if spared.

We quickly learned the mechanics of subservience. The officers, red-faced and choleric French *garde-mobiles*, processed us quickly as we entered the camp, issuing yellow Jewish stars to be worn on our shirts or jackets and confiscating our valuables. Vouchers were given, along with admonishments not to lose them. Their intention was to lull us into false security, into fighting incipient hysteria which might lead to troublesome revolts. The Germans wanted to kill us when they were ready, and no sooner.

"Next!" the French police shouted, faces contorted.

"Keep moving!" they barked.

As quickly as they seemed to anger, they stopped just as quickly. They fumed by rote. When valuables fell to the ground, we picked them up quickly or suffered the officers' bullying. There was pushing in the line. An old man dropped his cane, and a policeman picked it up and hit him

157

with it. But, in the next motion, as the man raised his arm in pitiful self-defense, the officer simply handed back the cane.

Some of the newly arrived carried photos of loved ones in their satchels. The officers tossed them to the ground for the sheer bullying pleasure of it. The photos were the last remnants of a vanished life, and the message from the police was a crushing signal: Yesterday's world no longer counts for anything. Often, they tormented the elderly, some of whom were too frail to walk, or too terrified. There were no smiles, no kindness or compassion.

"Where are you from?"

Inside the camp, this was the inevitable first question from fellow inmates who had arrived weeks earlier and somberly awaited the next transport train out. They wanted to hear something familiar, some news from home, some sign that the world hadn't gone completely mad. And then, again inevitably, they asked, "How long do you think they'll keep us here?" They asked such questions as if, newly arrived from the outside, we possessed insights they lacked, as if we had huddled around a radio late at night and listened to something miraculous on the BBC. Mendel Spira had his radio; was he hearing reports about Drancy as he tuned in now? In fact, we'd heard reports at Rivesaltes, only they had drifted back to us as rumors. There were broadcast accounts of the massacre of seven hundred thousand Polish Jews. Two days before we reached Drancy, the underground French newspaper, *J'Accuse*, reported, "Boche torturers are burning and asphyxiating thousands of men, women, and children deported from France." A Resistance leaflet reported about trains in Poland: "Convoys of women, old people, the sick, and children; in short, all who were unfit for work were choked to death by poison gas." Within days of our arrival at Drancy, the communist *L'Humanité* reported experiments with toxic gas on a thousand Jews deported from France.

But I knew nothing of this, nor of the response from the Allies: U.S. officials mentioned "wild rumors." The British declared accounts of mass murders as "exaggerated." The great savior nations of the west decided there were more pressing issues than the assembly-line destruction of an entire people.

So I listened to questions from inmates who had been here for weeks, and shook my head: No answers, I said. I had no more access to truth than they.

"What will happen to us?"

I shrugged, not knowing a response, and then heard them answering their own question: "How bad can it be if children are coming along?"

They looked haggard and confused. Hearing no answers, they shuffled away. I reached for the little piece of paper in my pants pocket, the voucher issued when the police took away our valuables. Their voices came back: Don't lose these, or you can't get back your belongings. The vouchers became a sliver of hope: Why would they give us these if they wanted to steal from us, if they intended to slaughter us? Around the camp, I heard this echoed from those already beginning to be dead.

Drancy's diet was watery cabbage soup that led inevitably to burning diarrhea. There was almost no water to wash and no soap if there was water. We were ushered into unfinished rooms with straw piled on concrete floors, home for lice and other vermin. It felt like St. Cyprien, it felt like Rivesaltes. Soon it would feel worse. Pipes and electrical wires were exposed. The war had interrupted all construction efforts, and the five-story apartment buildings now looked neglected and dismal. They'd been warehousing Jews here since August of 1941. There were mass latrines, a horizontal line of holes in boards, without separations for privacy. Men, women, it didn't matter.

I began to think sentimentally of Rivesaltes, with its evening sea breezes carried inland from the Mediterranean. It seemed like a resort next to Drancy. Here, there were dozens of us in each room, and each seemed dark and prematurely haunted.

159

In my living area, to my surprise, I found Tony and Erich Gutfreund. My heart leaped when I saw them. Tony was the daughter of my Aunt Charlotte's sister. She and her husband Erich came from Vienna. I hadn't seen them in five years, and now we embraced, and wept openly, and talked long into the night. Where had it all gone wrong? No one knew. Tony was a petite brunette who wore a blue beret. She carried herself with dignity even in this squalor. Erich, slender and stoic, kept his emotions to himself. We sat through the hours and remembered better times, and Tony sewed the Jewish star that the police had handed us onto my jacket.

"Wait one moment," I said, as her fingers moved toward the final stitching. I'd hidden away an Irish half-pound note, received from my Aunt Olga Bretholz, who emigrated to Ireland in 1938. I'd managed to hold on to this note, and I slipped it between the Jewish star and my jacket as Tony finished her sewing. Who knew when I might need it now?

In the early morning hours, I mentioned escape. Tony smiled encouragingly, but Erich found the very notion too dangerous. I told them of my fear that we were all going to be killed.

"We are going to stay together," said Tony, holding tightly onto Erich's arm, "and see what happens."

They took comfort in each other, even as I took comfort in my own singularity. Goodbye to Anny, goodbye and goodbye. I was lonely for my mother and my sisters, and worried that I hadn't heard from them in months. But they were in their corner of hell, and I was in mine. I saw Ditta standing at the hospital window, looking as if her heart was breaking. But now I was alone, and Ditta was out of my reach. My responsibility was only to myself. This gave me emotional liberation. I was burdened by nothing but my own inhibitions, and my captors' desire to keep me here.

In the morning, I walked outside and saw people shuffling about. A few guards glowered from a distance. Again, the echoes: Where are you

160

from? What do you think they will do to us? Sometimes questions led to arrogance, and ranks developed even among us internees.

"My credentials?!" snapped a man who wore a suit and tie, trying to imagine loopholes for himself. He'd fought for France in World War I, he announced, and his grandfather served under Napoleon III. This sort of indignity became a recurring theme among the French, who imagined they weren't like the others, the German Jews, or the Austrians or the Poles. The French authorities were running these camps for the Germans; surely, French citizenship, French blood, meant more than this unfortunate business of a man's religion. Mistakes had been made; credentials would be uncovered; exceptions would surely be made.

An elderly man spoke Yiddish to his wife, who wept softly. *"Wein, wein. Nor es wet gornisht helfen,"* he said. He spoke gently, but seemed slightly distracted. Weep, weep. But it will not do any good.

Children walked about, searching for familiar faces. They'd been pulled out of nurseries, out of kindergartens, plucked from grammar school classrooms and told to come with the authorities, told their parents were waiting for them. Many were toddlers. Their clothing was badly soiled. They were frightened and confused and wept openly.

At Drancy, they were put by the score into bare rooms with buckets to be used as toilets, because many of the children couldn't walk down long hallways to bathrooms, or were too frightened to go without adults. They needed to go badly. The steady diet of cabbage soup gave many of them severe diarrhea. They soiled their clothing and the mattresses on which many of them lay whimpering day and night. When their clothing was removed for washing, the children lay on their beds naked, with the autumn air growing colder, waiting for their clothes to dry. They wore little wooden dog tags, so someone would know who they were.

At night, we heard them crying from their distant rooms. They called for their mothers, or cried simply because the world had been unbearably cruel to them, and crying was the only language in which they knew how to express it.

One day I saw a woman reach down to a little boy, perhaps four years old, and ask, *"Quel est ton nom?"* What is your name?

"Sais pas," he said, looking into her eyes. Don't know.

What were any of our names now? The world had forgotten our names and our faces and our history. The past had closed up behind us. Behind these barbed wires, we had ceased to exist.

There were old people in worn out shoes with no laces who asked, in Yiddish, *"Wu is Gott?"* Where is God?

I had no answer, and turned away to see a face that looked vaguely familiar. I followed this man across a gravelly expanse and tapped him on his shoulder.

"Are you Epstein?" I asked.

"Yes, Arthur Epstein."

"You worked as a tailor's apprentice for my father in Vienna."

Epstein, startled, threw his arms around me and hugged me, and then looked me up and down. He was fifteen years older than I. I was nine when I'd last seen him, on the day my father died.

"Mon dieu, tu es Leo!" he cried.

He recalled my sisters, and mentioned their curly hair. I was touched that he remembered. In her last letter, I told him, my mother had sent me a photograph as a birthday present. But that was last winter, I said, and there were no letters since.

Like me, Arthur had fled Vienna for France in 1938. He had no family with him. I remembered him as a frail young man with sparse hair and a sad demeanor. Now he was thinner, and the war had turned him downcast and dour.

"From what we hear," he said, "it does not look good."

My stomach turned. He said he'd been here for a few weeks. As we walked through the compound, I glanced around and saw no guards hovering nearby. I mentioned escape.

"Don't be foolish," he said quickly.

162

He took me to a corner of the yard, somewhat hidden by a small concrete structure. Here, he said, some men had talked of a starting point for a tunnel to the outside. My heart jumped at the prospect.

"And?" I asked.

"And," he said, "nothing. It's all just talk, Leo."

As the days passed, I moved about the camp and looked for more familiar faces among the thousands of detainees. There were Tony and Erich, and there was Arthur, and Albert Hershkowitz, still nearby, still humming pieces of Italian opera.

Outwardly, Albert was nonchalant, laconic. It belied the inner turmoil we felt in the two weeks we spent at Drancy. We eyed the guards in their towers, relieved that they stayed out of the yard, but wondering when

Interior of the camp at Drancy, 1943. All internees had to wear a yellow star marked "Juif." A gathering of more than four people was against the rules. This and many other restrictions were diligently enforced
(National Museum of Auschwitz-Birkenau, courtesy of USHMM).

they might descend and have their way with us. Each time I saw them, I vowed for the thousandth time that day to escape.

As November arrived, tempers snapped at unforeseen moments.

"What will happen to us?" someone asked.

"How should I know?"

"When will they come for us?" someone else asked.

"Don't ask me."

Many stayed in their rooms, lying on the concrete floors with dazed, dejected expressions, faces frozen, oblivious to the days turning shorter and chillier. Children wandered about, sometimes tended by women, sometimes alone and inconsolable.

The oldest inmates knew what others denied. They understood euphemisms. "Resettlement" was not for them. "Work details" were for stronger bodies. The elderly and the sick dragged themselves through the camp in rumpled clothing that hung from their bodies and knew the end of their lives was approaching.

Their age gave me emotional distance. I was not one of them. I was not old, I was not a child, I had neither mother nor sisters nor Anny. In my mind, I was never not imagining fantastic escape. It was my constant companion, the wondrous fantasy that got me through days and nights, that kept me from going out of my head with panic. I was alone now, and that was my lightness and my opportunity.

One day internees arrived from the north of France. They talked of rumors out of Westerbork, the Dutch deportation camp. People there had returned from a railroad detail somewhere in the east.

"But there were no killings?"

"Hard labor," they said, "but bearable."

"Food?"

"They had rations. Regular food. Better than this soup."

But they'd also heard stories, variations of things we'd already heard. At Auschwitz and Birkenau, they said, selections were made. Some would live, and some would die. Some would work, and some would vanish. But which stories were true, hard labor or death? Rumors took on a life of their own. If you believed the mildest, you embraced hope; if you believed the worst, darkness descended on you.

One night I lay on my bed of straw and turned to the man next to me. He was twice my age, and fatalistic, and given to speaking in clichés: What will be, will be, he said softly. But I was on fire with the need to escape, and to tell people about no longer hearing from my mother, as if strangers might have reasonable explanations and calm assurances that everything would be fine.

Standing in line for soup one day, two young men in yarmulkes talked about their families. One mentioned a sister who'd been arrested in Paris.

"An aunt of mine lives there," I said, hungry for a human connection.

"Yes?"

"And two sisters, living in Vienna. I haven't heard from them since February. I think bad things are happening."

I wanted to be told that I was wrong. I had become like everyone else, wanting assurance from people who knew no more than I. The young man pointed his right index finger to the sky. This, he was saying, was where his trust rested. I saw him later in the camp square and told him I was frightened enough to attempt escape, I just needed an opportunity.

"If God wants it, he will create that opportunity for you and make it succeed," he said.

"And you," I said. "Would you attempt escape?"

"I have family here," he said softly, and added, "I will test God."

I met a fellow named Manfred Silberwasser, in his late teens, who had grown up near my home in Vienna. Manfred was arrested in a raid on the forced residence assigned to him by the Vichy government and sent to Rivesaltes. He was a frail fellow, perhaps undernourished even in better times. He had curly blond hair, and teeth that had gone yellow, and an expression always on the edge of a smile.

165

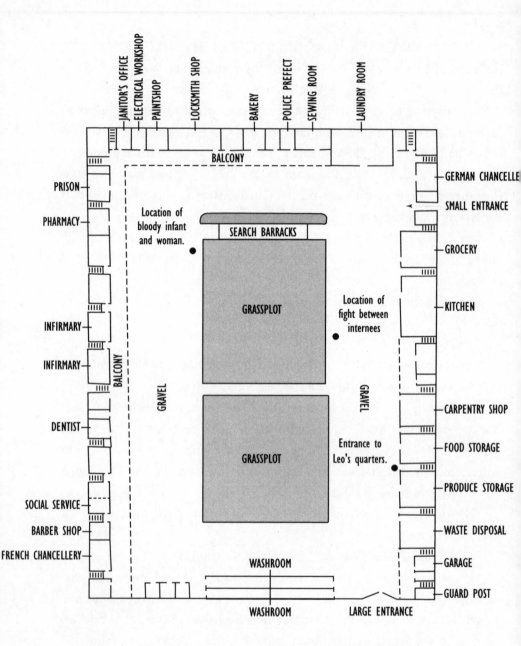

Layout of transfer camp at Drancy in the northeast section of Paris. The camp was established in August, 1941. Deportations began on March 27, 1942, and continued until the eve of liberation, August 11, 1944.

One morning we heard the shrill sounds of whistles outside our second-floor room and went to the open window shells. In the assembly square, we saw two young fellows being led away, their arms held behind their backs by several guards. Others were being sent back to their rooms. There had been a fight in the yard, a violation of rules posted on bulletin boards around the encampment. Now the two men would pay for it.

"I don't envy them," said Manfred.

He said there was a cell at the far end of the camp, to which troublemakers were taken for disciplinary measures. He said he'd seen people led off twice before. Always, the same thing: fighting among the inmates. Intolerable, the Germans said. Yes, yes, fighting was certainly unacceptable in the middle of a war.

"What happens to them?" I asked.

Manfred didn't know, except that they didn't come back. He shuddered. He feared the future and said he felt caught in a web. He mentioned escape. It forged a bond between us. Escape, of course, but when?

Then, a few days into November came the arrival of the future. A woman had given birth. Already, there were more than three hundred babies at Drancy. Manfred and I were looking out of our window opening when we heard a gunshot from the yard below us. We saw people running to one corner of the compound, and guards pushing them back. When Manfred and I reached the yard, we saw a bleeding child lying on the ground, and the child's mother, also bloody, lying motionless on top of the child.

We were sent back to our rooms, and in the coming days heard stories that spread like tremors around the camp: that a guard had held the newborn child aloft, that he'd thrown the child into the air, that he'd fired his gun. And that the mother, out of her head with grief, rushed the guard with the gun and he killed her.

In Vienna, I saw people on their knees in the street and stood there impotently. In France I watched from my own knees as Anny was pushed

167

against a wall by a bullying officer. At Drancy, I was now helpless again, in a community of doomed people unable to stop the murderous conclusion of their own lives.

In a few days came the call for our deportation to Auschwitz. The final chance for escape was here.

10

November 5-6, 1942

On November 5, two weeks after our arrival at Drancy, came the order to gather our belongings, came uniformed men to shave our heads, came the barking of the French officers: Go here, stand there, move faster.

But this time there was no passion in their voices. Gone was the casual abusiveness of our arrival day, when the officers had been brusque and bullying, as though building up an inventory of intimidation to last for the coming weeks. Now they were crisply efficient, workers on an assembly line, going through the motions of another day on the job while the German guards observed from several yards away.

"Go here."

"Stand there."

"Faster, faster!"

My heart raced at the speed of the guards' orders, and I trembled uncontrollably.

"*Nouvelle colonisation,*" some whispered as we gathered. "Resettlement. How bad can it be after this?"

Such words came from dreamers. Resettlement, indeed. The phrase was a fraud, slipped into our ranks to keep us mute, to keep us from mass, panicky revolt. So we were caught between rumors of benign resettlement and work camps, and the dreadful hints we'd been given in the perfunctory brutality against random inmates.

In the camp square, the ground was a mix of gravel and hard surface. I kept my eyes down as I moved along. Inmates wept, but muffled the sound. Who knew if weeping was now considered a capital offense? Mothers tried to hush their children. The day was raw and chilly and gray. Near two o'clock, they shuttled a thousand of us onto old buses and army trucks with camouflage gray-green tops, rifle butts at our backs, voices crying, *"Vite, plus vite!"* Faster, faster, faster! My shivering would not stop. An old man fell and was helped up by another prisoner. Others moving too slowly were jabbed with rifles or shoved by guards. Orders to move faster were constant.

"But I have to relieve myself," came a cry.

"Move faster, faster," came the response. Guards belittled us, screaming "dirty Jew" or "kike" to impress the German overseers as much as to insult us.

But it was still harsh. No relieving oneself, no consideration for women who'd given birth only days earlier, or those in their menstrual cycles. Faster, faster. The feet moved, and the mind whirled, and in that whirl it searched frantically for the tiniest crevices of escape.

Each vehicle held about forty of us. We were taken to the train station of Drancy-le-Bourget, less than two miles away, not far from the airport where Charles Lindbergh had made history only fifteen years earlier. Where were Lindbergh's cheering crowds now? As we rode silently through the streets of Drancy, most of its residents seemed oblivious to us. Convoys such as ours were simply another little splinter of the war, of which they had grown weary, from which they turned away to take care of their own lives. The trains heading east were no business of theirs. Here was the outside world from which we'd been removed, and it took no particular notice of our misery.

Now and then came a slight flicker of humanity. Someone on the street waved a hand in our direction. On our truck, a few shy hands waved back, hoping a connection could be made to prompt some last-minute rescue by incensed French citizens who hadn't yet surrendered their souls to the Germans. Then on our truck came something unanticipated, a word here and there, a hint of melody. When I realized what was happening, it lifted my heart. A moment of defiance had arrived.

"Allons enfants de la patrie…"

The words of *La Marseillaise* trembled out of one mouth, and then a few more joined it, and then in a moment the singing filled the truck, and my heart raced. We sang to embolden ourselves, to declare that we were still here. Maybe, if we sang loudly enough, our voices would carry to the streets, rousing the souls of the indifferent French and inspiring them to come save us. But, in a moment or two, the singing faded away and our sense of dread returned. The silence on the truck was awful. The historic French love of liberty had taken a leave of absence.

Arriving at the small railroad station minutes later, we saw only the freight train that was to take us to Auschwitz: transport No. 42. At six in the evening, we were the only civilians in sight. Now began the final count-off, fifty to a freight car, the divisions based strictly on numbers. Some of the elderly were carried on stretchers. I thought of Arthur Epstein, slumped dejectedly, long removed now from my father's tailor apprenticeship. He'd been taken from Drancy two days earlier and deported to Auschwitz. I saw Manfred Silberwasser, still with that inexplicable expression bordering on a smile. I saw pregnant women, and mothers nursing their newborn babies. There were small children who toddled along, prodded by guards to keep moving. Some of the children whimpered, but held onto traces of dignity. Many cried openly, holding little toys and dolls close to their bodies. Some were helped along by women, instant surrogate mothers who saw to it that the children didn't wander away. I'd never seen such compassion before. They seemed to know that something final had already begun.

A little boy stared into space. Was he searching for the face of God? Another little boy and a little girl clung to each other for comfort, as if they sensed the trauma to come. Some children comprehended the moment's severity and tried to act like adults. Some consoled younger brothers and sisters, who tried to climb into cattle cars under their own power. In recent days, several women had given birth. They'd been attended by camp nurses, and their departure from Drancy postponed until today's transport. Now I saw infants in cardboard boxes covered with dirty diapers and clothing. Everywhere there were infants in makeshift cradles. Lives that had just begun were now about to end. One cradle was placed next to an old man in the final hours of a long life. Now they would depart together.

There was too much sadness to absorb. As I waited to be assigned to a freight car, I heard commotion from the car in front of mine. A boy was separated from his family. He screamed to stay with them. The guards would not permit it. The boy kicked his thin legs at a guard holding him around the chest.

"Prends moi!" he screamed. Take me! Get me!

The family cried back. The guards would not be moved. The father— broken, emasculated—pleaded for his son's return, arms extended. The boy was shoved into one car, his family into another. In Vienna, Ditta was separated from my mother, and I hadn't been there to plead her case. I saw my mother with her own arms extended, and this man's cries became her cries.

I was powerless, and hated myself for it. The sickness in my heart became a paralysis, a dread that any outburst would lead to punishment, public humiliation, or worse. I vowed never to be emasculated again. I would run and run and run. Nothing would hold me—not the guards, not loved ones, not the war. My eyes filled up, and I turned away from the weeping family, and wondered frantically when I might find my moment to run.

It would have to wait. We were herded into our freight cars, again with orders to move quickly, rifles at the ready. Twilight was descending, and inside the train it took a moment to adjust my eyes to the fading light.

There was barely room to stand or sit or squat. I took a deep breath, and then another. Children cried fearfully. Some of the men wore suits and ties, clinging to some false sense of stature, reaching for fading elegance. I thought of Uncle Isidore, waiting in a three-piece suit in his apartment for the Gestapo to come for him. Many of the women wore lipstick and fashionable dresses. When we arrived at our next destination, they would show that they'd come from homes with civilized people, and surely this stature would count for something.

"That boy and his parents will be reunited," someone in the crush of bodies muttered. An optimist, surely. From somewhere else, a voice whispered a prayer to God. Another optimist. The war was vast, and God seemed to have more pressing concerns than the Jews. In this cattle car, we were surely his lost tribe.

The train did not move. The gray of evening turned into night and sheer darkness. I felt like part of a herd. Someone turned a small flashlight on, and then quickly back off. In the middle of the car was one bucket to be used for relieving ourselves. In an hour or two, the bucket overflowed. There was no place to empty it, so now there were sounds of the desperate relieving themselves on the floor.

The stench in the car filled our lungs, and we struggled not to vomit. Some were unsuccessful. The vomit clung to clothing, and then the air became worse. "Where is God?" someone cried. I remembered the nuns on the train out of Vienna four years earlier, and wondered if their God had a clearer way of making his presence known. People were pressed against each other. I itched beneath my trousers and in my armpits. Unbuckling my belt, I found tiny critters embedded in the seam of my pants: body lice. Never mind questions of God, my body was crawling. I wanted to tear the skin from my bones.

The smell in the car grew thicker, relieved only marginally by air coming in from two small windows. One was diagonally opposite me, at the front of the car on the right-hand side. The other, above me at the left-hand side of the rear of the car. Each window had two iron bars running horizontally across it. Toward morning, urine began to slosh on the floor.

"*Légion d'Honneur*," muttered a Frenchman, wearing a suit and tie as if his esteemed position in the world still mattered. He tried to convince himself that a mistake had been made, that his history meant more than his bloodlines.

"*Croix de Guerre*," came another voice.

Such sounds filled the long night, a word here, a child's sniffling there, someone claiming that a mistake had been made, he shouldn't be here, and someone else saying "shut up." Once, in the crush of bodies, two wives had to separate their husbands from fighting. Past midnight, a woman's shrill cries divided the air. Then another woman, trying to cope with a feverish baby, cried loudly. No one tried to stop them. Crying was a safety valve for all of us. The train stood all night on the railroad siding. We heard the footsteps of officers, guarding not only against any attempts at escape, but also watching that no notes slipped out of the train that might leave traces of our last hours.

We'd each been given a slab of grayish bread, a wedge of *la vache qui rit*, Laughing Cow gruyère cheese, and a can of sardines. There was nothing to drink. At Drancy, we longed for Rivesaltes' relative ease. But this was worse than Drancy, where at least we could see the sky. We waited, and fought back claustrophobia, and in the waiting our despair grew and grew.

My mind raced for thoughts of escape. As early morning light slipped through our little windows, I saw the ashen faces of fellow passengers. I saw Tony and Erich, still holding comfortingly to each other. Anny and I held hands in another lifetime that had ended only weeks ago. I saw an old woman with a crutch, her leg amputated at the knee, holding a small child who did not seem to be her own. Was some stranger holding Ditta, now that my mother had been taken from her?

Many in the train seemed dazed. Some mumbled to themselves. A misty drizzle fell outside. One man repeated an unintelligible phrase and seemed to hallucinate. Albert leaned against a wall, dressed in an open-necked shirt covered by a sweater and sports jacket, his head shaved. He worried about his sister and her family, whom he'd last seen in Bagnères. He looked characteristically calm and now, in his way, he started to sing softly, half to himself and half to remove himself to some earlier, grander time when his world was a stage and not the inside of a miserable cattle car.

"Nonta scordati me, la vita mia legata te," he sang. Don't forget me, I have given you my life.

I listened, and shifted my body for some comfort, and in a while heard muffled voices outside. It was about nine in the morning. The voices were in German and in French. Then came a thud, and then movement, and people braced themselves against each other. The large beast of a train finally roused itself.

"Ça y est," someone cried dejectedly, pronouncing the beginning of the end.

Some old people moaned. "Hush hush," a mother whispered to her weeping child. A young man with a bandaged leg, badly infected, possibly gangrenous and beginning to smell horribly, huddled beneath a blanket with his girlfriend. The two embraced. Tenderly, he kissed her eyes and her forehead.

Manfred gestured toward the girl, and I shook my head. Without speaking, we both felt the same. We wished to be unencumbered, we were drowning men swimming for air and wished no anchors for ourselves. Goodbye to Anny, and goodbye and goodbye.

175

Within the car, people's lips moved in silent prayer. An Orthodox man stood against the eastern wall of the train, his head shaved but his beard untouched. His arms reached toward heaven, his body swayed, and his voice rose imploringly, "*Oy, ribono shel olom*, master of the universe..."

"If God allows this to happen...," a voice muttered back, barely audible over the rumble of the train.

"Let him pray," came another reply.

We were a congregation of the doomed. I thought of my bar mitzvah, eight years earlier, when Rabbi Murmelstein placed his hand on my head and declared, "May the lord bless thee and watch over thee." What did such words mean now? Where was God in the lives of so many innocents? In Germany they burned synagogues, and God must have perished in the flames. I glanced at the old woman with the crutch, as she tried to soothe the little boy in her lap. The boy trembled in the morning chill. He looked drugged and dreamy. Was my mother caressing Henny now, or had they been torn from each other and moved to their own ghastly freight car?

The train's rickety movement brought an odd sense of relief. At least they weren't leaving us here to suffocate. We could feel traces of the morning air filtering from the window near the front of the train back toward us. We were moving, and movement would bring fresher air, and change, and who knew what else?

I thought of my childhood, vanished in some previous, safer life where I dreamed of trains taking me to places beyond my sweetest imagination. Such thoughts now seemed cruelly naive. I heard the weeping of frightened children, and snatches of dialogue: misgivings about not hiding from the police, conjecture about the future. The languages were French, Yiddish, German, and from all corners of eastern Europe, forming a melting pot of the condemned. But many seemed too tired to talk, too resigned to their fate.

Manfred and I stood beneath the little window near the rear of the left-hand side of the train. Clearly, here was our last chance. We saw trees

176

along the French countryside, birds perched on telegraph wires, vineyards, farms, cattle grazing in fields when we stretched ourselves high enough.

"The window," I said.

"When?"

"Before we get to Germany," I said. "Toward nightfall. When we can hide in the dark."

"What are you talking about?" came a man's resigned voice over the swaying of the train. "You can never...."

"Go ahead," came another voice.

"You can get killed, trying to jump," said a third.

Other voices joined theirs, all of them men, none of them loud, none overbearing, simply a small, scattered, random conversation that no one yet took entirely seriously. Escape? Who was kidding whom? What about the others who'd tried to escape, someone asked. There were stories of men who'd tried to jump from trains, who'd been killed in the jump, or run over by another passing train, or captured by the guards and tortured. Who did we think we were?

The rhythmic clattering on the rails sounded like a dirge, but had its comforts. As long as the train moved, we were alive and could still attempt escape. Time and darkness could be our allies.

The old woman with the crutch stared at us and cuddled the boy in her lap. She covered him with her coat. The boy was four years old and would never see his family again. The woman, gray-haired, in her sixties, had been alone. The two of them never knew each other before fate had simply tossed them together. Now, in their final hours, they'd become each other's only family.

"If you escape," a man said, "they'll take it out on the rest of us."

"What are you saying?" came another man's hoarse voice. "They're going to kill us anyway."

"Then why have they given us these vouchers for our valuables?"

Even now, some were still buying into that fraud. I looked at Albert, who leaned against a wall. He patted me on the cheek, an older brother

177

offering comfort. Now there were more voices, more opinions, everyone an expert. Go, don't go. My head swelled with too many people's words. I longed for some open space on the floor to lie down and sleep until everyone went away from here. I closed my eyes wearily, and then I heard a woman's voice saying, "If you jump, maybe you'll be able to tell the story. Who else will tell this story?"

I wasn't certain who had spoken, but looked up to see the old woman with the child in her lap. She pointed her crutch at me. Her eyes, ablaze with passion, locked onto mine. She was finished listening to all of the arguments and all of the fears and, like some biblical judge, she was now delivering her verdict. From this broken body, from this wretched soul cloaked only in the wisdom of her years, there came the last word.

"Allez-y, et que dieu vous garde," she declared in a voice ragged with exhaustion. Go ahead, and may God watch over you.

In that moment, she was a mother sending her sons to safety. She was every mother. She was the mother of us all. I thought of my own mother, four years earlier, urging me to leave Vienna as the Nazi presence grew more ominous, and I knew there was no longer a choice for us.

I looked at Albert. I motioned to the window above us. He gestured to his waistline: too large for the narrow opening. I weighed about one hundred twenty pounds, small enough if we could loosen the iron bars. He was considerably heftier. But it was more than his size; he was simply exhausted, and resigned to his fate. It was one thing to cross the Alps, another to squeeze through the eye of a needle. He gestured to the window, as if saying, "Go ahead."

I reached up to one of the bars and tugged. The bar did not move. Manfred did the same; nothing happened. Futile, someone muttered. All this talk, said someone else, and it comes to nothing. The two of us struggled more ferociously to yank the bars apart. Blood pounded through the veins in my neck. The bars would not budge. Here was our last hope, and it came to nothing. We needed to escape in darkness, arriving in several hours, and needed to escape while we were still in France, where there were still places to hide. But these cursed bars would not move.

"Sweaters," someone said.

"Pardon?"

Yes, sweaters. We removed them from our bodies, tied them around the bars like tourniquets, and twisted them back and forth. Nothing happened. Curse the sweaters, curse the idea, curse our lives. We tried belts, but the belts were too slippery. Curse the belts, curse the futility of it all. We thought of rope, but had none strong enough. We needed traction, we needed to dampen the sweaters to tie them tighter around the bars.

The floor!

On the floor was all the water we needed: the collected human waste of our fellow travelers, sloshing about with the movement of the train.

"Let's do it!" Manfred cried.

I hesitated for an instant. The train rolled through the bucolic French countryside. Fighting back revulsion, I bent down and dipped my sweater into the urine. Bits of fecal matter floated about. I felt degraded, felt it was the most disgusting thing I'd ever done. In order to save my life, I would first have to violate it beyond previous imagining.

We wrung the sweaters out, and wrapped them around the bars. Holding onto both ends, I twisted again. The sweater gripped the bar more tightly than before, but the tugging squeezed the urine out of the sweater and sent it down my upraised arms and onto my neck. The stench was overbearing, and I wanted to stop and try something else. But there was nothing else. This was our final possibility to save our lives.

Manfred and I took turns at the bars. We were exhausted, and heard more voices telling us to stop, telling us it was futile. The train rumbled and shook. My throat was raw with thirst, and with excitement. The sweat poured from our faces, and the urine dripped steadily out of the sweaters and down our bodies as time ticked away. Below our rolled up shirt sleeves, bits of fecal matter congealed and dried on our arms, sticky

179

and smelly and nauseating. I wanted to wipe the sweat from my face, but with what? My hands and arms and shirt were all covered with waste.

But now, miraculously, in our fatigue and our exasperation, we saw something else on our arms. It felt like gravel. It was rust particles from the point where the iron bars met the window frame. The bars were loosening ever so slightly, and the rust was our sign: Don't give up.

The hours raced by—five hours, maybe more—and the train slipped through the Champagne region of eastern France. Soon darkness would fall. We pulled and twisted and our arms grew weary. We heard more words of discouragement from others, who looked at us, these two puny young men, trying to change the course of the tides. But the bars bent and moved, and we realized that escape was possible.

The train grunted and tossed. We squatted on the floor and caught our breath. Around the car, voices became whispers. Manfred leaned against a wall, staring vacantly, exhausted.

"I'm a little nervous," he said, smiling wanly.

I wondered if freedom was really at hand. It was one month since I'd imagined I'd reached it at the Swiss border, only to have it snatched away. It was four years since I'd left home, and nine months since I'd heard from my family. Was there any way, in a thousand years of effort, that we would ever find each other again? My temples pounded and I vowed to go through with this attempt. But my stomach turned, and again I heard random murmurs telling us to stop, we could be caught, we could be hurt, they might punish everyone.

Eventually, many nodded into sleep. Their faces seemed prematurely ghostly. The pounding in my head gave way to a lightheadedness, a veiled and dizzying euphoria, and I shivered.

At about seven that evening, in darkness, sensing we were closer to the German border, we got to our feet. I reached for my backpack on the floor, and handed it to Tony, who seemed like a sister to me now.

She looked at me reassuringly. We were each other's last links to an extended family that was now only a memory.

"*Bonne chance et sei vorsichtig,*" she said, choking on words uttered in two languages. Good luck and be careful.

Erich waved goodbye from a few feet away, and turned his head. Manfred picked up his small duffel bag, and I turned to see Albert standing near me, speaking in Yiddish.

"So you are going through with it," he said. I nodded my head. He put his arms on my shoulders and pulled me toward him, and hugged me. In Switzerland, he'd had the heart taken out of him. My own heart was now thumping wildly.

It was a dreary evening, cold and raw. Manfred and I bent the upper bar up, and the lower one down. The space between them was less than a foot wide, but we assured ourselves there was room to squeeze through.

My mouth was dry and feverish, and a cold sweat covered my forehead. I pulled my cap from my shaved head, knowing the wind would blow it off, and I stuffed it in one of my pockets. I piled up some luggage to step on and reached for the opening. I stumbled and slipped back. I was grabbed by Manfred and Albert, who held one of my legs and helped me climb back—a climb of inches, a climb greater than all of the Swiss Alps.

My waist was now at window level. I reached through the window to a ledge outside, a metal drain spout just above the window where the side of the car met the base of the roof. I pushed my head through and felt the shock of cold wind across my bare scalp. I pulled with both my arms while twisting my body back and forth and sucking in my stomach. From inside the train, Manfred and Albert shoved at my legs, and I heaved myself forward an inch at a time.

And then air was all around me. My muscles tightened. I held on to the ledge above the window, and my right leg reached toward the

181

rear corner of the train until it hit the coupling that joined the car behind us.

"I'm okay," I called into the car, in a kind of stage whisper. I worried that guards would hear me. I worried about spotlights shining from either direction. I felt an exultant rush upon making it this far, and called through the window, "Hand me my backpack." I was amazed at the sound of my own words.

With my right hand, I held on to an iron stepladder leading to the top of the freight car, and with my left hand I reached for my backpack. Manfred followed me a moment later, boosted to the window by Albert. As he slid toward me, I inched farther to the right to make room for him.

In the darkness, clinging to the rickety stepladder, the wind rushing all about us, we cried simultaneously, *"C'est fait!"* We've done it!

We needed to time our jump at just the right moment, when the train would slow around a curve, when the guards' spotlights would miss us. The train moved at about forty miles an hour. The clanking of the couplings shook our bodies. We held on tightly not to slip, not to fall beneath the wheels of the car. Five minutes passed, at least. The wind sucked the breath out of my lungs while my mind became a newsreel of memories: I gasped for air in the River Sauer; I crawled breathlessly beneath barbed wire at St. Cyprien; I stood on a street corner on a drizzly night in Vienna, unable to find words to tell my mother goodbye. Four years had passed. I thought of Tony and Erich on the other side of the train's walls, and of Albert and the old woman with the crutch who had given us the final emotional thrust that we needed. Already, they seemed to belong to another life I once knew.

We wanted to jump from the left side, the north, where there were no parallel tracks. We wanted the train to curve enough to send any spotlights away from us, but we had no idea when the right moment might arrive.

182

"I wonder where my brother is now," Manfred said through the rumble of the train and the wind. He'd left him in Vichy-controlled France.

"I was just thinking of my mother and my sisters," I hollered back.

"I can't wait till my brother hears this," Manfred said.

We felt the train slowing as the track began to curve. The whole length of the transport was visible as we looked from one end to the other. The guards were using powerful lights, sliding them from the left-hand length of the cars to the right. Our moment was here.

I took a deep breath, like someone about to dive into water. I nodded at Manfred, and watched him jump from sight. An instant later, I leaped into the great darkness below.

11

November 6 - December 7, 1942

I n the darkness came calamity.

The sounds of shrill whistles split the night, and then the crackle of gunshots. I kept my body as close to the ground as I could. I listened for the rumble of the train, and heard nothing. Silence was all. The train stopped perhaps a quarter-mile beyond the area where Manfred and I had jumped. Then came more gunshots fired into the air. I held my breath and heard footsteps coming from the train, headed toward us, faster now, and I heard fragments of sentences in angry German voices.

"Let's look for..."

"Let's search..."

"...over here..."

Several minutes went by. The searchlights must have picked up shadows moving from the train, maybe mine, maybe Manfred's. Maybe someone else had tried to escape. God forbid, on a train carrying a thousand doomed human beings, that the Germans should cheat the ovens of a single Jew.

Minutes passed, minutes that felt like an eternity. "Over here!" came a cry. "Have you looked here?" came another. I looked for a place to hide, some unexpected hole in the earth into which I might burrow.

And then calm arrived, and I heard no more voices. Was it a decoy? I could run, but the guards might be hovering nearby. At Drancy, babies died who were barely old enough to cry. What would they do to me for defying the assembly-line power of the death camps?

Finally, another sound, not a voice but something metallic in the distance: the whine of wheel against rail, the heavy rumble of freight cars wearily creaking into motion, exhausted from the distance already covered and cranky about the miles yet to come. The train was pulling away.

I lay there in the sweet embrace of the earth until the train to Auschwitz faded in the dark and its clatter became a great silence in the eastern distance. I found I was lying in tall grass in a damp ravine. I took a deep, shuddering breath and wondered where Manfred might be. I moved a few muscles to see if anything hurt and put my beret back on my shaved head. I felt miraculously freer than I'd ever been in my life and wondered: Free to do what? Free to go where?

Manfred and I found each other in the dark and made our way to a country lane that ran beside the railroad track. Our hands tore at the incriminating Jewish stars on our lapels. Silently, we walked the lane for several minutes, still out of breath, chilled by the damp November night, clothing soggy from the ravine, rancid from the train, half-expecting German guards to leap out of nowhere to punish us for the foolish attempt to escape our fate.

We passed a few farms. Ahead, we saw silhouettes of some small buildings. The buildings became a village. We said nothing. There were no lights on the road, nor in any of the buildings. The silence was broken by a dog's bark in the distance. We saw a narrow sidewalk, and we waited out of sight when a few people walked nearby. We saw a bakery whose windows were painted deep blue, a defense against nighttime bombers. There was dim light behind it.

I rapped on the door, and we waited. No response. I knocked a little louder, fearful that each rap in the silent evening would rouse not only the baker but the town's entire population, any one of them a

Leo's Jewish star torn from his lapel.

potential traitor. The door opened, and a surly young man in a white baker's apron declared, "There is no bread until tomorrow morning."

"We don't want bread," Manfred quickly answered.

I wanted him to say it more softly, but not too softly. Too loud, trouble comes; too soft, it seems as if you're hiding something. In a war, every person suspects every other person who is a stranger.

"Where are we?" Manfred asked.

"You are near Mussy," he replied. "Are you lost?"

"We want to know where the village priest lives," I said.

The young man looked at the shadows of our faces. He said, "Wait a moment, I'll take you there," and closed the door. We waited nervously until he returned, wearing a jacket over his baker's outfit. We walked for a few blocks, the baker silent and taciturn, and Manfred and I quiet because we spoke French with Austrian accents.

As we approached the priest's sacristy, I thought of one more problem: To a priest, one shows respect. One removes one's beret. To remove one's beret was to show one's shaved head and thus announce: I am a fugitive, I am a Jew. But we had run out of choices. In a world in which one cannot trust priests, one might as well flag down the next train to Auschwitz. So we trusted. He was a middle-aged man and looked perplexed to see us standing there.

"These young men asked for your house," the baker said. Then, not wishing involvement, he walked off.

187

"What's going on?" the priest asked.

"We escaped from the train," I said, pointing toward the tracks. It was no time to be hesitant. I took my beret from my head, and he saw my bare skull. I am weary of running, I thought.

"Ah, yes," he said softly. "Three times a week. We know about the trains. You escaped from that?"

"May we stay the night?"

He looked us over and closed the door behind us. Then he grimaced. We stank from all that time on the crowded freight train. We stank from sweaty hours twisting at iron bars. We stank from vomit and excrement clinging to our bodies and our clothing, and stank from our fears.

"What you first want," he said, "is to use some soap and water."

We were not only filthy and infested, but also ravenously hungry. The priest warmed a pot of milk on his stove, and then put bread and cheese on the kitchen table.

"Toward six o'clock in the morning," he said, "we have the patrols here. I will let you stay the night, but you have to be out of here before six."

When we'd eaten our fill, he led us to a bathroom to bathe, and then gave us beds with crisp sheets. In Trier, the monks had such sheets, and I slept peacefully next to a German soldier named Heinz. Now new German soldiers would come in the morning. Our train would arrive in Auschwitz soon, without us. Tony and Erich were on that train, and Albert and the little boy separated from his parents, and people still praying to an unseen God, and the old woman with the crutch, who told us, "Go ahead. Go ahead."

Exhausted, I fell into a deep sleep, and awoke before dawn hearing the voice of a gentle angel speaking French. It was the priest, saying: "It's time." I hated to leave that bed. There was warmth under the sheets, and security. I wanted to stay in this room forever, to wrap the sheets around me and call it a day. I wanted to close my eyes and hide in the darkness behind them until the war was over. But it was after five in the morning, and daylight was coming, along with the German patrols.

The priest gave us breakfast and a note. There was a nearby village, he said, and in the village was a friend of his, another priest. He gave us some food and a few francs. As we said goodbye, it dawned on me that we never learned his name, nor had he learned ours. For each of us, it simplified our crimes.

We reached the next village late that morning and found the priest's home there. A maid said he was away for a little while. We saw a cemetery nearby and assumed we'd be safe there. In a cemetery, people can visit graves without questions being asked. We wandered among the dead for a while, envying their tranquility, and waited for the priest's return. I thought about my family and wondered if they still walked the earth, and, if not, would anyone ever find their final resting place.

The priest gave us shelter that night in his stable. We slept between two cows, on straw spread across the floor, and listened to the cows chewing their cud. It felt cozy and I felt safe.

The next morning, a familiar routine: Time to leave, patrols might arrive. Then the priest handed us two train tickets to Paris.

"Is it safe?"

"It's Sunday," the priest said. "Even for the Germans, a day off from patrolling the passenger trains. You should be all right until Paris."

"And then?"

"And then," he said, "if you escaped from that train of yours, you will have no trouble on a train going to Paris."

He sounded like the policeman in Luxembourg, joking about my swim across the River Sauer. Everything is relative: If you can swim a river, you'll be fine on dry land. You can escape from a freight train to Auschwitz, you'll survive a passenger train ride to Paris.

In Paris, I could look for my Aunt Erna. She was my mother's youngest sister. She'd moved to Paris in 1930 to marry. I'd last seen her in 1936, when she and her son Paul had come to Vienna. Now Paul was hiding in the mountains somewhere in France, and Aunt Erna had found a safe place with a priest who knew a friendly police lieutenant. I knew the address where I could find her.

"Manfred," I said, as our train headed toward Paris, "thirty years from now, when we'll think about this, it will seem like a dream."

"Are you crazy?" he snapped. The goofy little grin he wore even in the worst times vanished from his face. "You're a fool."

"Why do you say that?"

"Thirty years from now," he said sarcastically. "How can you think of thirty years from now when we don't even know what tomorrow will be?"

"Because," I said, "nothing is impossible any longer. After that train, nothing."

"Nothing," he mimicked me. "We don't even have papers. We don't even know where to go when we reach Paris."

"Rue St. Maur," I said. "No. 49."

We reached Paris on November 9, one day after the Allies landed in North Africa. It was precisely four years since the night Becker stopped his car along a road to see the blazes of Kristallnacht set the sky on fire. Now German occupation had reached across Europe. At Paris' East Station, German soldiers arrived on furlough, while others headed out. The city was taking on the character of its conquerors. We turned away, hoping to avoid all eye contact, and saw the unimaginable: German soldiers in tight embrace with French girls.

"Don't tip your hat to them," I said sardonically.

To remove our berets was to show our skulls in public. We had no papers, and we had no hair on our heads, and we wore no Jewish stars on our lapels. We walked the Paris streets until we found Aunt Erna's apartment, in the eleventh *arrondissement*. It was late afternoon.

The eleventh district always had a large Jewish population, but deportations had considerably reduced it. We saw some people with yellow stars on their jackets. We'd seen them in Drancy, but Drancy was a camp. This was Paris, the home of Hugo and Zola and Pasteur, men of compassion. This was the City of Lights, now the city where Jews were marked for the killing.

No one answered my aunt's buzzer, but a door opened on a second floor landing and a woman asked, "Who are you looking for?"

"Madame Szerer," I said. "I am her nephew."

The woman's name was Madame Angel. She walked toward us, examining our faces. "She is not home today," she said. "I don't know where she is." Then, warily, "I didn't know she had a nephew."

"She is my mother's sister," I said. "Is my cousin Paul with her?"

I knew he wasn't, but I hoped to gain her trust by name-dropping. Madame Angel seemed to relax a little. She was gray-haired, plump, and dour. She turned, walked into her apartment, and returned a moment later in an overcoat and scarf.

"Wait here a while," she said. "I'll see if I can find her."

Half an hour later, Aunt Erna arrived. *"Mon Dieu, mon Dieu!"* she cried. As we embraced, she wept. Madame Angel and Manfred watched us. I'd only seen my aunt three times before, but her embrace swept away the unfamiliarity. She was thirty-five years old and a pretty brunette. Her husband was a prisoner of war who'd escaped, come back to Paris, and been arrested again and deported. He never returned. Manfred and I went with Aunt Erna to her tiny third-floor apartment.

We stayed up late that night, and she told me about Paul. She'd sent him away when the French police started their mass arrests. He was living on a farm. "I miss him, but I want him to live," she shrugged.

Our clothes were infested with vermin. Aunt Erna took them from us and put them in a bag and then sprayed something into the bag. In the morning, she washed and steamed our clothes and gave each of us new shirts. They were her husband's. Then she showed us the way to the public baths, near the Place du Temple.

"To clean your *schmutz* away," she said.

"Is it safe to go back outside?"

191

"I'm afraid you must," she said. "The bath won't come to you."

There was no bath in her apartment or in her entire building. The toilets were located in a hallway. Aunt Erna's apartment was small, but she wanted me to stay with her. She was alone. Our family was scattered across Europe now, and neither of us knew who was alive and who was not.

"We want to get to the south zone," I explained. I was bursting at my seams from hiding in attics, from lying in crawl spaces, and from riding in freight cars crammed with people who couldn't fit themselves through windows with iron bars.

We stayed in Aunt Erna's apartment for about two weeks, biding our time and reading the daily newspapers to catch up on the war. German troops had now marched into all the unoccupied areas of France except the Mediterranean coast. Hitler told Marshal Pétain that Germany could no longer preserve the armistice, that new measures would have to be taken to stop Allied aggression. Within days, Prime Minsiter Pierre Laval vowed to collaborate even more fully with Germany. He said Britain and America were "tearing France limb from limb....The *entente* with Germany is the sole guarantee of peace in Europe."

Aunt Erna Szerer, c. 1950.

In the streets, life seemed in some ways to resemble peacetime. The French theaters were open, as were the racetracks and the stock market. At the Place de la République, and in Montmarte, we saw more French girls walking arm in arm with German soldiers. They nuzzled openly, certain that they had wisely chosen the winning side of the conflict.

One morning my aunt mentioned identity papers. She knew a man named David Rapoport, in the Rue Amelot, not far from her. Rapoport was legendary in the underground, a man born in the Ukraine who'd become a militant in the ranks of the Zionist–Socialists. He settled in Paris, where he helped Jews who were clinging to their last bits of freedom and dignity.

"He will know about false papers," Aunt Erna told me. "But I don't know why you can't stay here with me."

We saw Rapoport the next day. He was about sixty, small and stooped and gray. He seemed gentle and fatherly. He looked us over and invented new selves for us. Manfred became Roger Savary. I was Marcel Dumont.

"How did you pick such names?" I asked.

He shrugged. "You look like a Dumont, and he looks like a Savary," he said. And that was that. We picked up our papers the next day, along with fifty francs Rapoport slipped us, and never saw him again. Armed with our new papers, Manfred and I felt newly invincible. Rapoport gave us an address in the center of France, near Tours, on the Loire River. We would find help there, he said.

Once more, a final hug. Manfred stood by, eager to be going, as Aunt Erna and I embraced. Be careful, stay in touch. It was my mother's farewell all over again.

"Don't forget me," Aunt Erna said.

"Never."

We arrived in Tours that afternoon, and went to a restaurant to look for a man at an outdoor table reading a newspaper. We quickly found the restaurant, but no one was eating outside because the weather was too chilly. We walked inside, and found several people seated. A blond, freckled man worked on a newspaper crossword puzzle. He wore work clothes and smoked a pipe and told us to follow him. We walked toward the outskirts of town to a two-story farmhouse by a country lane.

"In the morning," said the man, "very early, we'll go across the Loire River. To the south."

After dinner, we listened to Radio Free France. Admiral Jean-François Darlan was telling Frenchmen, "Fight at the side of the

American and Allied forces." As battles raged in North Africa, his words sounded like a bugle call for a nation torn in its allegiance, and it renewed our confidence for the next day's journey.

We walked to the Loire River before dawn, and reached it in about twenty minutes. The morning was cool and misty. A fog hung over the river, making it easier for us to slip across undetected in our little row-boat. We crossed in less than half an hour, and landed at a sloping bank. This was the "free" zone. Our false papers would keep us safe, and we might now spend the war in some semblance of sanity, trying only to avoid detection.

Our man gave us directions to a nearby bus stop by a town called Joué. We watched him row several yards across the Loire, and he slipped back into the fog.

Manfred's intention was to reach the Dordogne, where his brother lived. We would stay together until we reached Limoges. My intention was to reach Bagnères. I had fled there only weeks earlier, but had nowhere else to go. Besides the Frajermauers, Milly Cahen, and the Spiras, I knew no one else in the Vichy-French zone, and Jews were being hunted everywhere. In Bagnères, I might still find the Spiras. I'd left some of my belongings with them, and I might find lodging for a little while until I figured out where else I might go. It seemed safer than Paris, and closer to Anny.

We found the bus stop in a few minutes. Children were there with school books in their arms. My little sister should have been in school. A few women chatted with each other. My mother should have been there. We stood among them, attempting to look innocuous. A pleasant morn-ing sun was burning away the fog. Then two gendarmes approached.

"Oh, God," Manfred said, choking back panic. I shot him a look that said "stay calm." Routine checks were made near the demarcation line, but we were well beyond the line, with French identity papers. This would merely be our first test. *"Papiers?"* one of the officers inquired. They skipped the children, but checked the women and a few working men who'd arrived. They politely thanked everyone else for their cooperation, but with us they stared silently at our papers. They asked us to step aside. The others at the bus stop gawked at us. The gendarmes asked us to move away.

"Look here," one officer said to the other. He seemed amused. "Can you believe this? Another Dumont." I told myself not to panic. The name was common. So near the demarcation line, they were surely seeing lots of Dumonts, Duponts, Duvals.

"Please come with us."

A sense of defeat knifed through me. In silence, we were taken to a police station near Joué. There, a simple question: Your real names? In Luxembourg, the truth had worked. In Switzerland, it had not. I produced my Belgian papers. Where had we come from? Paris. The mood was businesslike. We were not on our knees, begging for mercy, looking for hands to kiss. We decided to tell them the whole truth.

"We escaped from a train," I said.

"Ah, a train."

"From Drancy."

"Ah, but you're in free France now."

"Yes," I quickly agreed. Free France, not occupied France, not Germany, not Switzerland, and not Auschwitz. Distinctions could be made. This was not the Gestapo, these were merely French gendarmes under the Pétain regime, and this was "free" France.

But their language began to bother me. They used words I had heard before. They said we had been arrested, and our case must be processed through normal channels. Not to worry, they said. I worried. They used the word "disposition." They used the name "Centre d'Acceuil."

I knew what such words meant: internment camp, and then deportation. Most likely, back to Drancy, where death was waiting. They were playing us for fools, giving us a *laissez-passer,* a safe-conduct document, authorizing us to travel specifically from one location to another, without police accompaniment.

"You merely have to register when you arrive," an officer said.

"Yes, yes," we said, as though agreeing that it was a mere formality. It was part of the grand deception being played on Jews throughout Europe. Let your guard down, we won't hurt you. They hadn't enough men to accompany us, so they wished us to feel too comfortable to want to escape.

We were given travel passes and two days' worth of food coupons. Yes, we agreed, we would present these papers at the Centre d'Acceuil. Why should we run, when everyone was being so civilized?

At our first moment of freedom, Manfred and I ran for our very lives. We took the first train we could find and headed farther south. The world seemed to have spun wildly off of its axis, to have survived so much in these few hours, and to find ourselves on one more train, headed in one more direction.

And then, within hours, came a parting of the ways. In Brive-la-Gaillarde, south of Limoges, Manfred headed his way, and I went mine: to Bagnères and the Spiras, where I might discover if Anny was still near-by. Manfred and I shook hands firmly, and he gave me his brother's address. We said we would see each other again. Already, we had lived beyond our expected lifetimes in each other's company.

I watched him leave the train at Brive-la-Gaillarde, and I stayed on. It was the night of November 27. The Spiras might still be in Bagnères, and Anny might only be a few miles farther away. I carried sweet memories of afternoons strolling through streets with her hand in mine. I walked through the train station to a darkened sidewalk outside, where a policeman waited to take me away.

12

December 1942 – September 1943

Not so fast, young man."

For a moment, I pretended not to hear.

"Pardon, monsieur."

The gendarme was louder this time, and more insistent. The game was up. This time, I thought, they will shoot me on the spot and finally be done with me. "The rucksack," he said. He wanted to examine its contents for black market items, eggs or coffee or wine. I had none. But I had no legitimate papers, either, and I saw the next train to Auschwitz waiting for me, and this time there would be no escape.

"Open it up," he ordered.

The street was dark in the wartime blackout, with only a dim light coming from inside the small railroad station. I unbuckled my backpack. The gendarme looked inside but couldn't see in the dark. About fifty feet away, another gendarme inspected a man's suitcase. He carried a flashlight. I glanced about quickly.

"May I use your flashlight for a moment?" my officer called to the other.

"Come get it," came the reply.

As the officer turned his back to me, I bolted. I had never made a swifter decision. After the train escape, this felt like child's play. I was now a miraculous athlete, a professional escape artist, a young man in perpetual flight. I was indomitable. Also, I was too terrified not to run for my life.

I ran into the darkness. It was better to take a chance than to face Drancy and the train again; better to outrun these dim, middle-aged men in uniforms than to risk the unknown.

I never heard footsteps behind me, never heard a voice calling after me. The policeman was a thousand years old, or perhaps thirty-five. It was all the same. I was young and trying to hold on to my one single life. I ran until I reached the Spiras' house. The gate was locked. Breathing heavily, sweating profusely, I used its ornate ironwork as a foothold to climb to the top, and then jumped over. I tore my trousers on the way down, and when I landed felt an old, familiar ache: my hernia. When I staggered to Mendel Spira's door, he looked stricken at the sight of my face and loudly called to his family as he pulled me inside.

We talked through much of the night, and I told them of Switzerland and the unyielding officer at the border, and of Rivesaltes and Drancy and the train to Auschwitz, and of the priests who sheltered Manfred and me, and of the gendarmes at the train station who were looking for me at this moment.

"And all of you?" I asked, smiling at their comforting presence.

"We are well," said Spira.

"And the Frajermauers?"

"Still in Cauterets."

So Anny was in Cauterets. It was mere hours from here, but it might as well have been as far away as America. I mustn't try to go anywhere, Spira said. I mustn't try to leave this building. At the moment, with my hernia throbbing, I thought only of sleep.

So we settled into routines familiar from three months earlier. We read newspapers by day and listened to the radio in the evening. One night came news of Sir Anthony Eden, the British foreign secretary. He told the House of Commons, "Germany is now carrying into effect Hitler's oft-repeated intention to exterminate the Jewish people of Europe." So it was no longer a secret to the rest of the world. The Jews from the occupied nations were being sent to eastern Europe, Eden said, where they were "worked to death in labor camps or deliberately slaughtered in mass executions."

In the Spiras' modest dwelling, the walls closed in a little more. At night, I slept in Madame Leroy's attic with the Spiras' teenage girls, Recha and Susie. They shared a double bed, and I slept on a mattress on the floor. One night, stirred from sleep, I felt movement against my thigh and a tug at my blanket. When I reached down, the movement stopped. Again, I felt wiggling and a kind of struggle. I reached down and grabbed fiercely until all wiggling and all life ceased: a rat, which I squeezed with my hands until it died. I fought back every sense of revulsion and lay sweating in the dark. The rat was disgusting and loathsome, but it was only doing what rats do, scavenging, trying to survive, and dying because those around it wanted it to be dead.

I grew increasingly restless. I asked Spira about Broca, a kindly Bagnères baker who had given me extra helpings of bread when rationing was tight. "Don't be foolish," Mendel Spira said. "You can't go out there." I scarcely heard him. Broca was a first step. If I could go to him and then come home safely, perhaps in a while I might venture even farther, perhaps one day to Cauterets to look for Anny. The escape from the train had emboldened me. I could outrun anything now, including my own fate.

So, against Spira's better judgement, I ventured out. The day was sunny and brisk, and I passed an outdoor market where farmers displayed produce and housewares. I tried to blend into the crowd. I was there for only a few minutes. By the time I saw two gendarmes on bicycles, it was too late to run very far. One of them shouted, "I'm sure it's him," and I ran into a nearby apartment house, where the two of them cornered me. I was no longer the immortal athlete. Now I was that miserable rat unable to escape while its captors prepared to squeeze the life out of it.

"Where do you think you're going this time?" one officer asked. It was the one from the train station. I was handcuffed and taken to a holding cell, and within an hour I faced a captain's questions. I felt stupid and ashamed. The captain seemed interested, almost sympathetic. I told him about the train to Auschwitz and suspected I was winning an ally.

"But the escape," he said resignedly. "It was the occupied zone. Out of my province."

I had broken the law when I'd left Cauterets, my assigned residence, so many weeks earlier. *"Abandon de résidence assignée,"* he said, and nothing more. He returned me to my cell, and two visitors came for me in the morning: a gendarme and an attorney named Hippolyte Saliou.

I found it astonishing that there might be the rule of law, that there were still oases of civilization in Vichy France. Saliou was a short man with glasses and thinning black hair. He spoke softly, and I listened intently. He said the law was clear and that the penalty for abandoning an assigned residence was one year in prison. He said we would plead guilty.

"A year in prison?" I said, heart dropping. I felt claustrophobic inside an entire apartment; a jail cell might drive me mad.

"I have your best interests at heart," he said. He meant, as a Jew. Saliou saw a year in jail as a year off the streets, away from the risk of more serious arrest and internment and deportation.

"By the time you get out," he said, "this war could be over."

On a chilly early December morning, exactly one year after being denied a United States visa, two gendarmes took me by train to Tarbes and a stone building with a sign reading "Maison d'Arrêt de Tarbes." I was fingerprinted and strip-searched and filled out papers detailing the contents of my life. I was issued a jail uniform of coarse brown cloth. My meager money was taken from me, as was an envelope with photographs of my mother and my sisters. No one bullied me. I was merely a piece of routine business in a calm, orderly warehouse of human beings, while a war played itself out around us. Here, I would await my trial.

A guard walked me down a ground-floor corridor to a cell, and called into it, "Liebetrau, you have a companion now, someone to talk to."

"Thanks, Palisse, I was getting lonesome," a voice inside the cell replied.

The heavy cell door clanked behind me. I longed for the grand freedom of Mendel Spira's small house; or the open space of the stinking beach at St. Cyprien; or even the cramped confines of a train to Auschwitz with its tiny window I could slip through. I wished once again to outrun my pursuers...and this time never stop running.

I saw two cots in front of me, and a small sink, and a window with bars overlooking a prison yard. There was a small toilet. The steel door that closed behind me had a small square opening through which food and mail could be passed. Liebetrau nodded hello. He looked about forty, and the stubble on his cheeks showed hints of gray. His face was ruddy and pockmarked, and his teeth were broken and crooked.

"Why are you here?" he asked.

"Born Jewish," I shrugged. "You?"

"Manslaughter," he said.

I wondered if I would survive the night. He was bigger than I, and no doubt stronger, a real criminal surely hardened by years behind bars. I imagined a knife across the throat in the dark. I imagined my best hope was to establish my own credentials as a hardy fellow, and told him of my adventures. When I came to my arrest by the Swiss officer, he was furious.

"I am ashamed of this," he announced.

He was a Swiss national, imprisoned because he'd murdered his faithless French girlfriend in a moment of passion. Incarcerated for years, he was awaiting parole. He'd been a model prisoner, he said, and was certain release was coming.

201

When I awoke the next morning, I was relieved to find myself still alive. We were given weak tea, virtually tasteless. Only cold water came from our small sink. At lunch each day, we were served either vegetable or bean soup. The bean soup provided daily diversion for Liebetrau and me. We counted the beans to see who had the most. Often, we tied.

"They must be counting them out in the kitchen," I said.

"It's their diversion, same as ours," said Liebetrau.

On Sundays, we were served rations of meat which disappeared in a bite, and bread and cheese during the week. And always, the tasteless tea. "A bromide," Liebetrau said. He meant that it controlled sex drives. "Believe me, I've been here long enough."

I passed some time by writing brief notes to the Spiras and the Frajermauers. The attorney Saliou visited one afternoon, and reiterated plans for me to plead guilty at trial.

"I understand," I said, "that there is safety inside a cell. But what if conditions change? The Germans have been known to take prisoners from jails and make examples of them." He nodded his head, but seemed nonchalant. "This is constantly on my mind," I persisted.

"Let's hope it won't happen," he said.

When Saliou left, I was led back to my cell by Palisse, the jailer who had originally brought me there. He was an agreeable fellow who called me "Kid." Tall, heavy, and paunchy, Palisse shuffled his feet as he walked. There was another guard, Griffe, a tall, gangly fellow whose face seemed perpetually on the edge of a smirk. And there was Lebon, dour and demeaning, who could not crack a smile had he been paid for it.

On the morning of January 8, I waited in the warden's office to be taken to my trial. A female prisoner was brought in, arrested for dealing in the black market. We were handcuffed together until, after a short train ride, we reached the courthouse back in Bagnères. Saliou was waiting for me there, and so were Mendel Spira and his daughters.

The trial was so brief that I barely had time to absorb my surroundings. Saliou explained that I had fled my assigned residence out of fear of deportation. The judge, listening dispassionately, muttered into his legal papers, "One year in prison."

Heart sinking, I stood in the courthouse corridor minutes later and saw Mendel Spira walk past me. He nodded toward a nearby men's lavatory, and walked into it.

"May I go there?" I asked my guard. He'd seemed sympathetic to my plight, and loosened my handcuff.

"I'll be waiting right here," he said.

Inside, Spira handed me fifty francs. "You might need it," he said.

"A year," I said, as though uttering a curse.

"In a strange way, you'll be safe there."

"What if the Germans clean out the cells? What if they need an act of retribution and come to the jails?"

There was nothing Spira could say. A moment later, in the hallway, I was handcuffed again to the woman charged with black marketeering.

The courthouse where Leo was tried as it appears today in Bagnères (courtesy of Susie Spira-Pernitz).

A small crowd gawked at us. Recha and Susie Spira waved timidly, and I waved back, trying not to show my gloom.

A train would take us back to Tarbes, but it wouldn't leave for two hours. The two gendarmes decided to wait inside a bistro, and the woman and I, cuffed to them, sat down, too. The guards ordered red wine. Only in France, I thought, pretending it was the wine I myself helped make earlier in Carcassonne. The four of us sat at a table, and the guards talked about the boredom of their jobs. I thought of the months of confinement awaiting me. They talked of arriving home late from work. They took more notice in the woman than in me, and I thought about escape.

"The men's room," I said. "May I use it?"

"Don't be long," said the officer who had allowed me to go at the courthouse. He was being kind, but he also made me wear the hand-cuff on my wrist, and where could I run with such a thing dangling so clearly?

I didn't care. I found a window in the restroom, and quickly lifted it and climbed through. A light rain was falling in Bagnères. I ran just to run, to put distance between my captors and me. I thought of the Spiras, and knew to avoid them. To run to them was to endanger them. My temples pounded. I thought of the Frajermauers: too far away. A pounding heart became a light head, which became nausea. I ran until I came to a grocery store and reached for the front door. In that instant, I vomited, and my vision blurred, and then all went dark.

When I awoke, the storekeeper and a young clerk were wiping my clothes and putting water to my lips. I sat in a chair in a kitchen area behind the store. They fed me tea and asked questions, and I trusted them enough to tell the truth. "I have friends in Bagnères," I said. On Route de LaBassère. The grocer's expression brightened.

"You don't mean Spira?" he said.

"Yes," I said, feeling a surge of strength. "You know them?"

"Know them?" he said delightedly. "They shop here."

By sheer luck, I had chosen the best place to faint in all of Bagnères.

"You will stay here," said the grocer, "until dark."

He had a hacksaw, and in minutes I was free of my handcuff. The young man was sent into the rain to bring a message to the Spiras: Leo is safe. The Spiras sent a message back: Do not come here, and do not write from any fixed address. Within hours, police came to their home, as Mendel Spira expected the moment he heard of my escape.

Where to go? I thought about Toulouse, a city large enough to get lost in. Also, Leon Oesterreicher might still be there after freeing me from St. Cyprien, and there were friends of my Aunt Erna near Toulouse who had fled Paris a few years earlier. As darkness fell, I thanked the grocer and slipped into the evening rain. To Toulouse, I would go. But, as I passed my friend Broca's bakery, I looked in the front door and saw he had no customers.

"Monsieur Broca."

"Mon Dieu, Leo!"

I thought I had given the poor man a heart attack as I opened the front door. The last time I'd been here was ten months earlier. I told him about the courthouse, about my escape from the bistro.

"You?" he said. "I heard that a young refugee escaped from the courthouse."

"Not a refugee," I said. "I am a fugitive. And it wasn't the courthouse, it was a bistro. The police must be embarrassed."

"Can I help you?" he asked.

"Bread would help," I said. "But I have no ration cards."

Broca smiled. He wrapped bread in a piece of cloth to protect it from the rain, and handed me twenty francs. We embraced, and then I fled again. I walked all night in the rain. I grew tired, but feared the gendarmes searching for me. I sat under a tree and napped for a little while, and awoke and walked again. I watched carefully for signs, hoping I was headed for Toulouse. I ate some of Broca's bread. I longed for some tea to wash it down. I came to a fork in the road and, having no idea how to find my way to Toulouse, veered to the right and hoped for the best.

At dawn, I saw a sign marked Capvern, which was about ten miles from Bagnères. My heart sank. Walking all night, I'd moved only in circles. Rain began to fall again, and I found shelter in an abandoned shack with farm tools lying about. I was exhausted and wet, and bathed in defeat. I had no idea how to survive the brand new day.

When the rain stopped, I walked again. I came to a small village and entered a tavern. My clothes were soaked. A voice in my head said that there might be dangerous people in here. And another voice replied how, at this moment, jail seemed a kind of haven. The tavern owner stood behind his bar. I could have a drink, he said, but the kitchen was still closed. It was eight o'clock in the morning. I asked whether there was any food at all. He brought out a plate of beans, which I ate with Broca's bread. I watched the proprietor eye me.

I no longer had strength to run. I walked to the door, and saw rain falling steadily, and felt I could go no farther. I walked back to my plate to finish my beans and saw the proprietor on the telephone. He turned his back to me, hung up the phone, and walked into his kitchen.

The coward can't even face me, I thought. What have I ever done to him? He doesn't even know me.

As inevitably as I knew the gendarmes would come, I could not move from my seat. Exhaustion consumed me. In minutes, two gendarmes walked through the door and put handcuffs on me. One officer looked at the beans on my plate and asked if I wanted to finish them. The proprietor walked into the room.

"Let him have it," I said. "I'm no longer hungry."

"Did he pay you?" the officer asked.

"Not yet."

"I didn't have a chance," I said, gesturing to the telephone. "He was too busy."

206

"Where is the money?" the second officer asked.

I froze. I had money from Spira and Broca. How to explain this to the gendarmes? I was not supposed to have any money on me, since they had taken all my money when I'd arrived in jail a month earlier. I had to protect my friends. I motioned to my pants pocket, which was impossible to reach while handcuffed.

"Where did you get this money?"

"I had it on me."

"Impossible," an officer said. "Your money was taken from you in jail."

"I hid some of it in my rectum," I said.

"We'll tell this to the warden."

Then we were walking in the rain once again. Before returning to an overnight cell, I was strip-searched, heaping humiliation upon arrest. They would make me pay for my previous deception. In the morning, a train took me back to Tarbes. Two guards rode with me, neither saying a word. The silence seemed ominous. At the gendarme post, I was greeted with raw anger. I'd made their friend look bad. He'd been severely disciplined for letting me escape.

Half a dozen officers formed a tight circle around me. A few of them shoved me. I told them I was sorry. They mocked my apology. The shoves became hard punches. Who gave you the money? I tried apologizing again. Who helped you? I am sorry for what I did. Why did you lie to us? I am sorry, I am sorry. I told them I had acted alone. I told them I had walked in circles and was lost. The punches turned to kicks, and I looked for some section of the floor on which to fall and curl myself up into a ball.

"So you ran," an officer said. "Fast legs, have you?"

He stepped toward a fireplace and grabbed an iron poking rod. I raised my arms to protect my head. "Fast legs," he said again. His face contorted with anger. He slammed the poker across my thighs, and then across my calves. "Fast legs!" I slumped to the floor. Boots stomped across my back, my torso, and my legs and my groin. This was beyond

207

punishment now; it was revenge for a friend, a lesson to be told mournfully to all others with notions of escape.

Two men finally lifted me by my arms, handcuffed me, and took me back to jail. Again, I was humiliatingly strip-searched and handed prison garb. This time, I was taken to a cell on an upper level with no one else there. I was back under the watch of the guards Palisse and Griffe and Lebon.

I stretched out on a hard cot and felt the bruises on my throbbing body. Sleep, I thought. Withdraw into sleep, and let your body heal itself. But there was no sleep, only the turning of a key, and into my cell walked Lebon. So they've sent the bully, I thought. I stood to greet him: prison rules. He asked how I felt, with no sign of particularly caring.

"I'm hurting," I said meekly.

"So, you're hurting. Do you know why?"

"Yes, sir, I do."

"How about the money?" he asked. "Who gave it to you?" He wasn't waiting for an answer. "You'd better tell us. The sooner, the better." The words kept coming, and now he began to crowd me. "I am waiting," he said. I thought of Spira, who had taken a chance for me, and Broca who had been generous to me. My body hurt badly. Lebon twirled the keys on his chain.

"Nobody gave me the money, sir, I always had it on me," I said.

Lebon formed a fist around his keys and stepped closer to me. I felt a sharp thwack, his fist against my right temple. "Liar," he said. The word seemed to come from some faraway place, and it echoed around the cell. "Liar."

"No, sir, I..."

"You had it on you, right," he sneered. "You want me to believe that?"

He hit me again. My head bounced back from the impact. I reached for a nearby wall, determined not to fall down, feeling sharp pain under my right eye.

"This is the truth," I said.

How long could this go on, I wondered. Will he hit me until I am dead? Lebon held his fist in front of my face.

"We stripped you," he hollered. "We searched you when we first brought you here. Where was the money?"

"Here, sir," I said, pointing to my rear end.

"What a pig!" Lebon cried, and he grabbed me by the shoulders, turned me around to face the wall, and kicked me with his knee in the small of my back. Then, in one swift motion, he pulled my pants down. "Let me see what you have hidden in there this time," he said.

He is going to kill me, I thought. He will break all the bones in my face and leave me here to die. I turned my head and saw him aim a large key at my exposed buttocks. He will cut me open. I will bleed, and he will cut me more, and then I will die right here in this cell.

"Don't do it!" I heard myself shriek. "Don't do it, don't do it. You won't find anything."

Lebon kicked me in the buttocks with his boot, and then he turned me around. He kicked ferociously at my groin. His boot landed at the spot of my hernia, and a dagger of pain sliced through me. Then, a second kick between my legs, and I writhed in agony. Lebon turned away in disgust and walked to the cell door.

"I'll be back, pig," he sneered.

I picked myself up from the floor and struggled onto my cot. My groin throbbed, and every move I made invoked pain through my entire body. I lay there until dinner arrived that evening: herbal tea, and a slab of bread. I dipped the bread in the tea, and used it to moisten my face. Then I lay in the darkness, and waited for sleep that never came.

During the night, a turnkey peeped through the cell door. I feigned sleep. What if Lebon came back, I wondered. In the morning it was Griffe. My body felt worse now, and moving to the toilet across my cell seemed a long journey. "You asked for it," Griffe said, with no particular affect in his voice. I stood at silent attention. He said the warden had decided to keep me here, in solitary confinement, for one month. For one week, I would eat only bread and soup. There would be no daily walks in the prison yard. I could receive mail, but send none. And my date of departure would now be September 9, 1943, two days' extension of my original sentence to make up for my escape and brief freedom.

The next day, the good-natured Palisse was back on duty. He slipped my bread and soup through the small opening in the door and shook his head at the sight of me. I felt a painful swelling under my right eye. My buttocks were too sore to sit down, so I paced and paced. You are safer behind bars, Saliou had told me. Stay off the streets, Spira had told me. Stay with me in Paris, Aunt Erna had pleaded with me. There were so many voices smarter than my own, but I hadn't listened to any of them. Trust no one, my mother had said. Where was she now, and where were my sisters who loved me, and where was Anny?

In a few days, the prison barber visited me. My hair was growing back, and it had to be shaved again. I winced as he touched sensitive parts of my skull where Lebon had beaten me. The barber's grip grew tighter.

"What does my face look like?" I asked.

"Not pretty," he said.

He swept the hair off the floor and walked out of the cell. No more talk. But the sound of those few words seemed musical, and echoed through my head for a long time merely because they were sound itself. Time was my enemy. Boredom set in, and then dug its way deeper into my head, replacing everything, replacing fear and longing, replacing my mother and my sisters and Anny, replacing the gendarmes and Hitler's army and the war itself.

Day by day, my body healed a little at a time. This pain diminished, and then that one. Only the hernia nagged at me, angrily one day, then not so bad the next, and then pain the next. I had one goal: Not release, but release from solitary confinement, and moving to a new cell with

210

another human being. Perhaps a cellmate would have access to a radio or a newspaper, or at least access to a rumor from someone who had once seen a newspaper or listened to a broadcast and remembered what was reported.

One day, a letter came from Susie Spira. She said they'd heard of my plight and would send food when my solitary confinement ended. They were still in Bagnères, and the Frajermauers were in Cauterets. So the world wasn't deserting me; loved ones were still nearby. I lay on my cot and imagined letters to write from my new cell. I remembered Milly Cahen, standing at the barbed wire that last night at Rivesaltes, and Manfred saying goodbye as he departed the train. Maybe I could write to them both from my new quarters.

I stopped sleeping. The nights became endless, broken only slightly—and with great mercy and novelty—by the quick sound of a barking dog, a snatch of conversation in the yard outside my window, the clanking of a metal door. Two weeks into my confinement, I asked Palisse for relief from my boredom. Could he get me paper and ink for drawing? At lunch he brought several sheets of paper, a pen and a bottle of ink. I spent my last two weeks in solitary translating drawings and doodles and random bits of the inside of my head onto paper.

Finally, I was transferred to a ground floor cell with another prisoner. He was civil, and three days later he was gone. Taken to court one morning, he never returned. Then another cell mate, doing time for black marketeering. He stayed for a few weeks. They came and they went, half a dozen cell mates over months and months.

I was now allowed daily morning walks in the prison yard. The fresh air invigorated me. My legs were still hurting, but the exercise helped. My face was still sore, but slight breezes felt healing. One morning I saw Liebetrau in the yard, and we greeted each other as old friends. His release was imminent, he said, and he would return to his native Switzerland.

"What happened to your face?" he asked.

211

One of the drawings Leo doodled while in solitary confinement.

I hadn't seen a mirror in more than a month. I told him about the beating. He pulled the lid of a tin can out of his pocket, which he had polished until it reflected like a mirror. I was horrified at the sight. My face was a grotesque palette of colors, dark blue around my eyes, green and yellow elsewhere, vestiges of Lebon's brutality. All this, after a month.

My contacts with other inmates were minimal. In one section of the prison, I saw women's faces peer from their cell windows. I hadn't seen a woman since I'd been handcuffed at the bistro near the courthouse. I thought of Anny and wondered if she was still in Cauterets.

One day a letter arrived with a name I'd never seen: Marie-Louise Larrouy, from Tarbes. She said she'd heard of my situation from a friend, Anny's Aunt Rivka. She said Rivka was no longer in Cauterets. The family had been forced to disperse. I wondered miserably if Anny had now vanished from my life. A few days later, I received a package from Miss Larrouy: assorted fruit, biscuits, toothpaste, socks, and handkerchiefs. They were wrapped in paper which advertised a breakfast beverage. Its colors were bright. The paper became a work of art to hang in my cell. When I tired of its designs I took it down, cut it into smaller pieces, and used the blank reverse side for drawing.

In late spring came word that the Frajermauers had moved from Cauterets in another raid. This time they were looking for all Jews, no matter what identification papers they carried. Anny was now in Nice, living under the name of Marie Benedetto. She was hiding in a convent. In Trier, the monks had sheltered me. In Nice, the sisters were hiding Anny. I learned that Anny's parents and Netty were living under the name "Labatut" in Mégève.

Meanwhile, the plight of Jews across Europe worsened dramatically. In Poland, poorly-armed, starving Jews fought off thousands of tank-supported SS troops for weeks, but finally succumbed. The Warsaw ghetto was turned into a cemetery. In Germany, Goebbels boasted that Berlin was now "free of Jews." In France, there were seventeen transports from Drancy to Auschwitz in 1943, seventeen thousand Jews delivered to the Germans by the Pétain government.

On July 14, Bastille Day celebrating the nation's grand history of liberty, there was no playing of *La Marseillaise*. We were served a small portion of meat for dinner. It was the sole sign that the day was different from any other.

213

Liebetrau was gone now, but another cellmate mentioned his enjoyment of crossword puzzles. We created our own, and exchanged them, trying to stimulate our brains and pass the endless hours.

In late summer, sores broke out on my body, painful boils under my chin, on my arms and lower back, behind my knees and around my groin. I couldn't sleep. I tried wetting the areas with the warm tea that arrived every morning, but the sores persisted and the pain grew worse. Lebon was on duty following a difficult night. When I told him about the sores, he stared at me coldly and said, "Let's go to the infirmary."

Leo and a cellmate created crossword puzzles to pass the time in prison.

214

The photograph of Anny Leo received while in prison.

Furunculosis, I was told. I was given one salve, and then another when the first was ineffective. At night, my skin was so tender I couldn't cover myself with my blanket. The boils began to smell badly.

One day I received a letter from Manfred. Then came a letter from Milly Cahen, and a letter from Anny with an enclosed photo. She would soon rejoin her family in Mégève. I felt every letter was a life preserver thrown to me from a distant and fading world.

On the first day of August, I fashioned a calendar grid marking the final weeks of my prison stay. Where in the world would I go now? If I was safer in prison than outside, should I stay here? No, I would lose my mind. I grew nervous with anticipation.

Early on the morning of September 9, Palisse took me to the warden's office. Two gendarmes were there. I was handed my civilian clothing and my meager belongings, and gendarmes took me in handcuffs to an overnight holding cell at a nearby post. My new freedom, I thought. I was too frightened to ask where they were taking me.

The next morning, the gendarmes took me to a train, and the three of us went to my new destination. It was not freedom at all. It was a hard labor camp.

13

September – December 1943

At the village of Septfond, our train stopped at a station with one narrow building, two benches for waiting passengers, and one ticket window. But no one was there to buy, to sell, to come or to go. It looked like the last outpost of the inhabited world.

A gravelly country road led to the front gate of the camp, behind which there were twenty barracks and flat, desolate land surrounded by barbed wire. I sensed I had been here before. Drancy was ringed by barbed wire, and so was Rivesaltes before it, and St. Cyprien before that. Maybe I could escape this place the way I had escaped the others.

The gendarmes left me with an examining officer who looked at a manila folder containing the history of my various incarcerations and escapes. He did not seem pleased.

"Escape from a train," he recounted aloud, as though I needed reminding. "Crossing the Loire...eluding officers of the law...arrest...escape after sentencing...prison...." Looking up, he declared without a hint of congratulation, "This is quite a dossier, young man."

A sliver of youthful pride shot through me, which I concealed behind a mask of tame humility. Show them you've been chastened, Leo. Don't make them angry with you. Show them you're a harmless boy, frightened into submission, so that no one brings another boot into your genitals in the isolation of another empty cell.

Shuffling my papers absentmindedly, the officer explained that this was a work camp, and I would be assigned work. The work would be meaningless, except that it would keep me occupied. Also, I would obey rules. One of the rules was "no more escapes." I nodded my head earnestly and without a trace of conviction. I was taken to a barracks where twenty cots lined two walls, with two large windows leading only to the campgrounds. No escape route seemed available.

In the coming days, I found we could move about freely within the camp, though work details occupied us for most of the day. I was assigned to a group of six inmates whose job was to break large rocks into small stones. We gathered along a dirt path and listened to a sullen guard explain the intricacies of such occupation: take a hammer with a square peen; strike the boulder until it fragments; break the fragments into smaller fragments; and then break those into smaller pieces. Not all prisoners were assigned such tedious and tiring work. Some had a different kind of tedious and tiring work, such as hauling wheelbarrows bearing large rocks to our work area, and carrying off the small stones we had created. One day I was assigned wheelbarrow work.

"I have a hernia," I explained. Quickly, a camp doctor confirmed this, and I was relegated to the continuous breaking of rocks, which added back pain to my hernia discomfort. Millions were riding freight trains to their deaths, and I had been given a hernia as a measurement of my troubles.

Life at Septfonds was a vast improvement over previous incarcerations. I had fresh air around me, and not merely four walls. The guards were talkative, and thoughtfully brought water to us in the hottest hours of the day. Like us, they were prisoners, too, miserable and bored in this lonely outpost, and some seemed to identify with us. Conversation was relaxed and, in odd moments, took on the mood of old acquaintances chatting easily about events of the day.

218

One guard was more talkative than most. His name was Kaufmann. As we hammered our rocks one morning, he walked slowly past and muttered, "Italy. Out of the war." I looked up, trying to put meaning into his words. "Never could trust them," Kaufmann said, still identifying with the German cause. He was Alsatian.

Thus we received our cryptic bulletins on the war, a war we dissected endlessly, and found hope or despair depending on the latest rumors, or our mood of the moment, until the next scrap of outside information arrived and brought us a new round of light or darkness.

In the evening, I wrote short notes: to Manfred, to Milly, to the Spiras, and to my Aunt Erna's friends Jacques and Genia Estrajch, who lived in Blagnac. I no longer knew where the Frajermauers lived. Though I wrote many letters, I received none. I suspected everyone had forgotten me, or had been taken to fates worse than mine. In my new isolation and abandonment, I needed to break through the barbed wire around me.

One Sunday morning that fall, a visitor arrived: Manfred, looking slightly heavier than I'd remembered, and healthier. He smiled that silly smile of his that he wore even when leaping from the freight train into darkness. Now he'd emerged from the dark, and I was once again in custody. I smiled across the barbed wire that separated us. Manfred said he and his brother had moved, and he gave me a new address. He said the war was beginning to go better. Then he said he could get papers for me.

"If you were free," he said softly, glancing about.

"I am thinking about it," I said.

Manfred departed in a few minutes, and I returned to kitchen duty with a German Jew named Werner, who had fled to France with his wife and two children. He was arrested by Vichy officers and brought here while his family hid nearby. He worried constantly that they would lose each other.

"They will move," Werner said, "or we will be moved. One or the other."

"We?" I asked.

"Septfonds is not forever," he said. "This is only a transit point."

I'd imagined it was a last stop before release. Werner mentioned Drancy. I told him that I'd been there, that I'd escaped from the train. He seemed stunned.

"I would escape before I would go back to Drancy," I said.

Werner, agonizing endlessly about his family, could not indulge such thoughts. I said I hadn't heard from my family in over a year and a half. "This is our history," he said. "It's in God's hands." He was a thoughtful and religious man and, though I respected his sentiments, I had no patience for them. It was in God's hands, but God seemed to have washed his hands of the Jews, and of all innocents, and of all humankind. I was breaking rocks in a miserable labor camp for the crime of trying to stay alive. My mother and my sisters were dead or alive, no thanks to God. Werner worried frantically over the fate of his loved ones, and was ready to leave them in God's hands, but I had no such intentions.

One Sunday morning in mid-October, Kaufmann came to my barracks with a list of fourteen names. Werner and I were among them. We were to depart the next morning for a work detachment on the Atlantic coast. To me, this meant coastal fortifications and heavy construction work. I knew my hernia wouldn't hold up. I would be considered useless and might be sent to Drancy.

"If I have a chance, I'm going to try to escape," I told Werner, trusting him to stay quiet.

"You are overly alarmed," he said. "Don't take foolish chances."

"Werner, I've been there," I said. "It frightens me."

I could not challenge fate a second time at Drancy. It was a nightmare that still visited me in the dark, with weeping children wandering about, and families beginning to die in each other's presence, and ghosts prematurely haunting the landscape. At Drancy, a sickness crept into the soul and never left.

The next morning, as we gathered in front of the barracks, four guards with rifles slung over their shoulders led us to an open truck. We headed for the little train station at Septfonds, leaving clouds of dust behind us on the same gravelly roads that had brought me here weeks earlier. The guards wore no ammunition belts. I wondered if their rifles were loaded. Kaufmann leaned his face close to mine.

"Today, I am guarding you," he said. He knew my history. "Forget about escaping."

"Mr. Kaufmann," I said, "I ran away to save my life. Is it a crime to wish to live?"

"No, no, of course not."

"Whether I escape or not is entirely up to me," I said, feeling a frisson of boastfulness run through me. Kaufmann said nothing.

Our train from the Septfonds station took less than an hour to reach Toulouse. I'd been here after fleeing the camp at St. Cyprien: Lift the barbed wire, crawl under, run to Anny. I'd been here again after that miserable trip to Marseilles, when I'd missed by only hours my chance for America after the bombing of Pearl Harbor.

As we stood on the railroad platform now, fourteen of us huddled together, the guards unshouldered their rifles. Kaufmann, I thought, you would shoot me? They held their rifles at the ready. Kaufmann, who brought me water as I broke rocks under a hot sun, you would harm me now? Passengers walked past, eyeing us warily, but without alarm. In Vichy-France, who would care about a few more dead? Kaufmann, I thought, don't shoot, I'm not escaping yet.

We were led into an old European train with several doors opening into a corridor, and the corridor opening into separate compartments. Each compartment had a window. Windows meant possibilities. Two prisoners were shuffled into each compartment. I shared mine with Werner. In my mind, I'd been issued a ticket to freedom. When the doors closed behind us, the four guards lined up outside the car to ensure no escapes occured on the platform side. Werner and I looked through our window and saw Kaufmann chatting with the other guards.

"Werner, look here," I said, pointing to the window behind us. "This is easy. You can come with me."

"No!" he said adamantly.

"You don't know where this train is taking you."

"No," he said. He was rigid with fear, and I knew I had to leave before the fear clutched at me.

"Then do one thing for me," I said. There was no time to debate him. "Stay at the window. Be my lookout. If a guard starts to board the train, shout at me, 'Stop!'"

Such a shout would clear Werner of any complicity. For me, it would be a cry from hell, a warning signal to run faster. Werner was too frightened even to respond. I backed my way toward the other side of the train. I knew this moment. I had invented this moment. I thought of Manfred, and wanted him to see this. I lowered the window and saw a train paused on a parallel track. After Drancy, Manfred would think this was child's play. I climbed through the window opening. The train to Auschwitz had rumbled in the darkness. Here, I could see everything around me. The trick was not letting anyone see me.

I let myself fall to the ground. My beret fell, and I picked it off the ground and put it back on my shaved head. I ran between the two sitting trains and felt a gnawing in my groin. The landing had jarred me, and my hernia was acting up. I threw myself to the ground and crawled beneath the second row of trains, heart pounding, sweat running down my face, dirt clinging to my clothing.

A platform led to a stairway. I heard no whistles behind me, no calls to stop. The stairway led to an underground passage. Avoid the main exit, Leo, and avoid all passengers and ticket takers and find a doctor one day who will look at this hernia sending bolts of pain through you. Until that day, avoid all eye contact with passing strangers.

I saw a sign marked "Baggage" and entered a storage area. A clerk in a uniform stood behind a large table. All uniforms were to be avoided. The clerk handed a carton to a passenger. I pretended to search for a luggage stub in my pocket. The clerk ignored me. I walked across the room to a door, heart pounding, and opened it to find the city of Toulouse in front of me.

I turned down a small street and ducked into a doorway to catch my breath. Kaufmann would be counting noses by now. A search would be under way. About ten minutes had passed since I climbed through the window opening. I resisted every impulse to run madly through the streets. Attract no attention, Leo. Walk briskly, mind your own business. I wanted to hide from the whole world. I wanted to lose myself in a vast crowd, or a vast emptiness. I wanted to find a way out of this city. In a moment of coherence, I thought of nearby Blagnac, where my aunt Erna's friends, Jacques and Genia Estrajch, were living. I stepped into a bistro and asked the bartender where to catch a bus to Blagnac. In front of the train station, he said. My heart sank.

"That is the only one?"

"Near the market is another," he said, "not far from the Rue du Canal."

"The market," I repeated dumbly. I left quickly. The last bartender in a bistro had reached for a telephone and caught me in my exhaustion.

The bus ride from the Rue du Canal took perhaps half an hour to Blagnac, a small town on the northern outskirts of Toulouse. I was hot and sweating and my hernia was worse. I found the Estrajchs' house in the Rue Felix de Bax a few minutes from the bus stop. Jacques opened the door. When he saw me, his face turned pale.

"A gendarme was here half an hour ago," he said, pulling me into his apartment. I should have known. I'd written Jacques several times from jail, and they'd probably kept his address on a list.

"Wait a minute," I said. "Did you write to me at Septfonds?"

"Yes, twice."

"I never got mail there. From anyone. They must have kept every-one's address."

We both felt very vulnerable now. Jacques was a tailor, slender, balding, in dark-rimmed glasses. I saw a garment spread on a sewing machine in the kitchen.

"I was doing an alteration for the gendarmes when they arrived," he said, pointing to his work.

"Pardon?"

"They are my friends," he said. "They came here to tell me you escaped."

A dispatch had been sent to police offices in the area. They had already cast a net for me. Staying here was too risky, Jacques said. Genia had gone to the market and would be home soon. Their daughter was gone, staying at a Catholic school for girls, a safe place until war's end. My mother wanted a safe place for me. Now I was hiding with people whose own safety was threatened because I was here.

I was exhausted. The gendarmes would come for me again, and take me back to prison, and this time they would beat me beyond repair for embarrassing their guards again. "You'll rest for a while," Jacques said. He took me upstairs to an attic. Don't come downstairs, he said, without a signal from him. I fell asleep quickly, and was awakened a few hours later. There had been a second visit, Jacques said, from another officer.

"If he comes here," the officer said, "you must turn him in or jeop-ardize your status as a registered Jew."

The officer went away. Jacques brought me downstairs and told me that staying here would be impossible. Genia arrived home and made a warm supper, and they told me they had friends who had come here from Paris, Mr. and Mrs. Marx, who would let me stay with them for a short time. I felt relief, and guilt for exposing more people to danger. The Marxes lived five minutes away and had a small extra room.

Jacques and I walked quickly through the dark, empty streets, two men afraid of our own shadows. He took long strides, concerned about gendarmes who could appear anywhere. When we reached the Marxes' apartment, they greeted me as if they had known me for years. They were in their sixties, diminutive people with gray hair and glasses. They both wore slippers. A sense of coziness prevailed.

They showed me a bedroom with a window opening to a garden: a window with no bars, and a garden with no barbed wire in an apartment occupied by strangers making themselves vulnerable for me.

I wrote immediately to Manfred, remembering his talk of false papers. I felt I had landed in luxury fit for a prince. I had my own bed, and hot water for bathing. I hadn't known such cleanliness in a long time. Mrs. Marx gave me some old towel rags, which I stuffed into a sock to make a truss to support my hernia. In the evenings, we listened to Radio Free France. I wondered about the thirteen others in Toulouse who had stayed on the train when I jumped. Were the guards still looking for me? In a place where all Jews were considered guilty by reason of blood, why would they waste their time on such a meaningless fellow as me?

One day in November, a letter arrived from Manfred, with a birth certificate—mine! I was no longer Leo Bretholz. For the duration of the war, I would be Max Henri Lefèvre, born October 28, 1925, at St. Jouin-sur-Mer, Seine Inferieure, to Marie Antoinette Desbouilles and Marcel Auguste. The birth certificate was all that I needed to apply for a French identity card. Four days later, I had new papers and my new identity was certified. With the identity card, I was given ration cards for food and clothing. I wrote to Manfred to thank him, and never heard from him again. I wrote to Aunt Erna, who told me to come back to Paris, and reminded me that I never should have left in the first place. I thanked the Marxes, and once again I ran.

I arrived in Paris on the day before Christmas, 1943, and found the city calm. Paris had learned to accommodate the presence of German soldiers. I walked through the streets feeling uneasy, not wishing to test my new identity papers. My hair was growing back, and I wore no

Jewish star on my jacket. At nearby Drancy, there had been two convoys to Auschwitz in the previous two weeks.

"Such hardships to endure," Aunt Erna cried when she saw me.

It wasn't sympathy she was offering, but anger. So many troubles could have been avoided, she yelled, waving her arms dramatically. Why couldn't I have listened to her and stayed in Paris?

"If Paris is so safe," I asked, "why did you send Paul away?"

"He is just a boy," she cried.

The forged birth certificate used to give Leo his new identity in France—Max Henri Lefèvre. With the certificate, Manfred Silberwasser also sent instructions to contact a man in St. Vallier who helped Leo establish himself as a Frenchman. This man gave Leo his Compagnons de France uniform.

Identification papers under Leo's alias "Lefèvre."

There was more angst. Aunt Erna had news of her brother, my uncle. Uncle Leon Fischmann, whose daughter Sonja went to Birkenau and Auschwitz, was taken to the French internment camp at Gurs. Gurs was a terrible place in the Basses-Pyrénées, with wooden shacks that were leaky and cold and overcrowded with underfed inmates. Uncle Leon suffered an emotional breakdown there and was transferred to St. Luc psychiatric hospital in Pau. A letter came from the hospital. It said Uncle Leon was suffering from a delirium of persecution, and had ceased understanding the world around him.

I remembered him in better times, a man of high intellect who spoke several languages, who had been a successful businessman in Vienna, kind to my mother when she was widowed. He was her younger brother. His daughter Sonja, behind barbed wire for fifteen months, was trying to hold on.

When I looked at the ruined lives of my family, I realized I was running one step ahead of all manner of potential executioners. I walked the

227

streets feeling increasingly isolated. I saw Jews wearing yellow stars marked "Juif," but wore no markings of my own. They were pariahs, and I was merely a fraud, a man temporarily passing by pretending to be someone he was not, pretending to believe in a God who was someone else's. Everyone pretended, though. The Germans were pretending that the killing of Jews was valid by sheer reason of birthright. Humanity itself was pretending to be sane when all around was evidence of madness. And the Jews like Uncle Leon were said to be suffering from "delusions of persecution." What delusions?

In January of 1944, there were four straight days of air raid alarms in Paris. Allied planes one day, Germans the next. Once, we watched planes attack each other. I looked around and noticed few people scurrying for safety. They looked skyward, some of them waving their arms, as if they expected to be seen from above. Some stood on balconies, waving and shouting, expressing joy at seeing the Allies. It felt as if some grand national holiday had arrived, with the war fought in the distant heavens as some deadly spectator sport.

One day I received a letter from Anny. She'd left Nice to join her family in Mégève, once under Italian control and thus relatively safe for Jews. But the Germans had moved in, so Anny and her family fled elsewhere, to the village of Châlus, near Limoges in central France. Like me, she was still running. Once, she had protected me. Now she was vulnerable, and I was nowhere near her.

"Aunt Erna," I said one day, "I am leaving again."

I loved her for sheltering me, but my heart was with Anny and her family, which had replaced my own. Maybe, I thought, we could wait out the war close to each other.

On the second day of March, I left Paris for Châlus, with one stop planned along the way: Pau, a resort town in southwest France, to see Uncle Leon in the psychiatric hospital there. On the train, I sat near two German soldiers. I feigned sleep and heard them talking. They said they were hungry and took some cans of sardines from their backpacks, but they had no can opener. One soldier unsheathed his bayonet to cut open the tin.

"This Frenchman," one of them said, gesturing toward me and imagining I didn't understand him. "He must be thinking, 'Is this what the victorious Germans look like?'" The gesture of self-deprecation made me wonder if the war had now turned to the Allies' side. But, when I saw Uncle Leon, I saw damage that could never be undone.

I presented myself at the hospital as Uncle Leon's friend Henri Lefèvre, hoping he wouldn't reveal our true relationship. I hadn't seen my uncle in six years. I waited in a small room and remembered him as a dapper, kind man in a Homburg hat, fastidious to a fault, speaking refined German in a soft voice. I saw a different person enter the room. He stared and never blinked. His face was gray and stubbly with unshaven beard. I held back tears. The nurse said nothing. Uncle Leon looked neglected and incapable of coherent speech. I wondered if I should leave, and looked to the nurse for guidance. She shrugged her shoulders. Then Uncle Leon turned to her and declared, in perfect French, "This is my nephew."

I wondered, how will I get out of this? Will the nurse call for assistance and have me arrested for impersonating a gentile? I looked at her, and she winked at me. I smiled conspiratorially. We were telling each other, this is clearly a crazy man, and here is a figment of his insanity.

In fact, these were among the few sane words Uncle Leon would say during the hour I sat with him. The nurse left the two of us alone, and I told my uncle that I'd seen Aunt Erna. He didn't seem to understand. Your sister, I explained. He said nothing. I searched for safe conversational ground. Uncle Leon hollered fragments of sentences.

"Family," he growled. "Erna. Your mother, whom I loved. Martha the humanist. My own daughter Sonja. Don't tell me about family."

"What do you mean?" I asked.

"They are all against me!" he cried hoarsely, his face reddening. "They blame me for the war. The war is long over, and they won't tell me."

"Uncle," I said softly, "the war is still going on."

I told him the Germans would lose and everything would be fine. He would go home one day, and we would all go home, I said as gently as I could. I told him my mother and my sisters were missing, and so was his daughter Sonja. I told him his niece Martha was in England, and Erna was in Paris, and one day we would all be together again.

"No one is against you," I said. "Everybody loves you and wants you to try to get better."

Uncle Leon wept for several moments at the mention of Sonja's name. He put his face in the palms of his hands, and the weeping became sobs that shook his body. Some piece of him knew that his daughter was behind barbed wire, and also knew we were all trying to keep our sanity, and even when the end of the war arrived, there would be no grand family reunion.

I touched his shoulders and tried to calm him. The nurse appeared and told me my time was up. The two of us, Leon Fischmann and Henri Lefèvre, each of us missing our identities in our own way, each muddling through an endless war, hugged a wordless goodbye. I left wondering why the hospitals weren't filled with such men and women, Jews and gentiles who'd snapped under the war's relentless pressures.

Weeks later, a letter came to Aunt Erna from a hospital official, saying that Uncle Leon had been transferred.

"Two German police officers (Gestapo) came to pick him up for his transfer to Toulouse," the letter said. "We do not know anything about his situation since then. Although we have informed them of the deficient mental state of Mr. Fischmann, these German agents nevertheless took him with them, by automobile...."

A final irony: I was the last one in my family to see him alive; his daughter, Sonja, was the last to see my mother, in Vienna, before her deportation.

14

January - June 1944

In Uncle Leon's face, I saw bleak confirmation of my family's irrevocable decay, and took off for Châlus to seek solace. Anny was there, and I would hold her hand. Her father would be there, to embrace me the way no father had since my childhood. Her mother would be there. I needed a mother. For five years I had been running, and I was exhausted. When I looked in the mirror, I saw images of Uncle Leon in his ruin. I was twenty-two.

As my train slipped through the Limousin region, with its foothills, its rolling farmlands, and sprawling forests, I wondered about the Frajermauers. Eighteen months had passed since we'd all seen each other. We had new addresses and new names. I was Henri Lefèvre; the Frajermauers were the Labatuts. Our reunion should have been joyful, but we seemed estranged by more than our new names.

"Why didn't you look for me in Nice?" Anny asked me almost immediately.

Her tone was too strident. When she was in Nice, I was in hiding or in prison. When she was in Nice, she lived in a convent, pretending to be someone named Marie Benedetto. In Nice, the authorities stopped travelers at the railroad station and made them lower their trousers.

There were stories of those with circumcisions being shot immediately. To visit Nice was to invite catastrophe. I tried to slip past the moment's tension.

"What does it matter?" I asked. "We're here now."

But an aura of edginess hung over our reunion, a realization that much time had passed, and that many in our extended little clan who hid together in Cauterets were now missing. Some were deported to camps: Anny's cousins Willy and Joseph, and Joseph Frajermauer's brothers, Icek and Hillel, and Rachel's brother Jacob, and Albert Hershkowitz. Rachel's sister Rivka was now hiding in Vic-en-Bigorre under an assumed name, and her husband, Itzek, hiding on a farm, was discovered and taken to Drancy and deported. A funeral shroud hung over our reunion.

In Cauterets, Joseph Frajermauer was a confident man who seemed a tower of strength. We all drew life from him. Now, with his new name Labatut, he seemed to have a new personality as well, sapped of his old vitality. I wanted to connect with this family once again, but sensed changes in the atmosphere. The war gnawed at all of us. Perhaps I had imposed on the Frajermauers too much already. Perhaps I needed some distance of my own. I wanted to contribute to the war effort, and not merely to my own salvation. There was a Resistance movement in Châlus, but a bigger one in nearby Limoges.

"I'm going there," I told Anny.

I told her I wanted involvement in the Resistance effort, but I didn't tell her I'd been annoyed by her peevishness, and felt a cooling of my affection. I didn't want to be bound, not to Anny or anyone else. At Drancy, those bound to loved ones paid with their lives. At Septfonds, Werner had refused to leap with me from the train, and might have paid with his life.

In April, I said farewell and moved to Limoges, where I was given a name to contact: Rabbi Abraham Deutsch, who had fled there from Strasbourg after the German invasion. He was in his mid-forties, tall and lanky, goateed. When I went to his apartment, on the second floor of a rented house, there were several young people there, not much past adolescence, and much conversation filled the air, people coming and going, a sense of industry all about. So this was a piece of the Resistance.

Rabbi Deutsch and I talked for a few hours. I told him of my running, and found myself slightly breathless at the end. He nodded his head slowly, as if trying to relax me. "Henri," he said, "your running is over."

Wearily, I replied, "If you say so, it must be true." He wrote a name on a piece of paper: Madame Marguérite Bergeot, who owned a house at 13 Rue de Rochechouart.

Madame Bergeot was landlady and protective mother figure, what became known as a righteous gentile. A widow in her fifties, she was compassionate, gray-haired, and worried each day about those under her care. Her young husband had fallen in the last war, serving under French colors. She never remarried. She lavished all of the pent-up affection in her heart on those now trying to survive this war in her home. She embraced me without reserve and gave me a room with a twenty-year-old fellow with curly red hair and a freckled face named Bastinet.

"Formerly Bass," he laughed. "Eugene Bass."

He trusted me because he worked for Rabbi Deutsch, who had sent me here. I appreciated his openness, and we quickly became friends. Bastinet was from Sarrelouis, in the Saarland, the German state bordering France. His widowed mother was hiding in the small town of St. Junien, west of Limoges. "You have family?" he asked on our first night. I shrugged because I no longer knew.

In the morning, I met again with Rabbi Deutsch and Blanche Alexander, the rabbi's cousin and closest aide, to learn the nature of our work for the Resistance. Some days there were false identification papers to be delivered; some days, one item to be taken to a distant address; other days, a stack of papers to be taken to an orphanage or a hideout where children waited. In them, I saw the faces of my sisters. I whispered tiny prayers to a distant, apparently preoccupied God, asking that someone might reach them while there was still time.

235

Blanche coordinated much of our activity. Sometimes she would call a taxicab, and the two of us went together. Always, the same taxi driver in a Peugeot. Becker drove a Peugeot. The Peugeot, the River Sauer, the police in Luxembourg, all now seemed part of a distant era. Had I really swum that river? Had I escaped so many times since then? I no longer felt the energy for such exploits, and hoped I would never need it again.

I began to hear a term: The Sixth. It was mentioned rarely, and sometimes only muttered, but it was who we were, making connections with government officials, with police, with sympathetic souls who wished to defeat the Germans. We delivered false papers produced by people we never met, for people whose names and histories we changed for the war's duration. The genesis of the term The Sixth was found in another expression, Fifth Column, which caused so much derision from passers-by who saw it painted on the train cars coming from Belgium. Traitors were "The Fifth," so we were "The Sixth," trying to block their activities by forging identity papers, by bribing officials, or by buying official seals and stamps and attaching the right kind of names and backgrounds to people with strange foreign accents. I realized that my own forged birth certificate, obtained for me by Manfred Silberwasser, must have been acquired through The Sixth.

On quiet days, I strolled the streets of Limoges. Some week-

Members of The Sixth in Châlus, 1944. Leo is the first person from the left in the second row from the bottom.

236

ends I took a bus to Châlus to see the Labatuts. On a few occasions, Anny and Netty visited me. With Anny, however, it felt like a friendship more than an affair of the heart. The Resistance efforts were now my fulfillment.

"Don't be lulled into false security," Rabbi Deutsch told us on slow days. The Gestapo's regional headquarters were located in a hotel by the Jardin du Champ de Juillet, near the train station. I walked past it many times with Bastinet as we picked up young people slipping through Limoges. We took them back to Madame Bergeot's house, where they stayed in our attic room and slept in an old, upholstered armchair or stretched out on the floor.

On Friday evenings, we often gathered at Rabbi Deutsch's home. The rabbi's wife prepared sweet treats and we sang Hebrew songs. The last, always, was the *Hatikvah*, the Jewish anthem of hope. It bound us together, even as it reminded us of those whose hopes were extinguished. I choked on the lyrics. I had sung them with my friends only hours before Hitler's arrival in Vienna so long ago.

On Friday, April 28, 1944, the rabbi sent me to the local railroad station. A reliable source said prisoners were being transported east. Some had been in prison; others, at a hospital. Some were arrested in raids. Rabbi Deutsch wanted me to check faces, to see if any of the deportees were captured members of The Sixth. He hoped that with my Compagnons de France uniform I would not rouse many suspicions.

"Be careful," he warned.

Only a month earlier in Limoges, the Germans had executed about thirty men suspected of partisan activity or trading in the black market. Many others were arrested. Now we wondered: Were these the men being transported in the trains?

When I reached the station, I walked through the open wrought iron gate into the freight yard and saw a railroad worker stacking freight, but witnessed no other activities. One freight train waited at one of the sidings. I was pretty familiar with the station. There were restrooms on an upper level with windows that looked down to the freight yard, through which I could watch without anyone noticing me. From the corner of one window, I waited for the familiar sights: the uniformed Germans, the defeated prisoners, the sense of barely restrained cruelty in the air.

In a little while trucks arrived and orders were shouted. Prisoners were herded into the freight yard. I stood a couple of steps from the restroom window and counted about forty prisoners. An SS officer, in a black uniform, was in charge, and six German soldiers with rifles at the ready stood guard.

I saw that raw morning in Drancy again: the child separated from his parents, the women with babies in cardboard boxes, the old men on stretchers. Here in Limoges, we heard that the Germans were heading for defeat, that they hadn't enough manpower, hadn't enough transportation to move their troops into battle. But, to kill Jews, they always found enough trains.

Leo's Compagnons de France identification card. The Compagnons were a paramilitary youth organization trained and politically indoctrinated by Vichy-appointed leaders. Their slogan was "United to Serve." The card and his Compagnons uniform (see photo on dustjacket) allowed Leo to travel virtually unimpeded through France while on assignments for The Sixth.

I edged my face closer to the window and looked for familiar faces. The wrought-iron gate to the yard was still wide open. I saw supplies carried in for prisoners, and remembered the cheese and sardines we were given at the Drancy train depot with nothing to drink. I was once again watching, immobilized, at the edge of someone else's crisis: my mother trying to protect my sisters while I ran; Anny on the stairway with the sweaty gendarme while I hid breathlessly in the attic; a train-load of innocents heading for Auschwitz, while Manfred and I leaped from the train into darkness and lay terrified in the grass.

Then I saw the SS officer point to me. I was no longer at the edge of someone else's crisis, but in the heart of my own. Up there, he hollered, gesturing to my face in the restroom window. There was no time to run; two soldiers bolted for the stairway. I stepped to the near-est urinal and told myself to act as if there was no reason to hide. What is more natural than a man tending to his bodily functions? As the sol-diers strode into the restroom, I urinated as casually as I could.

They stood on either side of me. "Finish what you're doing and come with us," one said. I felt the other grip my shoulder.

"I'm only doing what I'm doing here," I said, gesturing to the urinal and hoping they wouldn't inspect me.

"You can tell it downstairs."

They took me down the steps, one guard in front of me and the other at my back. I pictured myself running for the front gate of the ter-minal, outrunning not only the soldiers, but their rifles' bullets, and out-running the fate of those prisoners about to climb onto the freight car. Suddenly, I bolted. I heard them shouting from behind as I ran to the wrought-iron gate at the front of the building. But I found the world had changed, and the hour of the end of my life had arrived once more: Someone had shut the gate and locked it.

Wrapping my hands around one vertical bar, I climbed. The soldiers shouted at me. As I scrambled to the top, I heard their footsteps behind me and an instant later saw rifles directly below me.

"Down!" one of the soldiers yelled. "Now! Or we shoot!"

I dropped to the ground and felt a sharp pain as I hit the hard sur-face. My hernia burned and throbbed again. It felt like serious damage this time. The soldiers grabbed my arms and took me to their com-manding officer.

"Papers," he ordered.

I opened my billfold and handed him my French identification papers. He glanced at them perfunctorily. I thought: He doesn't understand the language. And then I thought: The language doesn't matter, he wants to kill me merely for my insolence, for making his soldiers lose control.

"What are you doing at this station?" he asked in halting French.

"Waiting for a friend's arrival. I went upstairs to use the restroom. When I heard noise in the yard, I looked down to see what it was."

He handed my documents to one of the soldiers. If I didn't have these papers, I had no identity. If I had no identity, I was eligible to be taken away. I thought, they will kill me this time, but first they will punish me.

"You said that you were looking," the commanding officer said, "and I believe that you were observing us."

"No, sir, I was merely curious."

He looked about forty, and had a gold cap over a tooth.

"So, why did you run away?"

"I was scared, sir."

But I took courage. He was talking to me and allowing me to respond, which was good. He could have thrown me in with his prisoners. As the officer paced back and forth, I felt my hernia throb.

"You are lying," he declared. "Who sent you here?"

He spoke halting French, and I sensed that it made him uneasy. Because he couldn't communicate adequately, his anger rose. I am losing ground, I thought. I will be killed for the crime of this officer's problem in language skills.

"I know how to speak German, sir," I ventured.

"Ah, so?" he said, looking vaguely pleased. "How is it that you know German?"

"I was born in St. Jouin. My mother came from Mulhouse, in Alsace. When I was young, we lived there for a few years and I learned German in school. Some of it stayed with me. I hope you can understand me."

"You speak it quite well," he said.

Then another voice intruded: the SS officer.

"Du bist doch ein Jude," he said with a tone of finality. You are a Jew.

The muscles in my face went limp; this, I was trying to show, was the last thing I expected to hear.

"That's all I need now," I said.

He will laugh, I thought, or he will now put an end to my life with the simplest of commands to lower my pants. But he did neither. He turned to the soldier who was holding my papers and told him to hand them back to me.

"Don't ever come before my eyes again," he said. And, in a motion I never saw coming, he slapped my face with his palm, and then with the back of his hand. My head snapped sideways, and sideways again. I walked away with my face bruised and sore, and my hernia tearing, exhilarated to be allowed to go on living.

At that evening's Sabbath gathering, Rabbi Deutsch said a special prayer of thanks for the sparing of my life—and, in his wisdom, said thanks for the SS officer.

"He probably never meant to arrest you," the rabbi said. "But he couldn't lose authority with those under his command. It hurt your face, but it saved *his* face. If there is one good SS officer, you met him."

At Madame Bergeot's house that night, I climbed the steps to my room and felt the pain increasing in my groin. I put on my homemade truss before going to sleep, and wondered how long this problem could go untreated. I needed surgery, but who could risk surgery? My papers were false, my religion Jewish, and my secrets revealed beneath any hospital gown.

In the streets we heard rumors: an Allied invasion was coming, and an end to the German plague. For now, though, their presence was stifling, and those without papers hid in their little corners and waited. The Sixth worked with an agency known as the Organisation de Secour aux Enfants, the Organization for Help to Children, which operated a children's center near Limoges. I was to meet Blanche Alexander at her apartment on the afternoon of May 8, 1944, to take identity papers to the center and bring photographs back for processing to smuggle children out of the country.

Walking to Blanche's that day, I felt a searing pain on the right side of my groin. I tried to adjust my truss. I felt a lump growing beneath my fingers, and attempted to push it back into my lower belly. It would not move. I sat on a bench and waited for the pain to ease. Blanche was only blocks away, but I couldn't get up. The pain worsened, and I grew nauseous. I stretched out and closed my eyes. More nausea. I began to vomit, and with each heave the pain in my groin worsened.

It was a strangulated hernia, life-threatening. Maybe I should simply die here, I thought, and spare any hospital workers the chance to torture me for being Jewish before they kill me in some surgically twisted Aryan way. I lay back on the bench, and I heard a voice. A woman in a cape stood over me and said I looked sick. I tried to wave her off. She said I needed a hospital. I said this was not possible. But against my wishes, my life rested again in the hands of a stranger.

An ambulance arrived minutes later. The woman was a Red Cross worker. In the ambulance, I was given an anesthetic, and all consciousness floated away until I awoke the next morning in a ward of the Centre Hospitalier Régional de Limoges.

The hospital was staffed by nuns. I felt a drainage tube at my groin and a heated brick at my feet. In my drowsiness, I wondered what they knew of me. Surely, they had seen my circumcision. Would I now be handed over to the authorities? I opened my eyes, closed them, drifted off. I opened them again, saw two large black eyes staring at mine: the face of a nun in a white habit. I closed my eyes again. Hands reached beneath my covers and adjusted the brick at my feet. I moved my hands protectively toward my midsection.

"I am Sister Jeanne D'Arc," the nun said.

242

Joan of Arc? I imagined I was dreaming. This was the anesthetic, this was the war doing to me what it had done to Uncle Leon. I tried to focus my attention.

"As long as I am in this ward," she said softly, "you have nothing to fear."

I smiled weakly. Her words echoed like the voice of a guardian angel as I drifted back to sleep: nothing to fear, nothing to fear. When I awoke, I marveled that such a thing might actually be true, that I might be lying in a safe place with my hernia repaired, that I might slow down for a little while.

Then I wondered whether the sister was real. I thought about Blanche Alexander and the children waiting for papers that I hadn't been able to take to them. I thought of Madame Bergeot waiting for me to return to my room. I drifted back to sleep.

That evening, Sister Jeanne D'Arc came to my bed again. She assured me once more that I was safe as long as she was here. She smiled delightfully and walked away. But her walk was a lilt, a dance. As she moved through the big ward, with beds filled with the sick and the injured, Sister Joan of Arc whistled happily.

Blanche Alexander came to the hospital that night. She remembered my hernia troubles, how I'd complained after the train station incident, and she'd come here on a hunch.

"The war talk is good," she said. There were hints on the radio of impending Allied landings.

"Blanche," I said, "I want to be out of here when that day arrives."

It was May 9, precisely four years since I'd checked into a Belgian hospital for hernia surgery. The Germans had attacked that morning. Now, five hundred miles away, having run for so long, having worn out several homemade trusses, I wanted to be on my feet for the liberation.

"Rest," said Blanche.

243

"Yes," I said. It was safe here. The good sister, lilting through the ward, whistling reassuringly, had told me so.

I lay in bed late that night and thought of my friends gathered at Rabbi Deutsch's house. On Friday nights, there was the singing of the *Chant des Camps*, recounting the hardships and suffering of those deported to the east.

"Far away in the distance
Vast marshy fields stretch endlessly..."

I lay in that marshy field beside the tracks leading to Auschwitz.

"Not a single bird sings
In the barren and hollow trees..."

But the guards are there, searching for Manfred and me in the night, while freight trains rolled toward the east, filled with innocents in the last hours of their lives. I could see that moment, and hear it in the chanting of the song: the deportees with their bent backs, the contemptuous guards, the condemned prisoners forced to dig their own graves.

I wondered what my mother and my sisters had ever done to bring such sorrow onto their heads, and knew there was nothing in their entire blameless lives.

"But one day in our life
Spring will bloom again,"

The chanting continued: One day, one day. The sinister enemy would fade away.

"O, land, at last free
Where we can live again
To love, to love."

I had my backpack at the hospital, and in the backpack was a diary I kept through some of the war. In the hospital, I wrote, "Anny has not come today. Maybe tomorrow." But she never did.

In late May, I left the hospital and Sister Joan of Arc, and returned to my room at Madame Bergeot's. In the evenings, Eugene Bastinet and I listened to radio broadcasts from London. The news was hopeful. Amid the continued killing, and the continued deportations to the camps, the rumors of Allied landings gained credence.

Our room was more crowded with people on the run. On some nights more than a dozen people slept on our floor, and four or five more slept sideways on our beds.

On the night of June 5, we heard a broadcast about General Eisenhower and weather conditions. The report cryptically mentioned "activities" in the English Channel. It followed a week of broadcast pronouncements clearly offered in code: "Grandmother is riding her bicycle around the barn three times. We repeat. Three times." Or a nonsequitur such as: "If the rabbit lays an egg, sunshine will follow rain."

These were messages for the Resistance movement, guiding specific units toward special targets. Specially trained units decoded messages. Some of it seeped through to those of us at the lower levels. We heard of parachutes and equipment drops. On the night before D-Day, one of the coded instructions dealt with diversionary tactics such as sabotaging railroad tracks, setting up roadblocks, using all means to delay German troop movements.

On the morning of June 6, we learned of the invasion. First, we felt euphoria; then, reality hit. In the street, there were still the German soldiers. At the railway stations, trains still carried Jews to the death camps.

Three days after the Allied landing, the Germans massacred French citizens in Tulle, and the next day murdered many more in Oradour-sur-Glane. The German Panzer division, Das Reich, raced toward Normandy to meet the invading Allies, and civilians dared stand in their way. The commander of the division ordered the hanging of ninety-nine Frenchmen in Tulle. The bodies were hanged from trees and balconies and lamp posts, while families were forced to watch the savagery.

In Limoges, Bastinet and I prepared for trips to take false identity papers to Jews sheltered by farmers in nearby hamlets. Bastinet would go to Chabanais, since it was near St. Junien, where his mother was hiding. I would go to Oradour.

Early on the morning of Saturday, June 10, Bastinet took a commuter train to the station at St. Junien, where he was arrested by soldiers in an advance unit of "Das Reich." Their orders were to prevent any resistance: Thus, the coming destruction of Oradour, where I was headed.

Oradour, a bucolic hamlet on the banks of the Glane River, normally had a population of about six hundred fifty citizens. With families living there in hiding, though, the population was now about nine hundred. I left Limoges by train shortly after noon on June 10. On the road that ran parallel to the track, a few hundred feet away, I saw a German motorized unit. I had no idea where they were heading, but sensed something ominous. A farmer sat in a seat across from me.

"I don't want to travel in their direction," I said, gesturing toward the Germans.

"Yes," he said. "After yesterday in Tulle."

We both left the train at the station before Oradour, and I hitchhiked back to Limoges. The next day, news drifted back to Madame Bergeot's house: Those who had taken the train to Oradour were killed as part of a massacre of the entire village. The men of the town were herded into barns; the women and children, into a church. Everything was set ablaze. Those who tried to run away were machine-gunned to death. A handful of people escaped the fire with terrible burns; three survived. The mayor of the town, pleading for mercy for his people, was executed in the public square, La Place du Champ de Foire, on which all citizens were assembled before they were murdered.

The news horrified us, and then got worse. By Sunday, Bastinet still hadn't returned from St. Junien. At Madame Bergeot's, word of his fate arrived. Arrested by "Das Reich" soldiers on his way to his mother's hideout, Bastinet was searched. Incriminating evidence was found in his knapsack. Two bullets were fired into his head.

Madame Bergeot and I sat together and wept. The Allies had landed, but the war continued to bloody the whole earth.

15

June 1944 – January 1947

I went to Oradour-sur-Glane a few weeks after the massacre and found a shrine to the dead. Under a bright summer sun were tables bearing charred possessions of the victims: baby carriages, shoes, and toys that children had taken into the church before everything was burned. A handful of survivors remained of the hundreds who had once lived innocent lives there. Nearby villagers walked about with wintry, haunted expressions and told anyone who would listen what had happened.

"The mayor," someone said.

We had heard about the mayor in Limoges, how he had begged the Nazis to take his life instead of the lives of his people. But there was more to the story. They said the mayor was put on a table in the town center, and his two sons pleaded for his life to be spared, and so the Germans killed the sons. And when they finished that, they held down the legs of the father, the mayor of this little town, and with a saw they cut off his legs.

Some of us from The Sixth felt a special kinship with this town. A few times, we'd brought false identity papers here, so that these hunted souls could emerge from their hiding places and move about freely. Such efforts seemed to count for nothing now.

One night in July, after dinner with Blanche Alexander and her family, we listened to a broadcast of Radio Free France when a bulletin announced an attempted assassination of Hitler by his own officers. There was, in our little group, not a cheer but a gasp. We imagined possibilities. A flash of light had entered our lives. If Hitler's own officers were turning on him, then surely the organized brutality must be coming to an end.

In August, the French Resistance took control of Châlus, and issued a written proclamation: "We appeal to the patriots of Châlus to participate in the defense of the territory. Let us all stand up to pursue our liberation." The Frajermauers were living in Châlus. The proclamation told me they would not have to fear German raids anymore. And Châlus' liberation would surely spread. In Limoges there were still several hundred German soldiers, but they seemed less noticeable since the Normandy invasion. The SS still had its regional headquarters here, and soldiers still occupied much of a local hotel, but many had gone to Normandy after the D-Day invasion.

One day leaflets floated over the city. It felt like confetti falling on New Year's Eve, or rice at a wedding, or telegrams from God himself. They said the Allies were advancing toward Paris. Cherbourg had been liberated and troops were marching through the city. I felt weariness lift from my body. On the leaflets were photographs. One showed Winston Churchill on an inspection tour of Normandy, riding in an open vehicle while an admiring Frenchman reached out to light Churchill's cigar. Another showed Russian tanks on the move. We scrambled to pick up the leaflets as though they were freshly minted francs. Some landed in trees, which children climbed to snatch them out of the branches. Along the main avenue of Limoges, young people ran and shouted, and their parents happily waved the papers over their heads. A giddy sense of celebration erupted, and not a single German soldier showed his face. They were still here, but they were invisible. On this day, nine months before

250

the war in Europe ended, the glorious leaflets and the very scent of liberation filled the air.

One morning in mid-August, liberation came to Limoges. The combined forces of two Resistance operations, the Forces Françaises de L'Interieur and the Franc-Tireurs Partisans Français—which oversaw the operations of my group, The Sixth—converged and took over the German garrison. Several hundred German soldiers were led through the streets, surrounded by Resistance workers carrying rifles. The mouse was devouring the hawk. Here was the most ragtag outfit imaginable: ill-clothed, undernourished, some of them carrying rifles that had no ammunition. The Germans probably didn't care. They were exhausted by

One of the leaflets Leo
found floating over
Limoges, August, 1944.

the war, and demoralized by the turn in its fortunes. They marched in formation, arms raised, hands on heads.

Standing on a sidewalk, I marveled at the transformation in personalities. Only days earlier, these Germans were the masters, and the citizens of Limoges the meek. Now the soldiers seemed to tremble as they heard cries splitting the air: "Dirty Germans"; "Dirty Krauts"; "Remember Oradour."

I watched them march along a boulevard until they reached the train station, and then with a sense of spent emotion, I realized I didn't want to watch anymore.

One day I met a man named Julius Prinz, an Austrian Jew who had fled Vienna years earlier and joined the French Foreign Legion. He was now a captain, an advisor to the Resistance, whose job was to interrogate captured Germans.

"I want you to see these Germans," he said to me one day. "Just see them."

We went to an abandoned warehouse where German soldiers were held. Prinz wanted to show himself mastering the master race. They lay on beds of straw when we walked in, but quickly snapped to attention. Prinz was a diminutive man, but he knew how to swagger.

"How do you like being here?" he asked a German officer. There was no response, so Prinz asked again.

"How do you like it?" The officer shrugged his shoulders. What was the right answer? No one knew, any more than we Jews had known for the last six years, for there were no right or wrong answers, except to run.

"How do you like it here?"

I found Prinz's game gratifying. While I hated the memory it evoked of Jews cringing before Germans, I found it gratifying to see these German officers, once so contemptuous, now cowering in front of this little Jew.

The Sixth, in this summer of 1944, continued its work. Children had to be placed in orphanages. Families tried to relocate those who were lost. Children appeared, wondering where their mothers and fathers were. We also wondered.

Rabbi Deutsch assigned several of us to work for the Jewish Committee of Social Assistance and Reconstruction. Later, under Julius Prinz's direction, I searched for burial sites of fallen Allied soldiers. I wondered about my own family's grave sites, while clinging to faint hopes that they were still alive. I made inquiries, but to no avail.

One morning at my office I heard a familiar voice, and looked up to see a man I'd assumed was already dead: my old friend Werner from the camp at Septfonds, last seen as I escaped the train with him frozen in fear. We rushed to each other and embraced for several long moments. It seemed astonishing that he was alive.

"The train," I said after a while.

After my escape, they'd gone to the southwest coast of France, near Bordeaux, where they built air strips and ammunition depots. "Many did not survive," Werner said. "Bad health. Filthy conditions. And others...," his voice trailed off, "...to Drancy."

It could have been me, attempting to cheat fate a second time. A few days after the work detail ended, the Allies invaded. Werner was transferred to a camp at Merignac, near Bordeaux, where he was later liberated. Now he was going back to the house near Septfonds where his wife and children were still hiding.

"The train," I said again.

I wanted to know what happened when the guards found I had fled. Werner smiled. The guards boarded the train for a final count, and the numbers didn't add up. Kaufmann checked rest rooms to see if I was hiding.

"I wondered what he would do," Werner said. "He asked us all if we knew where you were. There was complete silence, Leo. I wondered if we would be held responsible. They could shoot us for helping you. And then, well, it was Kaufmann himself who broke the silence. 'This fellow Bretholz,' he said. 'He told me, 'If I want to do it, I will run away.'"

One day I met a young man named Freddie Knoller, born in Vienna, who was arrested in France and deported to Drancy in 1943. He survived Auschwitz and came to Limoges, where the two of us awaited emigration papers to America. My anticipated emigration caused my final breakup with Anny. We'd been drifting apart for months, at odds over inconsequential issues that masked deeper problems. I wanted to go to America, and Anny felt abandoned by me. I wanted to put Europe behind me. The continent was a graveyard, and I had escaped my own grave by inches, and in my head I was still running in ways I didn't yet understand.

Then, in May, 1945, the war in Europe was over.

I woke up in the morning and went to my office at the Jewish Committee for Social Work, where a frontpage newspaper headline announced that the war was over. Someone in the office turned on the radio, and this same story was all over the radio. The war was over. We felt a flash of elation, but it didn't last. At such moments, you wish to call your loved ones and share the joy. But my loved ones were gone, and instead of kissing their remembered faces I embraced a great emptiness. In the office, a few of us hugged each other warmly and congratulated ourselves on being alive to see such a moment. And then we braced ourselves. There were thousands of homeless all across the landscape, thousands of displaced people, and maybe some of them included our own families.

The end of the war was not like the end of a winning ballgame or the beginning of a new year. In Limoges, it felt like the winding down of an endless era of exhaustion, and the beginning of a great unknown. One day I visited the Frajermauers, and Anny told me they were returning to Belgium. "Maybe you will meet us there," Anny's mother said hopefully. I nodded, but we both knew I would not.

I wanted to find myself in America. From Baltimore, I received a letter from Aunt Sophie. Be patient, she wrote. She prepared an affidavit of support with help from the Hebrew Immigration Aid Society. But there were thousands like me, and the process was slow.

254

In August, 1945, when Japan surrendered, we felt more relief than elation. I spent my days helping the displaced find shelter, and my emotions turned toward America. On March 18, 1946, I received a letter from the American Consulate in Bordeaux, saying I had been given a low case number, 531. It made me feel important. My friend Freddie Knoller was in a similar position. He had no desire to return to Vienna. He had two brothers in New York who provided him with affidavits, and he waited in Limoges to assemble his travel documents.

In December, we received our French exit visas. A week later, United States Lines booked passage for Freddie and me on the liberty steamer *John Ericsson*, scheduled to depart on January 19, 1947.

I went to Paris to visit Aunt Erna, who cried, "You should never have left Paris."

"I'm alive, what are we complaining about?" I cried back. It was our traditional verbal duel.

Her son Paul was home, and he and I traveled to Belgium for a final visit. Eight years had passed since the night I'd arrived here with Becker in his crowded little car, and the list of the departed seemed endless.

In Antwerp, we met for a short time with the Frajermauers, but I never saw Anny. Excuses were made. She was away, she was very busy. And then, uncomfortably, came the news that she was engaged to be married.

Leo and Freddie Knoller head for the American consulate in Bordeaux to obtain their US visas, December, 1946.

255

"To be married," I repeated.

I expressed my delight for her, and swallowed the confused feelings that raced through me. All kinds of words and emotions were left unspoken. Once, I imagined spending my life with Anny. Now I was hungry for separation from this entire world I had known, and I simply wished Anny the best life she could find because my own seemed so confused.

Paul and I left the Frajermauers after a couple of hours and took the train to Brussels to see my Uncle David. Though he had survived the war, my cousin Kurt had not. I remembered the two of them on that hot day I had gathered my belongings in the camp at St. Cyprien. A few months after my escape, dysentery broke out in the camp. Guards who had once barely paid attention now turned away. One day the front gate opened and inmates ran to nearby farms and railroad stations while the guards let them go. Uncle David and Kurt returned to Brussels to rejoin their family. Kurt was arrested. He was taken to Auschwitz, where his life ended.

It was a different Uncle David I found now, a man who had never recovered from the news of his son's death and could not bear to hear the sound of Kurt's name. "Here," he said softly, handing me a small package. "Long overdue. Should have given it to you for your bar mitzvah. Open it, open it."

Inside was a signet ring with my initials. Uncle David and I embraced for the first time since I'd seen him in that noisy soup kitchen in Antwerp in 1938. We had a final family dinner, at which no one talked of the events of the war years. There were too many unhealed wounds.

Three weeks later, Freddie Knoller and I boarded a train in Paris bound for the steamer *John Ericsson* at Le Havre. Aunt Erna accompanied us to the train station. It occurred to me, she is the last member of my diminished family that I will see on this continent. Once, there were so many of us. The two of us wept openly, and as my train pulled away we waved to each other until we had each faded from sight—the way Uncle Isidore and Aunt Rosa waved to me in the train station that rainy night I left

256

Vienna, the way my mother and Henny waved to me at the bus stop that night, and the way Ditta waved to me from her hospital window.

Goodbye and goodbye.

It was stormy in January's North Atlantic. Huge waves swept onto the decks of the *John Ericsson*, and icicles formed on the guardrails and hung from life rafts. When we reached the gulfstream waters, where the temperatures warmed and the sea calmed itself, the icicles melted, and passengers, seasick the previous day, came aboard deck seeking sunshine. Most on board were young people, some of them women sailing to America to rejoin boyfriends they'd married during the war. It was a happy crowd. A dance band played, and a young Frenchman improvised jazz numbers on a piano that needed tuning.

Early on the morning of January 29, 1947, Freddie and I saw seagulls gliding through the air. An airborne welcoming committee, I thought. We were approaching the coastal waters of the United States. In the afternoon, the steamer entered New York harbor, moving past a fogenshrouded Statue of Liberty. Many of us stood on the deck and gaped, not quite believing we had finally arrived. Spontaneously, we applauded her welcoming figure.

My luggage sat in my cabin, to be taken by a steward to U.S. Customs. When he arrived, I was gazing through a porthole at a misty shoreline in the distance. He was a short fellow with dark eyes, about forty, with a cap on his head. He put my luggage on a handcart, and then joined me at the porthole. He wanted to introduce America to me. He peered through the opening for a few seconds at a scene he must have viewed many times.

"This is where I was born," he said proudly, gesturing into the distance. "Brooklyn."

"Brooklyn," I repeated.

"How do you like it?" he asked.

I didn't know how to answer. He was waiting for a response, and asked again, "How do you like it?"

257

He must have thought I didn't understand him. My English was still pretty rough. I didn't want to appear disinterested or impolite.

"It's nice, I like it," I said.

"Good," he said. And, to make sure I hadn't missed it before, he said, quite emphatically, "It's Brooklyn."

Brooklyn, in New York.

In the United States.

The steward picked up the handcart with my luggage, and as he departed my room he said, "Welcome to America." I smiled, then he turned to me one final time and said, "Good luck."

Epilogue

All these years later, such secrets we discover.

In France and Switzerland and Austria, half a century passes before the children and grandchildren of its participants peel away the war's final secrets: Yes, the neutral Swiss profited from the blood of the victims; no, the French weren't a nation of brave Resistance fighters; no, the Austrians weren't Hitler's First Victims, but his First Embracers; and, no, the churches generally did not reach out to their Jewish sisters and brothers in the darkest hours. Sometimes the world seems appalled at what it finds, and sometimes merely distracted, bored, unable to connect raw numbers with human faces.

I am a tiny footnote to all of this history, but such footnotes are the secrets which make the story real.

I reached America in 1947 and hid my story for the next fourteen years. Why had my life been spared when so many had been taken? Would some miracle arrive in the mail, telling me that my mother and my sisters were still alive somewhere in the wreckage of Europe?

Fifty years ago, my Uncle Sam Goldstein, Aunt Mina's husband, waited for me at the pier as I strode down the gangplank of the *USS John Ericsson*. Nine years earlier, in that little Luxembourg railroad station as the police escorted me away, it was Uncle Sam who had whispered, "Turn the visor around." Now I was turning my life around in a new country.

We arrived in Baltimore that night and gathered at my Aunt Sophie's home on Pall Mall Road. We were a little band of survivors: Aunt Mina the emotional; Uncle Sam the steady; Aunt Sophie who had tried for so long to bring the family here; her and my father's brother Osias and Aunt Olga, his wife. Aunt Olga had mailed me the Irish half-pound note that I'd slipped under my Jewish star the day I arrived at the internment camp at Drancy.

"Thank you," I said five years belatedly.

I said it in English. I started learning the language in Vienna, and I wanted it to be the language of the rest of my life. I wanted to be an American, even as I picked up the pieces of my old life.

The fate of my mother and sisters gnawed at me, robbed me of sleep, kept me emotionally bound to Europe. I was in America in body, but not heart. I began to think about going back. Then, three weeks after my

Leo's Aunt Sophie Albert, 1944.

arrival here, on a snowy night, Uncle Sam suffered a fatal coronary infarction.

Uncle Osias and I heard him scream from the bathroom, and found him with his head slumped to his chest, his face ashen, his eyes lifeless, dead at forty-three. Nine years earlier, he had helped keep me alive, but I was helpless to save him. I felt a piece of me die with him, and in the coming days thought increasingly about my own mortality. My father, Max Bretholz, died at thirty-nine. I saw him bending from the pain sparked by bleeding ulcers. I remembered him on his deathbed at the hospital. I wondered if his early death would be a precursor of my own.

In Baltimore, I found work at a clothing store on Hanover Street. Then I went to a textile distributor and became a salesman for them. Travelling on Maryland's Eastern Shore, I found my European accent openly ridiculed. During one trip I met with two other salesmen, Jewish fellows, one from Brooklyn and the other from Philadelphia.

"They mock my accent," I told them.

"Mine, too," they both said.

It was just America making fun of itself, and of its infinite varieties of people from all over the world who were now trying to find their way in this country. We were all thrown together in the same community of America, and laughing at each other instead of heeding someone's mad cries for Aryan purity.

One afternoon I drove my car along a road in northwest Baltimore. The city had been absorbing many new families from the south. They'd arrived during the war years to work in the local steel mills and waterfront. Hillbillies, some called them. Riffraff, others said. Outsiders—like me. I stopped for a red light on Liberty Heights Avenue, when a driver behind me honked his horn. I was still a pretty new driver. I looked up and noticed the light had turned green. I pulled over, and the driver behind me pulled up.

"Did I do something wrong?" I asked.

"Go back to Tennessee, where you came from!" he hollered, hearing my accent.

As he drove away, I thought: From Tennessee, how do you like that?!? That day, I think I truly became an American.

I met my future wife in 1951 at the wedding of our friends Herbert Friedman and Joyce Herman. I was best man and Flo Cohen was a bridesmaid. We were married in July of 1952. In August, I became an American citizen.

Slowly, I began to tell Flo about the war and its lingering effects. I needed to confront my past, she said. In April, 1954, we decided to go back to Europe, where the remnants of my family could meet my lovely wife, and I could try to make peace with myself.

In London, my cousin Helen Topor (now Meyer) waited to greet us. Helen—Uncle Moritz and Aunt Karola's daughter—escaped Vienna to Holland and then reached London while there was still time in the earliest days of Hitler's conquests. Her family was all gone now. Her sister Martha, whom the Gestapo tried to arrest on the morning after Hitler's arrival, had made it to Switzerland, but died not long after the war. Her sister Sonja, whom everyone said looked like my twin, died at Auschwitz with her three-week old baby Nicole. And Uncle Moritz and Aunt Karola, deported to parts unknown, were never heard from again.

Leo and his fiancée Flo Cohen shortly before their wedding in 1952.

"The war," I said.

"I don't want to talk about the war," said Helen. It was nine years after its end, but its losses still made her wince.

"My mother and your mother," I said. "You know, they wouldn't talk to each other." I remembered all the Friday nights I went to Uncle Moritz and Aunt Karola's home, and my mother never joined me. Whenever I asked her about it, my mother would dismiss me with a wave of her hand. "Why do you think?" I asked Helen. She, too, dismissed me with a wave of her hand.

One night we were joined by my old friend Freddie Knoller, who had taken the *John Ericsson* with me to America. He'd married an English woman a few years earlier, and they'd settled in her native land.

"You know," I told Helen, "Freddie and I sang in a choir once."

262

"My father had a good voice, too," she said wistfully. And then she caught herself, not wishing to touch on the past.

"Do you remember," I said, still laughing at the memory, "how people said they couldn't tell Sonja and me apart, we looked so much alike?"

"Who would like something to drink?" Helen asked, and we moved on to other matters.

Such secrets she kept inside her. Any touch of the past was simply too traumatic, and we left London without ever talking about the war years, or of those who had been lost.

In Paris, we saw Aunt Erna and remembered Uncle Leon. He'd sent a tormented letter to the Germans from the psychiatric hospital at Pau, telling them to come get him.

"Put an end to my hellish life," he implored them.

So the Germans accommodated him. From Toulouse, he was deported to Buchenwald, where his story seemed to have ended. But Aunt Erna unraveled a strange postscript. When the war ended, she said, she received a postcard from Uncle Leon, written in pencil, telling her he'd been liberated by the British. The postmark was Vienna. Aunt Erna contacted Uncle Leon's daughter Sonja Fischmann. They wrote to Red Cross officers and groups working with camp survivors. But Uncle Leon had vanished. Months later, Sonja received word from the Austrian chancellery asking her to come pick up her father's belongings. At the chancellery, she found a package containing a ring and some identification papers, and a portion of the 59th Psalm of David, written in perfect French in Uncle Leon's distinctive handwriting:

Deliver me from my enemies, O, God;
Protect me from those who rise up against me.
Deliver me from those who work evil,
And save me from bloodthirsty men.
For, Lo, they lie in wait for my life.

We left Paris and went to Brussels to see Uncle David and Aunt Olga. My cousin Hilde was now married, and Uncle David was

263

charmed by my new wife. But he darkened visibly when I mentioned my cousin Kurt, who was killed at Auschwitz. Talk of the war was impossible. Nine years after its end, we were all still wrestling with memories we wished to escape.

Flo and I took the train to Antwerp and met with the Frajermauers. The reunion was cordial, but nothing more. Anny was polite, but aloof. We talked about America and said nothing about the war years. An emptiness had opened up behind us.

We moved on to Switzerland and my cousin Sonja. She lived in Vienna, but I wasn't ready to face Vienna yet, so she met us in Switzerland. It was now sixteen years since that rainy night I'd left the city of my birth to begin my running, but it still had too many ghosts for me. Switzerland had its own troubling memories. I remembered my feet frozen and bloody in the trek through the Alps, and Albert Hershkowitz and I begging the guard Arretaz for our freedom, and Arretaz with a sneer on his lips. The last time I saw Albert, I was climbing out of the train headed for Auschwitz, and he was staying behind.

And I remembered, as Flo and Sonja and I walked around Interlaken, Switzerland, how I'd been the last to see Sonja's father, Uncle Leon, and she'd been the last to see my mother.

"Your mother was happy," Sonja said.

"Happy?"

"That you were in a safe place."

That I was in a safe place.

Sonja returned to Vienna, and in a few days Flo and I went to Limoges—where Madame Bergeot still lived, where the SS officer slapped me at the train station, where Sister Joan of Arc stood by my bed with words that seemed to come directly from heaven: I was safe with her. Flo and I strolled by the outdoor market, and in the afternoon crowd I spotted Madame Bergeot.

"There she is!" I cried.

We embraced long and hard, and wept, and embraced again. Madame Bergeot had been my landlady and substitute mother through all those months when Bastinet and I shared the upstairs room and brought in the various refugees one night after another.

"Oh, my God, you are here!" she cried now. "My son, my son."

By now, Flo was crying with us, and the three of us walked back to my former hideout. The attic room where I'd stayed for three years, in war and in peace, looked smaller now, but its intimate confines reinforced the sense of safe haven I'd always felt.

"Here is where Bastinet and I lived," I told Flo.

It was the only time his name was mentioned. Like me, Eugene Bass had been a surrogate son for Madame Bergeot, and we were not ready to speak of his murder, or the pain we felt when we heard the news.

As Flo and I headed back to America, I consoled myself with my cousin Sonja's words: At the end of her painful life, my mother was happy that I was safe. She felt she had done the right thing when she sent me away. But it was clear, after weeks of travel and so many reunions, that all of us were still struggling with our wartime demons, still keeping so many secrets.

For me, the war ended seventeen years after the killing officially stopped. The last announcement of war fatalities arrived in 1962, when I received a terse letter from the Jewish Community Council of Vienna with the final message about my mother and my sisters:

"This is to confirm that, according to our records, Mrs. Dora Bretholz, Miss Henriette Bretholz, and Miss Edith Bretholz were deported to Izbica on 9 April 1942 and that they do not appear on the list of returnees."

"They do not appear on the list of returnees." It took seventeen years to make this discovery and to form a euphemism for the act of murder. The letter was dated October 26, 1962. It was precisely twenty-four years since I'd left Vienna, and yet it was still shocking to think that the truth was now irreversible. They really were gone. It gave me a sense of closure, but it left me without the comfort of knowing their final resting place, which is a secret I will never know.

In the summer of 1970, twenty-five years after the war, the time came to confront the city of my birth. My wife Flo and our children Myron, Denise, and Edie traveled to Austria. I hadn't been to Vienna since that last rainy night in 1938. We stayed there for a week, and I felt like a stranger. What disturbed me most was the sameness of things: buildings, parks, the Vienna foothills on the outskirts of the city, places where I had played as a boy. All were there, as though the war had never happened. All were there, except the loved ones I'd known.

We visited the house where I'd left my mother. In the yard were the same mulberry tree, the same lilac bush, the horizontal wooden pole my mother used to hang mats and carpets to beat dust out of them, the same courtyard where the unemployed violinists had once played for a few coins. As I walked through the city, I sensed my family's shadows nearby, and was haunted by my memories. When we left, I felt as if I was leaving a graveyard.

We made our way to Strasbourg and saw Blanche Alexander, with whom I'd worked in Limoges. Her cousin, our Resistance leader, Rabbi Deutsch, had been installed as chief rabbi of Strasbourg. Our children listened to some of our old stories from the war, but seemed detached. To them, we were talking of ancient history.

We went to Luxembourg, to the Sauer River I had swum on that chilly autumn night in 1938 at the beginning of my journey. I remembered Becker telling me to take off my socks, and the two of us laughing afterwards. So many years later, I stood there with my family and beheld a narrow, rippling stream. Families with children enjoyed a sunny afternoon along the Sauer's embankment.

"Leo, be careful of the water," I heard my mother calling to me.

But there was scarcely any water at all now, and when I explained to my family how this was a rushing, torrential river in 1938 they nodded their heads, but I wasn't so sure they believed me.

In Echternach, I went to a small hotel-restaurant owned by Milly Cahen and her husband. I remembered Milly on that last night at Rivesaltes, when I was headed for Drancy the next morning, and the two of us stood by the barbed wire and wept because neither of us knew if we would survive. Now we learned that she was gone, killed in a car crash a few months earlier. She was one of the kindest people I had ever known.

We went to Trier and found the monastery where I stayed before crossing the Sauer. It was now a convalescent home. We went to Paris, and met my Aunt Erna there, and then my cousin Helen flew in from London. All these years later, it was getting a little bit easier to talk about our past.

In the spring of 1992, Flo and I again returned to Europe. Twenty-two years had passed since our last trip there. My cousin Helen had lost her husband; cousin Hilde was now seriously ill and confined to a hospital in Brussels; Aunt Erna was approaching ninety, but still lived energetically in Paris; her son, my cousin Paul, had died a few years earlier at age fifty-five; and cousin Sonja was still in Vienna. But there was a newly compelling reason to go back. I'd gotten a letter from England, from cousin Helen. She'd been convalescing from surgery, and she'd had much time to think about the past; about her father, my Uncle Moritz; and about her mother, my Aunt Karola, who never talked with her sister, my mother.

She sensed the years getting away from us all, and she needed to unburden herself. After all these years, such secrets we discover. She wrote:

> Our letters certainly crossed, one more sign that we are much closer, if not in distance, surely in our minds. Telepathy is what they call it.
>
> I can at last unburden the thoughts that have haunted me for years.... My father was the most likable bounder who could charm birds out of a tree—the feathered kind and others. He could win

the affections of the most innocent young and also those of more experienced ones, who fell for his charm.

Whilst my mother with her brood and our most faithful maid Lisl were packed off into the country, as food was very scarce in Vienna but quite plentiful on farms, your mother, Aunt Dora, was put in charge of our household. After an absence of three months—June, July, and August—we returned home well-fed and with loads of food for our bare cupboards, only to find that Aunt Dora had fallen for—or perhaps become the victim of—my father's charm, or call it what you will.

Mother's temper tantrums were well known and she certainly did not hold back then. A failed suicide attempt was hushed up and an immediate solution had to be found.

Max Bretholz, who for some time had done tailoring work for our shop, not very attractive, but a very decent fellow, was persuaded, with a lot of promises, plus a flat at the back of the shop and steady work, to marry Aunt Dora and to take financial responsibilities for the infant.

I can assure you, he was keener than she was, but it was the best solution in the circumstances. This was done with the approval of all the other Bretholzes.

When you were born, my father—after three daughters—was delighted to have a son. Martha, when she was older, knew of the situation, always covering up for our dad's misdeeds and always making excuses for him.

Well, Leo, this is the truth. I did mention all of this, years ago, to your friend Freddie. He implored me not to tell you, because of your close and wonderful relationship with the Bretholzes in the States. We thought it was better to lock those secrets up. I doubt whether any of that generation of Bretholzes is still living.

Whatever you think, you were a love child, and however hard it was, then, to forgive my father, I am glad it happened, because you happened—you, my half-brother.

I read the letter several times to make certain I wasn't hallucinating. "Well, this is the truth," Helen wrote. And it took only five decades of self-imposed silence to reveal it. I now knew the genesis of my life, and knew

"Uncle" Moritz Topor, c. 1910.

my true identity. In the war, I'd tried so hard to hide it from the enemy, to become Marcel Dumont and Paul Meunier, to become Max Henri Lefèvre. And all along my real identity had been withheld from me, as well. I now knew that my cousin Helen, for whom I had always had such fondness, was also my sister. I now knew why I bore such a resemblance to her, and to her sister Sonja who people said could have been my twin. I now knew why Uncle Moritz had taken me under his wing after Max Bretholz died, and I now knew why my mother and Aunt Karola never spoke to each other.

And I finally knew what the adults had whispered to each other on the day of Max Bretholz's funeral: Secrets must be kept.

And there was one more ironic postscript to Helen's revelations. In her letter, she doubted whether any of the Bretholzes of that bygone era were still alive. I received her letter on the very afternoon I returned from the funeral of Aunt Mina, who had cried so terribly at her brother Max's funeral—Max Bretholz, who became my father as an arranged afterthought to my conception. Aunt Mina was the last of her generation of Bretholzes.

Finally, Flo and I made the journey I had to make, to Drancy: the last stop before Auschwitz, the last stop before the assigned dying of the war years. We took the Metro there, and exited at a station with a large square called Place des Deportées. The camp was now a huge apartment

Leo and his "twin cousin" Sonja Topor.

complex with government offices on its ground floors. There was a memorial, marking the deportation and victimization of nearly eighty thousand Jews from France. A freight car was there, too, the kind that carried thousands to their deaths. We walked into a courtyard by the buildings that once housed people in the last days of their lives. Now, in the place where children once lined up for their final journey, there was a playground. On the ground floor, a sign proclaimed concern for children's health and safety. As I read it, a woman opened a window and asked if I was looking for anyone in particular.

"No," I said, "I'm here on a memory voyage. The sign in your window indicates the concern for children's safety. When I was here, in 1942, children were being...."

The woman slammed her window shut. Sometimes the world does not wish to hear of yesterday's pain, and sometimes it feels it has already heard too much.

Generations after the war's end, Austrian Chancellor Franz Vranitzky issued a statement admitting his nation's culpability. A few years later, the City of Vienna began to sponsor visits there by former Viennese citizens. Flo and I accepted an invitation to Vienna in 1996, and when we arrived I looked for Max Bretholz's grave. He was not my birth father, but until his death he had made himself my father, and my guardian, and he was the father of my sisters. At the cemetery where he was buried, it took me several minutes to clear away an overgrowth of weeds and ivy before

Helen and Leo, 1997, on her first and only visit to Baltimore.

I found his name on a weather-beaten headstone.

With head bowed, I recited *Kaddish*, the prayer for the dead, and placed a small stone on his marker. Goodbye and goodbye, my dear father. Max Bretholz was a good man, and I thanked him for showing me the love that a true father gives a son, and thus keeping his secret from me.

I thought about the blessings I'd been given in the midst of a terrible war, and wondered about those who had helped me survive. I wrote to the Centre Hospitalier Régional de Limoges, and asked to find Sister Joan of Arc. They sent me her last known address and suggested I try writing to her, which I did without knowing if she was still alive.

In your profession as a nurse, you have met and cared for thousands of people, I am sure. You would be hard-pressed to recall every case. But I shall never forget the moment when I first found myself in your presence. On May 8, 1944, an ambulance delivered me to the hospital with a strangulated hernia. My nom de guerre was then Henri Lefèvre. I was a Jew, working with the Resistance, hoping to survive under an assumed identity. I feared that during surgery my Jewishness would be discovered. When I awoke, a gentle, whispering voice, close to my ear, was speaking to me in these comforting and reassuring words: 'As long as I am in this ward, you have nothing to fear.'

I knew then that I had met an angel. It was you who had whispered these words of succor and compassion. I shall never forget them. Nor shall I forget your cheerful demeanor when you tended

271

your patients' needs, sometimes whistling lilting tunes. Do you still like to whistle now? I hope this letter finds you in good health and fine spirits.

I sent the letter as one tosses a bottle into the ocean with a message inside. Surely, no one would ever read its contents; surely, Sister Joan of Arc had long since gone to her reward. But, on a drizzly afternoon in November, 1997, a letter arrived at my home in northwest Baltimore from Castres, France, from Sister Joan of Arc.

You will never know how much your letter has touched me. And to think of the trouble you took to find my address. I was not able to respond immediately—and will you please excuse me—because I have changed my situation. I have gone from being a nurse to becoming a patient myself, which is not at all conducive to engaging in correspondence.

But, do believe me, I have not lost the feelings of friendship which bind me to the sick. I am happy to have been of help to you, to give you comfort and take you into my prayers, at a time when there was so much hatred around you.

I no longer can hear very well. I can't even hear the ringing of the telephone next to my bed. But it will amuse you to know that I can still whistle, and I am going to try it, right now.

On this pleasant note, thank you again for your memories. Think of me as one who no longer resembles the sister-nurse of many years ago, but as the infirm sister who sends you her affection, for the pleasure you have given her by remembering.

•••

All these years later, such secrets we uncover. In the summer of 1978, I found the French book, *Le Mémorial de La Déportation des Juifs de France.* The size of a telephone directory, the book contained lists and more lists of all of the convoys from France to the death camps. With trembling fingers, I found the convoy from November 6, 1942. It was No. 42. When I found my name, a cold shiver ran through me. Those who had survived the camps were designated with an asterisk next to their names. When I found my name, I stared at my own death notice: There was no asterisk.

I am listed as one of the ghosts of Auschwitz.

I am listed with all those who stood in the final hours of their lives in convoy No. 42, with their hunger and thirst and their fears, and their bloodshot eyes and their babies crying, and their simple desire to live out their natural lives, and were deprived of it by barbarians.

I think of my fellow deportees still: the child separated from his parents on the loading platform, and the old man praying to an unseen God; my friend Tony and her husband Erich, holding hands and consoling each other; the young fellow with the gangrenous leg kissing the tears from his girlfriend's face; my friend Albert singing one final bit of a sad folk tune; and the little boy sitting on the lap of the old woman, who lifted her wooden crutch into the air and cried to Manfred Silberwasser and me, "Who else will tell the story? Now go! Go ahead!"

And so we went.

And, after all these years, that is my final secret, which I now tell to all those who thought they had taken my life, and thus mistakenly listed me among the dead.

I am here.

And this is the story of my arrival.

About the Authors

Leo Bretholz finally arrived in the United States in 1947. He settled in Baltimore, married, and raised a family. After working as a salesman for a textile firm, Leo operated two bookstores for several years and spent two years managing a bookstore in Amsterdam. His essays have appeared in various publications, including the *Baltimore Sun's* op-ed page. He and his family have returned to Europe a number of times, looking for answers and closure to his personal Holocaust ordeal. Leo continues to lecture on the Holocaust at schools, universities, synagogues, churches, and to various groups.

Michael Olesker is a columnist for the *Baltimore Sun* and a commentator on WJZ-TV, the CBS-affiliate in Baltimore. He met Leo Bretholz at Leo's bookshop, and over the course of many years listened while the story that became *Leap Into Darkness* unfolded. Michael's previous book, *Michael Olesker's Baltimore: If You Live Here, You're Home*, was published in 1995.